IN TURNER'S FOOTSTEPS

Engraving of Marrick Priory, Swaledale by J.C. Varrall after Turner.

IN TURNER'S FOOTSTEPS

Through the hills and dales of Northern England

DAVID HILL

JOHN MURRAY

Designed and produced by
Breslich & Foss
Middlesex House
34-42 Cleveland Street
London WlP 5FB

First published in 1984 by
John Murray (Publishers) Ltd
50 Albermarle Street
London WlX 4BD

ISBN O 7195 4149 2

Editor: Nicholas Robinson

Assistant Editor: Mark Daniel

Designer: Peter Bridgewater

Maps: Olivia Hill

Typeset by Babel Translations and Electronic Village, London
Colour Origination by Dot Gradations, Essex
Printed by Cambus Litho, East Kilbride
Bound by Hunter & Foulis, Edinburgh

CONTENTS

Acknowledgements

Breslich & Foss would like to thank all the museums, art galleries, photographic agencies, collectors and others for permission to reproduce works of art in their possession and for providing photographs.

Acknowledgements are due as follows (all numbers refer to Illustration No.'s unless marked otherwise):

ASHMOLEAN MUSEUM, OXFORD: Pl.10

AUTHOR: 21, 28, 30, 33, 38, 39, 41, 46, 54, 60, 62, 69, 74, 80, 81, 83, 87, 91, 97, 102, 111, 115

BIRMINGHAM CITY ART GALLERY AND BRIDGEMAN ART LIBRARY: 92

BRITISH MUSEUM: 2, 4, 7, 8, 9, 12, 13, 15, 16, 17, 22, 24, 25, 26, 27, 29, 31, 34, 37, 40, 42, 43, 45, 47, 48, 49, 50, 51, 52, 55, 56, 58, 59, 61, 64, 66, 67, 70, 71, 73, 75, 78, 79, 82, 84, 85, 86, 88, 89, 90, 93, 95, 96, 98, 99, 100, 101, 104, 105, 106, 108, 109, 110, 114, 116, 117, 119, 120, Pl.1, Pl.6, Pl.15, Pl.20

CECIL HIGGINS ART GALLERY, BEDFORD: 65

ALAN E.COLE: Frontispiece, 35, 53, 68, 103

COURTAULD INSTITUTE GALLERIES: Pl.16

FITZWILLIAM MUSEUM, CAMBRIDGE: 57, Pl.2, Pl.3

GRAVES ART GALLERY, SHEFFIELD: 113

INDIANAPOLIS MUSEUM OF ART: Pl.4

LADY LEVER ART GALLERY, PORT SUNLIGHT: 94

THE MARCHIONESS OF ZETLAND: Pl.8

NATIONAL PORTRAIT GALLERY: p.9

PRIVATE COLLECTIONS: 3, 6, 72, 76, 123, Pl.5, Pl.13, Pl.14, Pl.19

TATE GALLERY: p.21, 11

TRUSTEES OF THE WALLACE COLLECTION, LONDON: 121

USHER ART GALLERY, LINCOLN: 1

VICTORIA & ALBERT MUSEUM, LONDON: Pl.9, Pl.18

WALKER ART GALLERY, LIVERPOOL: Pl.11

STANLEY WARBURTON: pp.14 and 23

DEREK WIDDICOMBE: 5, 10, 14, 18, 19, 20, 36, 44, 77, 107, 118

YALE CENTER FOR BRITISH ART, PAUL MELLON COLLECTION: 63, 112, 122

PREFACE

The subject of this book grew out of my doctoral research on Turner and Yorkshire at the Courtauld Institute of Art, London. This has been supervised by Professor Michael Kitson, whose advice, encouragement and patience has been invaluable. There is, however, more than a hint of prodigality in the use to which this has been put, and the result is more clearly the product of the pursuit of pleasure than of discplined scholarly enquiry. Turner provided the excuse for a series of expeditions to the hills and dales of northern England to locate the sites of his sketches. These were begun in snow-covered Wharfedale in 1976 and continued through all weathers and seasons until the summer of 1983, when I managed to retrace the entire 1816 itinerary on the same days of the year as Turner, though mercifully in better conditions. There is, I would argue, some interest in all this pleasure. Pleasure was clearly one of the main reasons for Turner's tour in the first place. His sketches have a remarkable personality, and because of this quality give an insight into the nature of his response to particular places. This response is the mainspring of his imagination. Furthermore, since his landscape paintings are, on the whole, pictures of particular places, familiarity with the landscapes themselves leads us to a far greater understanding of the man and his work.

This book would not have been possible without the help and information that has been given to me so generously by others. I owe my first debt to Stanley Warburton, Chairman of the Northern Branch of the Turner Society, and co-author of the *Turner in Yorkshire* exhibition catalogue. His enthusiasm and knowledge of this subject has supported my research throughout, and his contribution to this study is greater than individual acknowledgements can make clear. Evelyn Joll of Thos. Agnew & Sons located most of the watercolours for me and put me in touch with their owners. Andrew Wilton, Keeper of the Turner Bequest at the British Museum, has willingly given his time and his extensive knowledge of the Turner Bequest to suggest many profitable lines of enquiry. My thanks are also due to the staff of the British Museum Print Room for their unfailing kindness and attention in making works from the collection available for study.

Others to whom a special debt of thanks is due include D.J.Butler, County Archivist of Durham; Alan E.Cole; Dr. J.A.Edwards of the University of Reading; Trevor Farrer Esq., of Whitbarrow Lodge; Robin Griffith-Jones of Christie's, Dr.John Gage; Edward Jones; James Miller of Sotheby's; Angus Taylor; Henry Wemyss of Sotheby's; Andrew White, Curator of Lancaster Museum; Dr. J.Selby Whittingham, Secretary of the Turner Society; Brigadier Tryon-Wilson of Dallam Tower; E.H.Yardley; R.A.Yardley; and not least Peter and Ruth Annison of *The Rope-Maker's* at Hawes for making my stay in Wensleydale such a pleasant one.

David Hill, 1984

Opposite: *Pencil Sketch of Turner by C. Martin.*

J.M.W. TURNER

J.M.W.TURNER

Turner is popularly thought of as a painter of lurid sunsets, indistinct landscapes and storms at sea. In particular he is often remembered for having had himself lashed to the mast of a ship in a snowstorm, for painting two pictures—one of a steam train rattling over a viaduct, the other of an old ship being towed up the Thames to the scrapyard. He painted in a rather 'impressionistic' style, and possessed an over-developed imagination which indulged itself in strange pyrotechnics of a type not uncommon in the 'Romantic' age. Greater familiarity with his work, however, reveals him as one of the most prolific and wide-ranging imaginative artists of his age.

Turner was born on St. George's day, 23 April 1775, the son of a Covent Garden hairdresser, who made a decent enough living to be able to provide for his son's education and to do without his assistance in the business. By his 'teens the boy had decided to become an artist, completely mastered the techniques of architectural draughtsmanship, and by the time he was twenty-one in 1776 had firmly mapped out a career which would earn him the title of 'the first genius of the day' by the time he was forty.

It was a career with many different aspects. He was a topographer,a marine and country house painter as well as the artist of historical, mythological and genre subjects for the Royal Academy. His principal ambitions, indeed, were directed at the Academy and he was elected A.R.A and later R.A. at the youngest possible age in each case, was made Professor of Perspective there at the age of thirty-two, served on the Council and various committees for most of his career, and finally in 1845, aged seventy, was chosen to carry out the duties of President when Martin Archer Shee was ill. He had greater ambitions than gifts as a poet, but dealt with high literary themes all his life. He painted a succession of subjects from classical literature, and illustrated most of the popular poets of his generation: Byron, Rogers, Campbell and Scott. He would no doubt have been happy to tackle Wordsworth as well if a project in the poet's mind in 1834 had ever come to fruition.

Besides his grand exhibits at the Academy, Turner made nearly 1,600 watercolours, many intended for engraving and most of particular places that he had visited. He worked on producing watercolours in series for use as illustrations for the topographical books that were popular, catering for a market interested in British scenery while the Continent was closed to travellers by the Napoleonic Wars. Turner was an indefatigable traveller himself, and made sketching tours throughout his life. Of all the series he produced, none seem to be a more perfect image of his mind and sensibility, none balances more perfectly his virtuosity of technique with an interest in the particular spirit of place than the series of Yorkshire subjects made between 1816 and 1818 when the artist was exactly half-way through his career.

A great deal has been written about Turner. Ten years after his death George Walter Thornbury, 'a prolific journalist and writer of verse, novels, and topical miscellanies', produced the first full-length biography, a compilation of anecdotes, reminiscences and rumours, intended to portray the artist as he was: 'a great disappointed man, whose ambition was never satisfied, and who in despair of all other pleasures sought out Nature, and in her presence felt his only real happiness.' The picture that Thornbury painted was of a person whose physical appearance belied the beauty that he created. After recording himself aged about twenty-one years, Turner was afterwards always loath to allow his portrait to be taken. He seems to have had good reason to be sensitive about his appearance, for in 1826 even his most enthusiatic admirer could only say that 'Nature, in endowing his mind, appears to have been indifferent to his person.' Thornbury, however, felt that we ought to know the worst:

> His less enthusiastic friends describe him as having a red Jewish face with staring bluish-grey eyes and the smallest and dirtiest hands on record. His complexion was very coarse and weatherbeaten, his cuticle that of a stage-coachman or an old man-of-war boatswain. It was as tough as the skin of a rhinoceros, and red as the shell of a boiled lobster. That complexion told of rough days, when the rain had driven in his eyes as he sat on diligence roofs, or in boats lifting over enormous waves. The sea wind had buffeted him; the hot Italian sun had parched and browned him. His dress was always careless and often dirty; and his sleeves were long, so as to hide his small, pliable hands.

Some of the descriptions were, as Thornbury admitted, 'little more than effusion[s] of sheer spite' such as that of 'the late Mr Rippingille' who accused Turner of being 'a short, vulgar-looking man, with an ordinary head, and a coarse, red, 'pimply' face, utterly devoid of any degree of refinement or intelligence.

Thornbury's book also contains stories that indicated a miserly, taciturn, and misanthropic personality, who could charge seven hundred guineas for a picture and then return to say that he must also charge the coach fare for bringing it. Turner was certainly sharp in money matters. He charged his best friend interest on a debt for pictures, drove a hard bargain with engravers and publishers, haggled tenaciously for the best price for his pictures, and wasted nothing on needless luxuries. On the other hand he could be extremely generous. It is said that he lent money willingly to friends in need, and accusations of meaness are deflected by his scheme for a charity for artists less fortunate than himself, for which he saved money. At the beginning of his tour to Yorkshire in 1816, his hard-nosed attitude to business led to an unfortunate confusion over his religious beliefs. Turner had so exasperated the publishers, Longmans, that when he set off for Yorkshire to make his sketches, 'he took with him a letter of introduction from...[the]...London publisher [i.e. Longmans] to one in Yorkshire [i.e. M. Robinson, of Leeds], which concluded thus: 'Above all things remember that Turner is a GREAT JEW'. The story continues:

> The intimation was taken seriously and literally to heart, and down came the little man, looking 'the very moral' of a master carpenter, with a lobster-red face, twinkling staring grey eyes, white tie, blue coat and brass buttons, crab-

shell turned-up boots, large fluffy hat, and enormous umbrella. The next day happened to be Sunday; and after breakfast the publisher, signifying his departure to church, expressed a hope that Turner would amuse himself with the books and pictures till he returned. Turner was somewhat nettled at being thus obviously treated as a pagan, but preserved silence until dinner arrived; in the course of which some apology was made about an unlucky and *mal-a-propos* ham; whereupon Turner broke out—'What on earth do you mean, sir?'

And the unfortunate host had to explain as tacfully as he could that he thought he had been informed by the London publishers that Turner was Jewish in fact.

In the preface to the second edition of Thornbury's *Life* in 1877, the author observed that: 'When my volumes made their appearance, a certain sense of irritation and disappointment diffused itself through the artist world. The younger and more passionate admirers of the painter were mortified at discovering that, after all, their demi-god was only a little, ignoble man, with sordid views and low tastes, who lived the life of a soured miser and suspicious recluse.' However, Thornbury had allowed his vision of Turner to run away with him, for he forgot that an equal amount of his testimony described a much more fondly remembered person. A Mr Rose of Jersey recalled Turner:

Trudging down the avenue something after the manner of Paul Pry, by which I mean that an umbrella invariably accompanied him. Rain or sunshine, storm or calm, there was that old faded article tucked under his arm. Now, the umbrella answered a double purpose, for by some contrivance the stick could be separated from the other parts; this then formed into a fishing-rod, being hollow, with several joints running one into the other. I have seen him sitting patiently for hours by the side of a piece of water belonging to the property, his piscatory propensities keeping up his excitement, though perhaps without even a single nibble; yet it must not be understood that he was always unlucky, for when fortune favoured him in securing any of the finny tribe, it was not long before we were made acquainted with his success, at which he appeared as much pleased as a boy from school.

Fishing seems to have brought the best out in Turner, and his brother anglers were unanimous in their high opinion of his character. The son of Turner's friend, the Rev. H.S. Trimmer, told Thornbury that: 'To be appreciated, he required to be known. He seems, however, to have allowed few people to get to know him well,' and Thornbury's *Life* was perhaps coloured too vividly by those who were not allowed to do so.

The irritation that Thornbury's book caused, however, stemmed from a more serious criticism than that of simply letting his imagination run away with him. He appears to have distorted much of the testimony that had been given him, and falsified, if not invented, certain stories. *The Athenaeum* published a series of letters after 1862 from people supposedly 'quoted' by Thornbury, all claiming that he had falsified their information, and the editor of the magazine arrived at the conclusion that Thornbury was simply a 'circulator of falsehoods'. But it is going too far to dismiss the book altogether, for while it must be treated with caution, it provides a field from which many fascinating insights into his character may be gleaned.

Turner had to wait until 1939 for the first truly scholarly biography, the culmination of over thirty years research by A.J. Finberg. Finberg had an exceedingly dim opinion of Thornbury's work, 'whose personal contribution to the *Life*, he concluded, 'may best be described as deliberate falsification of current information, legends and gossip', and a 'a mass of turgid fiction'. Finberg unearthed the facts as they could be historically verified, 'made no attempt to dramatise scenes or events, nor filled up gaps in the evidence with vividly imagined details...The facts, I think should interest those who care for the works of England's great landscape painter.' The result of his labours he preferred to describe as a 'chronicle' or a 'chronicle-biography' rather than a biography, but despite his work's unimpeachable scholarship, it failed to satisfy everyone. Bernard Falk, whose own life of Turner leaves a great deal to be desired on matters of fact, criticised Finberg for lacking 'any pretension to literary art', and Jack Lindsay found fault with him for keeping only to 'the definite external facts of Turner's artistic career' and for stopping 'sharply at the outer edge of anything connected with Turner's personal life'.

Lindsay corrected this shortcoming by dealing with Turner's mind, psychology, and motives at length in his 'Critical Biography', but perhaps added less material to the chronicle of Turner's life. He did, however, stress the importance of Turner's sketchbooks as 'a far-reaching key to Turner's mind', and referred to them frequently to enrich his account. Finberg, however, had worked with the sketchbooks more scientifically than any other of Turner's biographers, and his pioneering work at the beginning of this century in beginning to catalogue the subjects of Turner's sketches and arranging them in chronological order in his *Complete Inventory of the Drawings of the Turner bequest*, published in 1909, has not yet been superseded. Finberg himself regarded his work as only 'a beginning or first installment of the task of putting the Drawings of the Turner Bequest into proper order and making satisfactory arrangements for their preservation and public use.' He was equally modest about the remarkable amount of work he had managed to accomplish in identifying the subjects of Turner's sketches, but there remained a very great deal still to do, and he concluded: 'the need for...[this]...kind of information...remains; its possession would add considerably to the interest, value and usefulness of the collection; and in my opinion the task of gathering this information ought now to be undertaken.' Unfortunately this task was not implemented, and only recently has work been put in hand to produce a new catalogue in the light of modern scholarship.

There are 541 oil paintings in all, many of which are unfinished, and of those which are finished only perhaps half have a literary, historical or classical theme. This is to be compared with 1,578 finished watercolours, and over 19,000 pencil sketches, colour studies and unfinished watercolours. The overwhelming majority of his work consists of pictures of places he visited. He spent his whole life making tours and recording them in sketches. While the works he completed for the Royal Academy reveal the literary imagination of the artist, the watercolours and sketches reveal the character and personality of the man. It is impossible to know Turner without knowing the landscapes with which he is associated, for it is only through them that we come to see him as an individual living in the way he chose. Turner's 19,000 sketches and drawings are a unique source of documentation for any artist and it seems likely that Turner was himself quite aware of their importance as the key to his mind and artistic practice. Artistic processes were something which he looked for in the work of his own favourite artists. 'Where...', he asked of his beloved Claude, for example, 'can we find a clue towards his mode of practice?' and it seems that when he conceived the idea of leaving his work to the Nation, he did so for the very reason that it would allow the interested public the opportunity of tracing his own 'mode of practice'. Thornbury recorded that Turner rejected an offer of 100,000 guineas for the contents of his studio, and Finberg mentioned 'unpublished memoranda preserved by his executors', which showed that 'at one time he thought that four different selections of his finished pictures might be exhibited annually, that a selection of his unfinished canvases might be shown every fifth year, and a selection of his "unfinished drawings and sketches" every sixth year.'

One of the innovations of the age was that the processes of the mind and the workings of the imagination were thought worth studying in their own right. Constable spoke of the gratification 'to admirers of intellect, to *watch* and *trace* the *general workings of minds*', Wordsworth's poem *The Prelude* was subtitled the *Growth of a Poet's Mind* and Coleridge turned his scrutiny inwards to the growth, development and working of his imagination in his *Biographia Literaria*. Turner's collection of unfinished works, sketches and drawings were, it seems from Finberg's account of the memoranda, intended by the artist to form the core of his deliberately assembled collection of finished works given to the Nation. Turner seems to have been ensuring that the study of the growth and general working of his mind would be possible too.

A clue to the significance that Turner's sketches held for him is contained in an account given by one of Thornbury's more reliable sources. Mr Trimmer recalled that 'Turner once went with my father and mother to see the pictures at Osterley House, collected by Mr Child. There was a splendid Gainsborough my father had once rescued from a garret. Of this picture Turner made, *memoriter*, a small pencil drawing in the evening, and also a sketch of a woman gathering water-cresses whom they had seen on the way, on which he had written, "*Checked blue apron*". "These," said my mother, when he had finished them, "are for me". "If you take them," said Turner, "I must do two more".' Turner preferred to hoard his sketches, they were not made as saleable commodities, and only ever disposed of to the closest of friends, people who had personal knowledge of, interest in, and care for his life. The sketches were the essential aids with which he could recall every aspect of his experience. Over a lifetime he constructed a complete storehouse of memory in which he had preserved his entire past and in mid-career, about 1821/22, he carefully went through all the sketchbooks and numbered and labelled them, systematising them so that he could retrieve at will any episode from his past.

The importance of memory in Turner's work may be illuminated by observing how it also forms a vital part of the work of Wordsworth and Coleridge. Wordsworth, perhaps, cheated a little by allowing his sister, Dorothy, to keep his memory for him in her *Journals*. Nonetheless, the close relationship between her records and his poetry, and the fact that the poems were often written several years after the event they describe, testifies to the way that his ideas often depended on their being transmuted in the imagination by the power of memory. Dorothy's record of a cold, windy, Spring morning spent by the shores of Ullswater on 15 April 1802 runs: 'When we were in the woods beyond Gowbarrow park we saw a few daffodils close to the water side. We fancied that the lake had floated the seeds ashore and that the little colony had so sprung up...I never saw daffodils so beautiful...' After re-reading this in 1804, Wordsworth composed his famous, but slightly distorted recollection, 'I wandered lonely as a cloud', and it was the capacity of the memory to move him, to give satisfaction, to restore spirit and *joie de vivre,* that forms the principal theme of the poem:

For oft when on my couch I lie
In vacant or in pensive mood
They flash upon the inward eye
Which is the bliss of solitude,
And then my heart with pleasure fills
And dances with the daffodils.

Coleridge's 'inward eye' of memory responded as much to literary as actual experiences, but he nevertheless kept volumes of notebooks crammed with his jottings, through which he could recall his past in books as well as in fact, and from them draw the material from which to fashion images of his imagination in his finished work.

No better images of Turner's imagination exist than his so-called 'colour-beginnings' or 'colour studies', where the raw material of experience derived from his sketchbooks can be seen taking shape under his hand. Turner's memory did not spring fully-formed from his imagination, like Athene from the head of Zeus, it required gestation and the opportunity to take shape gradually. Turner does not seem to have conceived finished pictures in his mind's eye, or to have had anything but a vague notion of what a picture would look like when it was finished. He told the diarist Joseph Farrington in July 1799 that he had 'no systematic process for making drawings—he[i.e. Turner] avoids any particular mode that he may not fall into manner. By washing and occasionally rubbing out, he at last expresses in some degree the idea in his mind.' The 'colour-studies' are the records of the struggles of these ideas to emerge and many might be referred to more accurately as unfinished watercolours than as either 'colour-beginnings' or 'colour studies.'

Turner had a remarkable memory because he trained it through sketching and because he constructed in the pages of his sketchbooks a framework of linked images of the places he visited and of incidents observed while he was there.

The strength of the landscape watercolours which developed from the sketches did not, of course, come from memory alone, but from its combination with a bravura technique used to create images of place, weather and light. But there is something more—a quality of personal association with the landscapes, which in the case of the hills and dales of north of England, is apparent as deep affection. Ruskin had this to say of it:

> The fact of his *feeling* this early affection; and being thus strongly influenced by it through his life, is indicative of that sensibility which was at the root of all his greatness. Other artists are led away by foreign sublimities and distant interests; delighting always in that which is most markedly strange, and quaintly contrary to the scenery of their homes. But Turner evidently felt that the claims upon his regard possessed by those places which first had opened to him the joy, and the labour, of his life, could never be superseded; no Alpine cloud could efface, no Italian sunbeam outshine, the memory of the pleasant dales and days of Rokeby and Bolton; and many a simple promontory, dim with southern olive, many a low cliff that stooped unnoticed over some alien wave, was recorded by him with a love, and delicate care, that were the shadows of old thoughts and long-lost delights, whose charm yet hung like morning mist above the chanting waves of Wharfe and Greta.

TURNER AND THE NORTH OF ENGLAND

Turner made his first tour of northern England in 1797 when he was twenty-two years old and already recognised as one of the most promising young architectural draughtsmen of his day. He had exhibited his first watercolour at the Royal Academy in 1790, when he was only fifteen, and since then had built a modest reputation as a talented painter of ruined abbeys and castles in the popular style of the day. He celebrated his twenty-first birthday, however, by signalling with his first exhibited oil painting, *Fishermen at Sea* that he had greater ambitions than this. In 1797 he exhibited two more oils, *Moonlight, a Study at Millbank*, and *Fishermen coming ashore at sun set, previous to a gale*, together with four architectural watercolours, two of Salisbury Cathedral, one of Ely Minster, and another of Ewenny Priory. The *Morning Post* of 5 May considered *Fishermen Coming Ashore* to be 'an undeniable proof of the possession of genius and judgement', and the critic of the *St. James's Chronicle* for 20-23 May declared *Ewenny Priory* to be 'one of the grandest drawings he had ever seen, and equal to the best pictures of Rembrandt.' In 1796 his work was considered by one critic to be among the 'Principal Performances' alongside paintings by the most eminent masters including Benjamin West, the President of the Royal Academy. Turner was still too young even to be considered for election as an Associate Royal Academician, for which the qualifying age was twenty-four, but already his work attracted notices such as his peers would have coveted. It is not surprising, therefore, that his work began to attract some of the wealthiest and most illustrious patrons of the day.

Edward Lascelles was born in January 1764, and was thirty-one when his father, Edward *Senior* succeeded to the Harewood estates. John Hoppner, friend of Turner, was one of the first artists to visit the family at their new property. On 14 November Farington recorded in his diary: 'Hoppner has been at Mr Lascelles at Harewood House in Yorkshire. Lord Harewood left Mr. Lascelles £30,000 a year and £200,000 in money.—Hoppner says they are very good people.—He went with young Mr Lascelles, who has a taste for the arts, & had practised a little, several excursions to see remarkable places. Bolton Bridge is a very picturesque spot.' Edward *senior* was created Baron Harewood of Harewood in June 1796 and took his seat in the House of Lords in March 1797. On 9 May that year he was feeling prosperous enough to make a gift of £300 to his son, and Edward *junior* immediately set about spending it on his taste for porcelain, furniture, gambling, books, the opera and pictures. He had already acquired work by Hoppner, Laporte, Sandby and Payne, as well as a 'plaister group' and 'a pair of Bronse cupids', and on 17 May 1797, just over a week after he received the money from his father, he 'paid Mr Turner for a drawing', a sum which would not have dented his allowance very severely, three guineas. The drawing was the *St. Erasmus's and Bishop Islip's Chapels* in Westminster Abbey that Turner had exhibited at the Academy in

Edward Lascelles, after a painting by C. Northcote.

1796. Lascelles would have known Turner's work through his friend Viscount Malden of Cassiobury Park, near Watford, who that year had bought a group of the artist's watercolours of his father's country property, *Hampton Court, Herefordshire*. Malden was buying works from a number of younger artists including Turner's friend, Thomas Girtin, and it was possibly as a result of visiting Cassiobury to play cards that Lascelles decided to take painting lessons from Girtin and to have Turner paint watercolours of Harewood.

Turner set off for Harewood shortly after the Academy exhibition closed in June 1797. It was the furthest he had yet travelled, and he decided to use the opportunity to make a tour of the North Country as a whole. The importance he attached to the tour is suggested by the sketchbooks he took with him. Two large, expensive, calf-bound books with numerous brass clasps. He obviously intended to fill them with work of some substance, drawings which would impress when prospective purchasers of finished pictures browsed through them to select subjects to be worked up. His tour took him through Rotherham and Sheffield, to Conisborough Castle and Doncaster, Pontefract, Wakefield, Kirkstall Abbey, Knaresborough, Ripon, Fountains Abbey, Richmond and St. Agatha's, to Egglestone Abbey and Barnard Castle. He continued northwards to Durham, Newcastle and Northumberland, exploring Warkworth, Dunstanburgh, Bamburgh and Lindisfarne, as far north as Berwick-upon-Tweed and Norham Castle, before heading south via Hexham to the Lake District. He made a comprehensive tour of the Lake District before crossing the sands to Lancaster and returning to Yorkshire and Harewood via Bolton Abbey. He must have stayed at Harewood for a few days for he made a comprehensive study of the house and castle from all angles, and made an excursion to Plompton Rocks, before continuing on to York, Howden and Beverley, and returning to London through Louth, Stamford, Boston and Peterborough.

Except for those in the Lake District, most of Turner's subjects were of architectural or antiquarian interest. By the time he came to make finished pictures from the sketches, however, his interests had begun to change. Though it seems to have been for his abilities as an architectural draughtsman that Turner was commissiond to make pictures of Harewood, he was much less interested in the building than in the landscape that surrounded it. In *Harewood House from the North-East*, one of two finished watercolours that Lascelles paid ten guineas each for on 21 November 1797, Turner took a view of the entrance front which in other hands might have seemed mundane, and set it in a living, populated landscape. *The Times* of 3 May 1797 in praising Turner's 'exquisite Architectural Views' in the Academy exhibition, described him as an 'admired Pupil of Mr Malton,' and it seems unlikely to be mere coincidence that Turner chose a similar view of Harewood House to his ex-master. The comparison is much in Turner's favour. Thomas Malton was a watercolourist of the old school, precise and mechanical, above all interested in refinement, with accuracy of detail, elegant figures and pale tints of colour. Turner's approach could not have been more different. He used his watercolours as *paint*, exploiting both opaque and transparent pigments for effects of intense luminosity and deep, saturated colour. It was for the relationship of the house to its setting that the picture was painted, and the trees, lawns and distant valley are made out with at least the same care as the buildings. Turner has, furthermore, banished the elegant figures and smart coach of Malton's watercolour and put estate workers in their place. Turner's figures are never merely picturesque staffage, they are always characteristic of the place. In this case one of the principal elements of the economy of Harewood was its timber, and Turner shows us the house near sunset in summer, for the sun is well to the north-west. A group of workmen rest in the foreground after their day's labour with spade, pick-axe and wheelbarrow, and are about to tuck into a meal, evidently just brought by the woman making off through the trees to the left. Meanwhile the result of their efforts, an enormous felled tree, is being led off in front of the house on its way to the saw-mill. Toppling it must have been a tiring business for instead of simply chopping it down it seems to have been necessary to dig out the roots, presumably for the sake of neatness, it being so near to the house.

The second picture was a view of the house from the south-west, and Lascelles was so pleased with the pair that he ordered two more, together with two views of the castle and others of Kirkstall and Norham Castle, also based on sketches made in 1797. In the pictures of the house Turner adopted much more distant viewpoints, so that he could concentrate on the lakes and the parkland, set against the blue valley of the Wharfe beyond and capped by the crag of Almscliff beyond the house. The landscape may have been the real reason that Lascelles wanted a set of views of the house at all, for Capability Brown's parkland, laid out in the 1770s, would just have been reaching maturity. The change in emphasis between the first and second pairs of views of Harewood, over the winter of 1797-8, however, indicates that Turner's art was now progressing towards pure landscape, with specific effects of time of day, time of year, light and weather, characteristic activities, scrutinised at length and in detail. James Thomson had described the pleasures of scrutiny in his poem, *The Seasons*, which Turner studied in detail, as 'the long review of ordered life...is inward rapture only to be felt' (*Summer*, 1645-6).

One of Turner's favourite themes, especially in the north of England, was 'the long review' of his own life, and his pictures often contain specific clues as to the personal significance of the subject. One of the subjects exhibited by him at the Royal Academy in 1798 was *The Dormitory and Transept of Fountains Abbey—Evening*. Turner was confident enough in his handling of effects to be precise about the time of day and often about the particular meteorological conditions depicted. In the same exhibition he included an *Autumnal morning* and a *Sun-rise after a squally night* and the following year still more specific effects, *Fishermen becalmed previous to a storm, twilight*, *Summer's evening twilight*, a *Hazy sunrise, previous to a sultry day* and a *Thunder-storm approaching at sun-set*. The *Fountains Abbey* was accompanied by lines from Thomson's *Seasons* which specify still further the effect it contained:

All ether soft'ning sober evening takes
Her wonted station in the middle air;
A thousand shadows at her beck—
In circle following circle, gathers round
To close the face of things.

Turner was equally specific, but less accurate, about the parts of the building shown, with the monk's refectory at the right, and the lay brothers' refectory and dormitory beyond spanning the River Skell. This is not, however, by any means the most obvious view of Fountains Abbey and, since he sketched much more characteristic views in 1797, of the choir and Abbot Huby's tower, and of the great east end with the tower and ruins behind with haymakers in the foreground, one is forced to wonder what took him to this damp, overgrown, irrelevant corner of the ruins in the first place, and still more why he chose to make a finished watercolour of it. It seems likely that his interest was more piscatorial than picturesque, for even today, there are some fine trout in the stream here. Turner was a devoted fisherman and we can imagine him casting a line in the evening after finishing his sketches in the afternoon. The sunlight streaming through the windows impressed him enough to set down his rod for a minute and pick up his sketchbook and colours and make a watercolour record of the effect. He remembered both aspects of the site in his finished watercolour, for there is both a fisherman and an artist sketching, introduced into the very centre of the composition.

Turner traced the origins of his success to his first Northern tour. In 1831 when revisiting Norham Castle, on the river Tweed near Berwick, he was observed to take off his hat and make a low bow to the ruins. When his travelling companion enquired the reason for this strange behaviour, Turner explained: 'I made a drawing...of Norham several years since. It took; and from that day to this I have had as much to do as my hands could execute.' The picture in question was one of his exhibits at the Academy in 1798, *Norham Castle on the Tweed, Summer's morn*, bought by Edward Lascelles, and on the basis of Northern subjects included in that exhibition, Turner began to press his case for election as an Associate of the Royal Academy in 1799. His election was confirmed on 4 November, and it is significant that in July Turner encouraged the support of Academicians Farington and Smirke by inviting them to choose subjects from his north of England sketchbooks of 1797. Smirke chose a view of Richmond for himself, and a view of Derwentwater and Lodore for Farington.

Lascelles's patronage continued until about 1808, when it was replaced by that of Fawkes, but in the meantime Turner's work had attracted interest from the opposite side of the Pennines. On 16 October 1799 Farington recorded in his diary that 'Turner called on me. He has made drawings of Whalley Abbey. Whittaker [sic], (I suppose the Author of the History of Manchester) is to be the Author of the work. Turner also made drawings of seals &c.' The drawings were for what seems, in fact, to have been Thomas Dunham Whitaker's first History, that of *Whalley*, published in 1801. During the summer Turner had toured the area sketching at Mitton, Whitewell, Browsholme Hall, Towneley Hall, Gawthorpe Hall and Stonyhurst. Farington had reported a month earlier on 11 September: 'Turner now engaged by C. Towneley to go to Lancashire to make drawings of Whalley Abbey for a publication', but Turner's relationship with Charles Towneley and the author was not an entirely happy one. In a letter to Mr Wilson of Clitheroe, Whitaker complained: 'I have just had a ludicrous dispute to settle between Mr Towneley, myself, and Turner, the draftsman. Mr Towneley it seems, has found out an old and very bad painting of Gawthorpe at Mr Shuttleworth's house in London, as it was in the last century, with all its contemporary accompaniments of clipped yews, parterres, &c: This he insisted would be more characteristic than Turner's own sketch which he desired him to lay aside and copy the other. Turner abhorring the landscape and contemning the execution of it, refused to comply and wrote to me very tragically on the subject. Next arrived a letter from Mr Towneley, recommending it to me to allow Turner to take his own way, but while he wrote, his mind (which is not infrequent) veered about, and he concluded with desiring me to urge Turner to the performance of his requisition — as from myself. I have, however, attempted something of a compromise which I fear will not succeed, as Turner has all the irritability of youthful genius.' The compromise was to hand over the task of making the drawing from the objectionable picture to James Basire the engraver; Turner's drawing was abandoned.

Whitaker's difficulties with Turner's youthful irritability seems to have dissuaded him from illustrating his *Histories* with any new work by the artist, relying instead on drawings made by the Rev. J. Griffith for the *Craven* in 1805. A more fruitful result of the project for Turner, however, was the patronage of Thomas Lister Parker of Browsholme Hall near Clitheroe, which Turner painted for the *Whalley*. Parker was four years younger than the artist and inherited Browsholme on the death of his father in 1797. The family had a history of involvement with the picturesque, for the father had toured with the Rev. William Gilpin whose writings on the subject had been extremely influential in the late eighteenth century. Thomas Lister Parker seems to have inherited some of his father's interests as well as a fine collection of about sixty pictures, and he built a gallery to house them in 1804-5, including a 'Landscape, by Velvet Breughel, from the Orleans collection', which had been presented to him by Walter Fawkes. Parker seems to have begun buying works from Turner soon after he came into his inheritance, and there are records in the artist's sketchbooks of a forty guinea picture of Lomond, dating from Turner's tour to Scotland in 1801, and a *Bowland* at the same price, of about 1803, neither of which can now be traced. Parker was on particularly good terms with a number of Turner's most prominent early patrons, including Sir John Leicester of Tabley Hall, Cheshire, who was his second cousin, and Walter Fawkes of Farnley Hall, though his first purchases seem to predate theirs. It seems possible that it was he who first introduced Turner to Fawkes.

Parker's interests included gardening on the grand scale, for he spent £100,000 on planting at Browsholme; touring, for he visited Russia, Italy and France in 1801 and 1802; and history, for he converted the house and gardens at Browsholme into one of the finest and earliest antiquarian houses in England. In 1807 he acquired another painting by Turner, a sea-piece, the *View off Sheerness*, but was obliged to sell it in 1811, probably to finance some other project, having first had it copied by A.W.Callcott. His extravagance finally caught up with him, however, and in 1824 he was forced to sell Browsholme to his cousin. He nevertheless maintained an interest in the arts in general and in Turner in particular, and by 1826 owned a watercolour of *Bolton Abbey* by the artist which came to him from Fawkes, possibly on the latter's death in 1825, as a memento of the times and interests that the three men had shared.

Turner's next visit to the north was in 1801, when he travelled through Yorkshire on his way to Scotland. At this stage of his career he was preparing his case for election as a full Royal Acadmician the following year when he would be twenty-seven, the youngest qualifying age, and he was in search of sublimities with which to make his mark at the Exhibition in 1802. He was mostly interested in mountains, therefore, developing themes which he had been exploring in North Wales over the previous two years. Nevertheless he took time to explore parts of Yorkshire that he had missed on his first visit in 1797, and one of his sketchbooks of this time shows that his itinerary took him to 'H[elmsley]', where he spent 17s., 'Pick[ering], where he spent 8s.6d., 'Scar[borough], £1.17s.d.', 'Wit[by], £1.12s.6d.', and 'Gis[borough], 8s.'. He made sketches *en route* at Helmsley, Rievaulx Abbey, Pickering, Scarborough, Whitby and Guisborough, as well as numerous studies of the waves breaking on the beach in a sketchbook labelled '30 Guisb[orough] Shore', though the shore appears to be that of Northumberland rather than Yorkshire.

Turner was duly elected a Royal Academician on 12 February 1802. In March the Treaty of Amiens was signed bringing a lull to the war with Napoleon, and for the first time in nearly ten years it became possible to go abroad. Turner seized the opportunity as soon as the Royal Academy Exhibition closed and went to Paris and the Alps for the summer. He brought back a magnificent collection of Alpine studies, together with the results of a prolonged study of Napoleon's art treasures in the Louvre. With his new status as Royal Academician to develop, Turner's exhibited works occupied virtually all his attention for the next five years or so, and he does not seem to have embarked on any but the most local sketching expeditions around London and the South Coast, until his next visit to the north, and his first to Farnley Hall, in 1808.

TURNER AT FARNLEY HALL

At the Royal Academy council meeting of 4 November 1812 Turner was not at his best. He complained to Joseph Farington 'of a nervous disorder, with much weakness of the stomach. Everything, he said, disagreed with him—turned *acid*. He particularly mentioned an aching pain at the back of his neck. – He said he was going to Mr Fawkes's in Yorkshire for a month, and I [Farington] told him air, moderate exercise and changing his situation would do most for him.' Turner had missed his usual summer tour this year and after fourteen months in London he was beginning to feel the worse for wear. Walter Fawkes's house, Farnley Hall in Yorkshire, had been Turner's regular retreat since 1808, and in that time the relationship between patron and artist had warmed into friendship and respect. Turner could have anticipated a cheering welcome, good company, bracing weather, breathtaking scenery and the sure restoration of his *joie de vivre* as he set out that late autumn for Yorkshire.

Joie de vivre was not the most frequently noted feature of Turner's character. In London he was mysterious about his private life, seeming to many to live the life of a recluse, socialising comparatively little, entertaining hardly ever, and taking care and pleasure only in his work. As we have seen, one of his early biographers told stories of a coarse and surly misanthrope, taciturn, mean, even sordid. A figure slovenly in speech and dress who, later in life, lived in near squalor, 'wallowed' at a brothel at Wapping, went under the alias of 'Admiral Booth' and sat alone at night in a corner of a pub called the 'Yorkshire Stingo'. These stories were collected from sources often tainted by the malice of professional jealousy and self-interest. Those few who properly counted themselves as his friends reported a wholly different personality, as even Thornbury admitted: humorous, witty, cheerful, even boisterous, fond of company, children and good conversation. 'Turner at Farnley was not the morose, slatternly self-indulgent genius that Mr Hamerton and Mr Thornbury depict', in fact he was quite the reverse, 'he shot and fished and was as merry and playful as a child.' It is impossible to know Turner without knowing him at Farnley. This was Turner at his best.

Farnley Hall stands at the top of sweeping parkland, commanding magnificent views over Wharfedale, about two miles from Otley. From its terrace it is possible to trace the windings of the river downstream towards Harewood Castle and Almscliff Crag, and upstream towards the grey roofs of the town and the great shoulder of Otley Chevin behind. Opposite stand Caley Crags where one hundred and seventy years ago goats and deer wandered free along the spruce and bracken-topped hill, and Turner sat with his sketchbook tracing every field and rock, path, road, riverbank, tree, hill, moor, barn, church, farm or manor house in the surrounding countryside. Farnley Hall is little altered since Turner stayed there, a spacious Grecian block attached to a mullioned Elizabethan manor house, surrounded by groves of tall trees sheltering it from the winds sweeping down from the wide stretches of moorland beyond.

Walter Ramsden Hawkesworth Fawkes was born on 2 March 1769 and inherited Farnley Hall and estates aged twenty-three years in October 1792. His father Walter Beaumont Hawkesworth of Hawkesworth Hall had acquired Farnley under rather unusual circumstances. Francis Fawkes was the last of the direct line, a widower with no surviving children, and one day in his old age he rode over to call on his cousins, the Vavasours at nearby Weston Hall. Mrs Vavasour was entertaining at the time and made it quite clear that the 'blunt squire' of Farnley in his muddy boots and breeches was a far from welcome visitor. Francis remounted and went to call instead on his distant kinsman Walter Hawkesworth at Hawkesworth Hall. 'Cousin Walter,' he is reported to have said, 'I'm out of money! Nay, look not surprised, I am here to borrow! Will you lend me three hundred guineas?' Cousin Walter ransacked his pockets and drawers, put the money in a bag, and the squire rode home to Farnley. A few days later the bag was returned unopened, and when Fawkes died in October 1786 he left the house, estates and a fortune to his charitable kinsman Walter Hawkesworth, on condition that he adopt the surname and arms of Fawkes and make Farnley his principal residence. Fawkes's first act was to commission John Fisher of York to carve a monument in Otley Church to his benefactor. His second was to commission John Carr of York to build him a more modern and spacious mansion at Farnley than the modest sixteenth-century structure his predecessor had inhabited. The plasterers, painters and decoraters finished their work in 1790 but Walter hardly had time to furnish the new house let alone enjoy it, for in October 1792 he died leaving the benefits of the unexpected inheritance to his son.

Walter Fawkes the younger led a carefree youth, spending his time at Cambridge in 'idle sports', rowing, sailing, singing, drinking and generally enjoying himself, occasionally finding time to study a little Tully, Maro, Payley or Locke. He shouldered his responsibilities as the new squire of Farnley however, and in August 1794 he married and set about ensuring the line of succession, fathering four sons and seven daughters before his wife died in 1813. Soon after his marriage he began to exercise his taste for the arts in developing the collections at Farnley, and in December he commissioned four oil paintings from William Hodges, but was so dissatisfied with them that he resolved to buy only watercolours thenceforth. His dissatisfaction was aimed only at modern artists for in 1796 he paid 300 guineas for a Ruisdael, and in 1798-9 he bought a number of pictures from the Orleans collection then being dispersed in London by the Lords Bridgewater, Gower and Carlisle. His taste at this time seems to have been conventional and correct, and he acquired works by or attributed to Van Dyck, Cornelius Jansen, Guercino, Guido Reni, Carlo Dolce, Snyders, Vandervelde, Backhuysen, Weenix and Cuyp, besides two sketches by Sir Joshua Reynolds bought, it is said, at the studio sales after his death in 1792 and a group of Swiss views by John Warwick Smith.

It is not known when or how Turner and Fawkes first met, but it was Fawkes's interest in the Alps that prompted his first commissions from the artist in about 1804:

Gt Devils Bridge causeway
Upper Fall of Riquenbach
Mt Blanc from St Martin

W. Fawkes G50e

Fawkes had visited Switzerland during his youth and his travelling companion the Rev. Henry Forster Mills recalled admiring the mountains from the shores of Lake Geneva while Fawkes 'sat and all their grandeur traced, Or sketched with magic skill the lake below.' It has been claimed that it was Fawkes who persuaded Turner to go to Switzerland in the first place, and that he even suggested many of the viewpoints. Whatever the case, Fawkes took an uncommonly close interest in the sketches that Turner made in 1802, and of the forty watercolours related to the tour, at least twenty-one hung at one time at Farnley.

The first watercolours were all on the grand scale, and so impressed was Fawkes with Turner's work that he broke his resolution against oil paintings, and bought six from Turner between 1804 and 1810, three sea pieces, two Alpine subjects and a view of London from Greenwich. With the exception of Turner's academic subjects, Fawkes built up a fairly representative collection of Turner's grand and sublime public performances, and most of the pictures were exhibited either at the Academy or at Turner's own gallery in Harley Street. In 1808, however, Turner resumed his sketching tours out of London to travel north to stay at Sir John Leicester's at Tabley Hall in Cheshire, where he was commissioned to paint a pair of views of the house and lake. He also had an invitation to stay at Farnley and in one of the sketchbooks used at Tabley he made a note of alternative routes to Otley via Manchester. Instead of taking the direct route, however, he seems to have made a detour to explore Ribblesdale and the Craven dales and he made sketches at Whalley, 'Ribblesdale Leap', Ingleton, Giggleswick, Settle, Malham and Gordale before travelling on to Farnley.

The purpose of this trip was to see the sites described by Whitaker in his *History of Craven*, published in 1805 with some poor illustrations by the Rev. J. Griffith. This seems to have piqued the 'youthful genius' whose work had been one of the most interesting features of Whitaker's earlier history, and he set about visiting and sketching most of the illustrated sites. He continued his exploration from Farnley by making a tour up Wharfedale to Addingham, Bolton Abbey, Bolton Woods, the Strid and Barden Tower, and taking his first views of Farnley from the crags of Otley Chevin, and of the Washburn Valley at Leathley and Lindley Bridge. In the sketches made this summer he came to terms for the first time with the landscape of Yorkshire, with its limestone crags and gorges, brown pebbly rivers and waterfalls, field-chequered valleys, blustery weather, gritstone outcrops and heather-covered hills—a landscape in which to take pleasure in the pure vivid sensations of feeling alive.

Turner's stay at Farnley resulted in Fawkes ordering a group of twenty watercolours at ten guineas each; ten Yorkshire subjects and ten Alpine. However, with one exception—the watercolour of 'Farnley'—none of the subjects have any particularly personal associations at this stage, and if the intimacy of Turner's subjects at Farnley may be taken as a barometer of his relationship with Fawkes, it was still on a fairly business-like footing. Fawkes's patronage at this time was generous in the extreme and the importance of his support should not be underestimated. Most collectors preferred the work of masters who were dead, and Fawkes's taste in the 1790s was typical of many still. Though Turner was relatively successful, he was by no means universally liked, and a number of his original patrons, including Edward Lascelles and the Earl of Essex had deserted him in the face of increasingly hostile and often abusive criticism. Turner's exhibited works do not seem to have sold well, either at the Academy or at his own gallery, and throughout this period it was on commissions from private patrons, particularly Walter Fawkes and the Earl of Egremont, that he depended. By 1810 he calculated that he was worth £11,350, quite a fortune for the son of a Covent Garden hairdresser, and £1,000 of that was owed to him by Fawkes.

After 1808 Turner stayed at Farnley virtually every year until Fawkes's death in 1825. From the evidence of his sketchbooks, however, his activities seem, during the period 1809-15, to have been mostly social. There are hardly any Farnley drawings which can be dated to these years, although he seems to have made a number of watercolours of Southern Coast subjects which were being published at the time and corrected proofs of the engravings.

He was, however, stocking his imagination. An incident recalled, by Walter Fawkes's son, Hawkesworth, from the autumn of 1810 reveals very clearly how his ideas for pictures took shape. 'One stormy day at Farnley, Turner called to me loudly from the doorway, "Hawkey! Hawkey! Come here! Come here! Look at this thunder-storm. Isn't it grand? isn't it wonderful? - isn't it sublime?" All this time he was making notes of its form and colour on the back of a letter. I proposed some better drawing-block, but he said it did very well. He was absorbed—he was entranced. There was the storm rolling and sweeping and shafting out its lightning over the Yorkshire hills. Presently the storm passed and he finished. "There! Hawkey," said he, "In two years you will see this again, and call it Hannibal Crossing the Alps".' Hannibal had spent about several years waiting in the wings of Turner's imaginations for a drama in which to make his appearance. In the end he was given only a supporting role, for the real point of *Hannibal Crossing the Alps* is neither Hannibal nor the Alps but the experience of witnessing the storm from the terrace at Farnley Hall. At that moment the reality behind the story of Hannibal's struggle against the elements was revealed, made more vivid by Turner's memories of his own adventures in the Alps eight years earlier, memories which would often have been relived in browsing through his sketchbooks with Fawkes, exchanging recollections and selecting subjects to be worked up into finished watercolours. Meanwhile the storm rolled and swept and shafted out its lightning, and Turner's imagination marched at the head of an army of elephants across the rocky sweeps of Otley Chevin. It is not surprising that he was so excited, and two years later the experience duly appeared on the walls of the Royal Academy, its elements set tumbling and whirling by the maelstrom of his imagination.

Arguments over the hanging of *Hannibal* at the Academy in 1812 were the least of Turner's worries that year for he was building his own house at Twickenham, and the Yorkshire holiday in November would have been a welcome opportunity to relax. Farnley had a reputation for 'mirth and sportive fancy' and visitors could ride, fish, hunt or shoot. A regular guest was Sir William Pilkington of Stanley Chevet, near Wakefield, a noted scholar and amateur artist. He, too, admired Turner's work and bought a picture of *Woodcock Shooting on Otley Chevin*, probably sketched on Turner's visit, which reputedly includes a portrait of himself. The pleasure in killing seems callous today, and while the Reverend Mills's recollections are humorous in expression, the content seems perhaps unworthy of his office:

...free to play,

We little sportsmen ranged the fields along,
Mark'd the poor linnet on his willow spray,
And stopp'd with thun'ring tube his dulcet song.

During Turner's two month stay in Yorkshire in 1816 he began to compile a pictorial record of life at Farnley. One of the projects was to illustrate a book of ornithology that the Fawkes children were keeping. Turner recalled in the year of his death that: 'A Cuckoo was my first achievement in killing on Farnley Moor, in earnest request of Major Fawkes [i.e. Major Richard Fawkes, as he became, seven years old in 1816] to be painted for the book,' and while the children pasted in feathers from the wings and back and breast, Turner made watercolour studies to stick on the opposite pages. Even Ruskin found himself at a loss to describe the exquisite colour and detail of the bird drawings: 'They seemed to delight him, especially the peacock's head, which he said was a marvel of colour and force, and the kingfisher, which he examined for a long time with a microscope, and he could not find words to describe its exquisite beauty. I asked if Turner had painted many birds, and he answered, "Nowhere but at Farnley. He could only do them joyfully there!",' and he carried the same feeling, accuracy and technique into drawings of fish, most probably caught at Farnley in the Wharfe or in Lake Tiny.

From Farnley Turner could walk or ride up onto the moors or down the glens to Lake Tiny, explore the banks of the Washburn, or make excursions up the Wharfe to Bolton Abbey, the Strid and Barden Tower, stocking his memory with all the effects of summer and autumn in Wharfedale: mists rising from the valley, sunlight sparkling on clear peaty streams, and clouds bringing cool showers from the west. After 1816 he again took his sketchbooks with him, and began to make a series of studies of the house, grounds and favourite spots in the area. Occasionally he would catch the bright flash of a kingfisher flitting out of shadow into light, spy a heron stalking fish in the Washburn or disturb deer or goats browsing among the rocks on the Chevin. He loved the life at Farnley and recorded every aspect: a deer being carried down in triumph to Caley Hall; or a shooting-party with the day's trophies being made ready for the spit, the dogs and beaters resting after their labours, the gentlemen swapping stories of their successes, the guns, the marquees and the beer-barrels, all the paraphernalia of the occasion, made out with relish and the recollection of an event enjoyed. On one of these occasions we are told that the artist provided even greater spectacle and amusement: 'On the return from shooting, nothing would satisfy Turner but driving tandem home over a rough way, partly through fields. I need hardly say that the vehicle was soon capsized, amid shouts of good-humoured laughter; and thenceforeward Turner was known at his host's by the nickname of "Over Turner".'

On wet days he might wander around the house examining and recording Fawkes's Civil War heirlooms, or making studies of the interior of the old house as it developed into a museum of the period. Fawkes had a collection of relics descended from General Thomas Fairfax, the commander of Oliver Cromwell's army, who had lived at nearby Menston Hall, one of the many outlying properties of the Farnley estate. The collection included Fairfax's sword, boots, candlesticks and wheelchair, which he had designed to get about in late in life, Oliver Cromwell's hat, sword and watch, General Lambert's sword, and the stone table brought from Menston Hall at which Fairfax entertained Cromwell and other Parliamentarian officers to dinner in the orchard two nights before the Battle of Marston Moor. Turner recorded every aspect of the museum as it developed, with bay windows, porches, panelling, chimney-pieces and furniture being brought from other Fawkes properties of the period, in an album called 'Fairfaxiana' which included emblematic frontispieces, as well as laboriously detailed drawings of objects in the collection, including most ingeniously, a drawing of a chest at Farnley, made with paper doors that open to reveal the painted relics inside.

On other days he would sit in the rooms of John Carr's elegant new wing, with its decorated ceilings and doorcases, and there are records of the ladies seated in the Library with Turner's own picture *Shoeburyness Fishermen Hailing a Whitstable Hoy* hanging over the fireplace. Another watercolour, of the *drawing-room*, shows three further Turner oils, *The Dort*, over the fireplace, with *The Victory Returning from Trafalgar*, and *Sun Rising through Vapour* to either side. On other occasions Turner browsed in the Library and made illustrations to Fawkes's favourite poets, Byron, Moore and Scott, or dreamed on classical themes. The classical theme at Farnley also found expression in architecture, and Turner designed the east lodges ('in a rather heavy Greek style' according to Effie Ruskin) for his patron in 1818.

The family took a keen interest in the artist at work, and an interesting survival from the time is a special drawing table that he would have worked at. A room is said to have been permanently reserved for his use were he would stretch cords from one wall to the other, 'with papers tinted with pink and blue and yellow, hanging on them to dry.' Hawkesworth showed us in a drawing how Turner would sketch standing up, and when one of the daughters ventured to ask his advice on a drawing she was told to put it in a jug of water. The damp papers hanging from the lines in his room might have helped convince her that this was serious advice, but it was Hawkesworth who had the most revealing glimpse of his working methods. 'One morning at breakfast,' probably in November 1818, 'Walter Fawkes said to him, "I want you to make me a drawing of the ordinary dimensions that will give me some idea of the size of a man of war." The idea hit Turner's fancy, for with a chuckle he said to Walter Fawkes's eldest son, then a boy of about fifteen, "Come along Hawkey and we will see what we can do for Papa," and the boy sat by his side the whole morning and witnessed the evolution of *The First Rate Taking in Stores*. His description of the way Turner went to work was very extraordinary; he began by pouring wet paint onto the paper till it was saturated, he tore, he scratched [and 'tore up the sea with his eagle-claw of a thumb-nail' according to another source], he scrubbed at it in a kind of frenzy and the whole thing was chaos—but gradually and as if by magic the lovely ship, with all its exquisite minutia, came into being and by luncheon time the drawing was taken down in triumph.' An evident interest in Turner's methods prompted Fawkes to buy some of the artist's most experimental work including a series of body colour drawings of Farnley and environs which were described as 'sketches' but which were, in fact, mostly studio works based on detailed pencil drawings—works contrived to give the appearance of having been made at the moment that Turner first confronted his subject. Fawkes's interest in Turner's sketching practice culminated in 1817 when the artist returned from a tour of the Rhine. When Turner produced a sketchbook containing fifty-one drawings coloured on the spot Fawkes bought the lot for 500 guineas and Turner immediately sent out to Otley for some glue wafers and stuck them in an album for his friend. This tour seems almost to have been made solely for Fawkes benefit, for apart from the oil painting of *The Field of Waterloo* exhibited at the Academy in 1818, and a few later watercolours, Fawkes bought all the other finished works made from the material he gathered, including a watercolour version of the *Field of Waterloo* and the oil painting of the harbour at Dordrecht, *The Dort*, which Walter Fawkes bought as a twenty-first birthday present for his son Hawkesworth.

On 13 April 1819 Walter Fawkes opened the rooms of his house in Grosvenor Place, London, to the public for the first time. It was announced: 'Mr. Fawkes's Collection of Water Colour Drawings is now thrown open, by tickets to the Public. It is well-chosen and judiciously varied; comprising some of the finest specimens which our artists in this branch have ever furnished. The whole is the work of British Artists, and therefore constitutes a delightful repast both for the Patriot and the Amateur.' Two rooms were hung with modern British watercolours, some forty in all, by Turner, Nicholson, Smith, De Wint, Hills, Fielding, Cristall, Cox, Gilpin, Prout, Robson, Smith, Varley, Atkinson, Glover, Ibbetson, Garrard and Heaphy. The rest of the exhibition, another sixty pictures, was all by Turner. In the Large Drawing-Room was Fawkes's entire collection of Turner's forty finished watercolours, the effect recorded by Turner himself in a watercolour engraved for the catalogue, and in the Small Bow Drawing-Room were 'Twenty Sketches made in Wharfdale, Yorkshire' also by Turner. The sketches were singled out for particular praise by the critic of the *Repository of Arts:* 'They appeared to us (at least many of them) to be done in distemper, and will perhaps by artists be preferred to the finished drawings in the adjoining apartment. As they are not classed in the catalogue, it is impossible for us to refer to them in detail; it will be sufficient to say that they are the best examples we have ever seen of the unrivalled powers of this artist in landscape views.'

Fawkes issued admission tickets, which advised that there would be 'No admission if the weather be wet or dirty', and visitors 'gave up their tickets in the hall, and were ushered up a handsome flight of stairs with marble statues in niches, into the suite of rooms in which the pictures were. Catalogues were lying over these tables, and thus every advantage was given for indulging in these fine works of art.' The catalogues were actually published in June, sometime after the opening of the exhibition, which allowed Fawkes to include a selection of the reviews as an introduction. One enthused: 'Turner is perhaps the first artist in the world in the powerful and brilliant style peculiar to him; no man has ever thrown such masses of colour upon paper; and his finest works have been collected in Mr Fawkes's house, and almost all from the Noblest scenery in the world:—THE SWISS ALPS—VIEWS OF MONT BLANC—CHAMOUNY—THE DEVIL'S BRIDGE—THE GREAT ST. BERNARD—THE MER DE GLACE—Mountains mingling with the Clouds, and rich with all the effects of Storm and Sunshine: Cataracts plunging into Invisible Depths; Lakes shining like blue steel, under the Alpine sun, or clouded by forests hanging over them from the hills; uplands covered with vines and olives, and solitary sweeps of splendid snow.'

Another visitor, W.P. Carey, recalled in 1826 that 'Turner the enchanter whose magic pencil had created the chief wonders of this temple, was frequently there. Nature, in endowing his mind, appears to have been indifferent to his person, but his brow is a page on which the traits of his high calling are stamped in capital letters, and his dark eyes sparkle with the fires of inspiration. He generally came alone; and while he leaned on the centre table in the great room, or slowly worked his rough way through the mass, he attracted every eye in the brilliant crowd, and seemed to me like a victorious Roman General, the principal figure in his own triumph. Perhaps no British Artist ever retired from an exhibition of his own works, with so much reason for unmixed satisfaction, or more genuine proofs of well deserved admiration from the public.'

There was no more sincere proof of admiration than Fawkes's dedication of the catalogue:

TO
J.M.W. TURNER ESQ
R.A.-P.P.

My Dear Sir,

THE unsought and spontaneous expression of the public opinion respecting my Collection of Water Colour Drawings, decidedly points out to whom this little Catalogue should be inscribed. To you, therefore, I dedicate it; first as an act of duty; and secondly, as an Offering of Friendship; for, be assured, I never can look at it without intensely feeling the delight I have experienced, during the greater part of my life, from the exercise of your talent and the pleasure of your society. That you may year after year reap an accession of fame and fortune, is the anxious wish of
Your sincere Friend

W.FAWKES.

London, June, 1819

What makes this exhibition particularly special is not simply that it was the first retrospective exhibition of Turner's watercolours, nor even that it was the collection of one man, but that every single picture was the product of a very special relationship between painter and patron. Fawkes would have been to most of the sites himself, and the two men could share their responses, memories, and associations. For most of Turner's traveller's tales in this period, it is possible that Fawkes was the only audience. When Turner went to Italy shortly after the Fawkes exhibition closed in 1819, he made thousands of sketches but there was no grand commission to fulfil, no series of engravings to produce, only a large tribute to Raphael for the walls of the Academy and a series of watercolours for Fawkes. Why then all these sketches? So that Turner could retrace his movements and recall every moment of the tour at will. Fawkes was the only one of Turner's patrons to show any interest in the sketches, however, and in order to cover the main sites of Turner's tour he bought a series of nine finished watercolours, four of Rome,

Frosty Morning *by Turner, 1812.*

two each of Naples and Venice, and another showing the artist's adventures on the return journey over Mt. Cenis in January 1820 when his coach capsized. He owned another of Turner's coaching scenes, one of the first, *Lancaster Sands*. Of all Turner's patrons, Fawkes took the keenest interest in his travels. Turner usually travelled alone, but the essence of moving experiences is that they must be shared, the knowledge they give communicated. Turner was a sort of professional Ancient Mariner with a heart burning to tell what it had learnt, and for twenty years Fawkes listened, the spellbound wedding-guest.

Turner's best pictures are often those illuminated by experience and whether or not the bracing airs of Farnley cured his 'nervous disorder' as recorded by Farington, that winter was brightened up by the *Frosty Morning* which he was painting for the exhibition in 1813. Turner said that he had sketched the scene while travelling by coach in Yorkshire, probably on the visit to Farnley in the late autumn of 1812. In the painting, a rising sun reveals a country road junction, frosted wheel ruts mark the passage of yesterday's traffic through the mud, and the frozen air, thickened under clear overnight skies, is thinning to show traces of blue through the mist. In the faint warmth and raking light the hoar frost glitters from every twig and leaf. The month is probably November, for the dried sticks of hedgerow plants are not yet broken down or rotted off by winter, and a cold cow still searches for food out in the field. It is perhaps nine o'clock in the morning and a group of figures have assembled. Two labourers have arrived with their cart and horses and have unloaded a wheelbarrow, a pick-axe and a spade. One of them, already warmed by the work, has cast off his cloak and is lifting the back from the cart so that they may begin to load it. Meanwhile a third man, evidently not a labourer (or he wears a good coat and long breeches and spats, and has the right to shoot game openly) stands lost in comtemplation of the work, with the sun warming his face. By his side a young girl wraps a still-warm hare around her shoulders, while a boy amuses himself by testing the ice on a large puddle in the hedge-bottom. Evidently the sportsman and the children have been waiting for some while, long enough for the girl to begin to shiver in the cold. What has brought the children out on a morning such as this? The answer has just rounded the corner in the distance, the morning coach. When it arrives, their wait will be over.

Similar carts appear in a number of drawings made at Farnley, and seem designed to carry heavy loads. One appears at the stone quarry on Otley Chevin, another by the east lodges in 1818. The cart in *Frosty Morning* is evidently being used to carry sand or gravel, which abounds in the Wharfe valley by Farnley, perhaps for use on pathways at the house. The figure in a green coat with a gun reoccurs throughout the Farnley drawings, shooting on Otley Chevin or on Beamsley Beacon, superintending the dead deer in the *Caley Hall* watercolour or, most prominently, in the foreground of *Shooting-Party on the Moors, 12 August,* next to the words 'W.FAWKES'. Other elements of the picture have long been recognised as having personal significance for Turner. His friend, H.S. Trimmer, reported that the artist had 'immortalised his old crop-ear in his "Frosty Morning",' drawing both horses from his own, and being particularly successful in catching the stiffness of the old model's legs. Trimmer also noticed that the girl 'reminded him of a young girl whom he occasionally saw at Turner's studio, Queen Anne Street, and whom, from her resemblance to Turner, he took to be a relation.' Turner himself said that 'he was travelling by coach in Yorkshire, and sketched it *en route*; and the coach is introduced in the picture.' Thus we know that the artist himself was on board the coach, and it seems likely that it is Fawkes at the roadside, with Hawkesworth and one of the girls, awaiting Turner's arrival from London. *Frosty Morning* was one of Turner's favourite pictures and it hung over the fireplace in his studio until his death, and a passage from Thomson's *Autumn* (just a few lines from the quotation that accompanied the picture at the Academy in 1813) might easily have summarised Turner's feelings for Farnley:

The happiest he who far from public rage
Deep in the vale, with a choice few retired,
Drinks the pure pleasures of the rural life.

(1236-9)

After Fawkes's death the whole direction of Turner's art changed. His art lost its sense of place. It gained in poetic feeling, mood, resonance, introspection and the truth of imagination, but sacrificed truth to place in the process. Turner could never bear to revisit Farnley, although he remained on close terms with the Fawkes family, for the rest of his life. It is almost as if he was unwilling to change in any way the memories of this happy time in his life. Ruskin said that 'of all his drawings those of the Yorkshire series have the most heart in them, the most unwearied, serious, finishing of truth.' It was on his friendship with Fawkes that this unique quality depended.

A GENERAL HISTORY OF THE COUNTY OF YORK

Thomas Dunham Whitaker.

On 15 May 1816 Farington reported in his Diary: 'Smirke told me that Turner had been engaged to make drawings for a History of Yorkshire: Longman & Co. to be the Publishers: and that he was to have 3000 guineas for his drawings. – ' Two days later at a dinner given by the Mayor and Lady Mayoress of London at the Mansion House, Farington had the opportunity to check the details with Turner himself: 'at 20 minutes past six we adjourned from the Drawing Room to dinner. – Turner told me that He had made an engagement to make 120 drawings views of various kinds in Yorkshire, – for a History of Yorkshire for which he was to have 3000 guineas. Many of the subjects required, He said, He had now in his possession. He proposed to set off very soon for Yorkshire to collect other subjects.'

This was the most valuable commission Turner had ever received, and one of the most ambitious projects being undertaken by any publisher at this time. According to the prospectus issued in 1816 it was intended to publish *A General History of the County of York* in seven folio volumes. The author was the best-known and most respected antiquarian topographer of the day, the Rev. Thomas Dunham Whitaker, LL.D., F.S.A., Vicar of Whalley and Rector of Heysham in Lancashire. The work was to be illustrated throughout with portraits, facsimiles, vignettes, woodcuts, and lithographs, a series of architectural subjects by John Buckler, and landscape views by the greatest landscape painter of the day, J.M.W. Turner RA. The illustrations were to be engraved by the most skilled craftsmen available, and subscribers would receive the work in parts, beginning with the sections dealing with the ancient district of Richmondshire, price per issue, two guineas on small paper, four guineas on large.

Thomas Dunham Whitaker was born at in Norfolk in 1759 the son a curate. The following year the family moved to Holme Hall in Lancashire, the ancestral seat between Todmorden and Burnley. The family had a lengthy pedigree of eminent scholars and churchmen, one of the most famous being the Rev. Dr. William Whitaker D.D. (1547-95), Regius Professor of Divinity at the University of Cambridge in 1579, appointed Chancellor of St. Paul's Cathederal by Queen Elizabeth I in 1580 and made master of St. John's College, Cambridge, in 1586. Thomas Dunham Whitaker embarked on his own academic career at the age of seven years when he was sent to study at Rochdale Grammar School under the Rev. John Shaw. In October 1775 he entered St. John's College to read Law, and graduated in November 1781 with the degree of Bachelor of Laws. His intention to enter the profession was frustrated by the death of his father in 1782 when he settled at the Holme and set about managing and improving the estates. Between 1784 and 1799 he planted no fewer than 422,000 trees, receiving in recognition the Gold Medal of the Royal Society of Arts for the greatest number of larch trees planted in one year. In 1785 he entered Holy Orders, and set about rebuilding the chapel at the Holme, an ancient chantry chapel of Whalley Abbey which had come into the possession of the family in the reign of Elizabeth I. He spent £470 on a new Georgian building with a handsome bell-turret and octagonal cupola, and completed the interior with seventeenth-century carved panelling and church furniture. In 1797 he was licensed to the perpetual curacy of Holme on his own nomination.

The association of the family with Whalley Abbey and the surrounding area prompted Whitaker's first major piece of historical research, *The History of the Original Parish of Whalley and the Honour of Clitheroe, in the Counties of York and Lancaster. To which is subjoined An Account of the Parish of Cartmell*, published, probably at the expense of the author and his patrons, in Blackburn in 1801. The project was very much in the eighteenth-century vogue for parish and county history, when no private library was complete without its large calf-bound, gilt-tooled volumes of local antiquarian topography, and the reviewers acclaimed it as setting new standards of scholarship. In 1806, with the first edition sold out a revised edition was printed in London by J. Nichols & Son, and sold through Payne, White &c and Edwards of Halifax. On 16 June 1810 Whitaker was writing to the printer to complain that 'The remaining copies of the History of Whalley, which were disposed of by me to Mr Edwards at £1.10s each have been nearly sold by him at 7 or 8 guineas per copy.' Whitaker's books were sought after, and both the *Whalley* and his second history, that of *Craven*, published in 1805, ran to second editions quite quickly. *Whalley* in 1806, *Craven* in 1812, and in November 1813 Whitaker wrote to Nichols to say, 'I am now at leisure to attend to another Edition of the History of Whalley, and sincerely wish that Mr Edwards would authorise you to set about it.'

Thomas Edwards of Halifax was one member of a family of bookbinders, booksellers and publishers, founded by his father William, and carried on by his three brothers, James, John and Richard. John and James opened Edwards and Sons in Pall Mall while Richard had a bookshop at 142 Bond Street and is notable for commissioning illustrations to an edition of Young's *Night Thoughts* from William Blake. Thomas, meanwhile, kept up the business in Halifax, which besides selling books and binding them traded in a whole range of picturesque commodities such as 'True Daffy's Elixir', 'Dr Walker's Jesuit Drops', 'Lignum Lotion' and 'Dr Balimar's Golden Spirit of Scurvy Grass'. Thomas is credited with having first introduced Turner to Whitaker, and it has been suggested that it may have been through the Edwards family that Turner first came to the notice of Walter Fawkes. James Edwards had a large house in London which 'soon became the resort of the gay morning loungers of both sexes. At the same time also invitation was held out to students and scholars, and persons of real taste, for the opportunity of seeing and examining the most curious and rare books, manuscripts and missals', and it is possible that Turner, though hardly a 'gay morning lounger', may have been a visitor at some stage. The Edwards were certainly well-known at Farnley. The Library contains a number of books bought from or bound by Edwards of Halifax, including a number with 'fore-edge' paintings, a technique reputedly invented by William Edwards. In 1805 one of the Edwards was at the centre of a piece of jollity which probably typifies the sort of society that Turner enjoyed on his Yorkshire holidays. 'You cannot think', wrote Lady Elizabeth Spencer Stanhope, 'how charmed I was with Mr Fawkes when we were at Farnley; he was so full of information and talent. He told us two stories which pleased me so much that I will endeavour to relate them—both facts...You have doubtless heard of Edwards, the great bookseller. He has quitted his shop in Town, and gone to reside at his native place, Halifax. He is a great miser, but being a man of talent often visits Mr Fawkes. One day he arrived upon such a miserable hired horse that they resolved to play him a trick. Accordingly, after dinner the Steward came in, with a solemn face, stating that instead of killing a horse that was meant for the dogs they had shot Mr Edwards's, that it was half-eat before they found out the mistake. Edwards was in a dreadful pucker; but at last, having condoled with him, they told him that the only difference between his deceased horse and one of Mr Fawkes's which they had meant to kill was that Mr Fawkes's horse had not a white spot on his forehead, and his legs were not white, but that by painting them it would look just the same, and that the people at the livery stable would never find out the mistake. Edwards was highly delighted with this plan, and, would you believe it, he was mean enough to hope by this means to cheat the man. You may picture what fun it was to Mr Fawkes and his servants to see him ride home on his OWN hired horse all bedaubed with paint, after which he wrote triumphantly. "The man at the Livery Stables has never found out the trick WE have put on him!" How they will all quiz him when finally they tell him the truth!'

This sort of outlook seems to have characterised Thomas Edwards's dealings with Whitaker, for it was only after the antiquary's books were already in print and successful that he risked any of his own money on them, publishing the second edition of the *Craven* in 1812 and the third edition of the *Whalley* in 1818. Whitaker, nevertheless, seems to have admired the family enough to incorporate their coat of arms in stained glass at Whalley church, and Thomas Edwards remained on good enough terms with Walter Fawkes for the squire of Farnley to sponsor the bookseller's son at his christening on 9 July 1816, his name bearing testimony to their association, Walter Fawkes Edwards.

Whitaker was remarkably industrious. Besides writing and revising the histories of Whalley and Craven he completed his Doctorate of Laws at St. John's College in 1801, became Vicar of Whalley in 1809, Rector of Heysham in 1813, and acted as Justice of the Peace in both Lancashire and Yorkshire. In 1812 he seems to have been feeling the strain for he closed the revised *History of Craven* with the words: 'Time has been when such a scene [as Fountain's Abbey] might have inspired and dictated another work. But the recollection of increasing years [he was only 53] and declining health, together with the demands of duty in a most serious and important charge, checks at once the unseasonable impulse, and compels him to resign a History of Richmondshire (*footnote:* Which has been suggested to the Author) to some younger and more vigorous antiquary...'

Whitaker's age, declining health or intended retirement was not reflected in his output. Sometime before 1810 he completed *An Account in Latin of John Home's 'History of the Rebellion of 1745'*, and in 1810 Edwards published *The Life and Original Correspondence of Sir George Radcliffe LL.D, the friend of the Earl of Stafford.* In 1812 he published *The Sermons of Dr Edwin Sandys, formerly Archbishop of York, with a Life of the Author,* in 1813 *The Vision of William Concerning Piers Ploughman*, and *Pierce the Ploughman's Crede, edited from the edition of 1553*. This was by no means all. He decided to edit a new edition of Ralph Thoresby's *Ducatus Leodiensis* (1712) and to write an accompanying volume himself: *Loidis and Elmete, or An Attempt to Illustrate the Districts described in those words by Bede and Supposed to embrace the Lower Portions of Aredale and Wharfedale, together with the valley of the Calder in the County of York*, a folio of over 400 pages. Thoresby's *Ducatus* was published by Longmans in 1816 and *Loidis and Elmete* by Hurst, Robinson & Co in the same year, but the two publishers worked in partnership and the volumes formed a pair. Longman's in fact paid for many of the illustrations for the *Loidis*, but the title that they gave to the work in their ledgers, after 10 July 1815, '*Whitaker's Yorkshire*' shows that Whitaker's grandest project of all was by that time underway. On the same day Longman's and Hurst Robinson bought the rights to the *Craven* from Edwards of Halifax, and with the *History of Richmondshire* that Whitaker mentioned at the end of the *Craven*, the publishers had rights on about half of the grand *General History of the County of York* they were building up. Whitaker's ambitions were not prepared to rest on so little, however. He also projected a history of Lonsdale (published with the *Richmondshire*), new editions of John Whitaker's *History of Manchester*, Horsley's *Britannia Romana* and Tim Bobbin's *Lancashire Dialect*, quite apart from a new and complete history of the Roman Empire. In his spare time he published ten sermons, one political speech, and contributed twenty-eight articles to the *Quarterly Review* between 1809 and 1818.

The *General History of the County of York* was an enormous undertaking. Apart from the *Craven* (2 Vols.) *Richmondshire* and *Lonsdale* (2 Vols.), *Ducatus* and *Loidis and Elmete* (2 Vols.) there would have been at least as many volumes more to deal with other parts of the county: lower Swaledale, Nidderdale, York, most of the North Riding, all of the East Riding, and the whole of the district around Sheffield known as Hallamshire. Whitaker was contracted for £1 per page, an agreement which, it is said, severely compromised his scholarly standards, and various artists were engaged, including John Buckler to take the architectural subjects and Turner the landscape. The decision to employ Turner cannot have been taken lightly, as Longmans had discovered already that he was not cheap, having been charged 25 guineas merely for the right to engrave an earlier watercolour, *Harewood House from the South West* for the *Loidis and Elmete*. It is said that Turner originally asked 40 guineas per picture, but was beaten down to 25 guineas, and even then returned to say that he had forgotten to add in the costs of the Bristol boards and colours that he would have to use. Even at the reduced sum Longmans had committed themselves very heavily, 3,000 guineas for the 120 watercolours alone, and at least another 9,600 guineas for their engraving at an average of 80 guineas per plate. Thus the Turner illustrations alone were likely to cost in the region of 12,600 guineas and this was quite apart from the costs of the rest of the book, the other artists and engravers, the author's fees, not to mention the costs of actual publication, paper, printing, binding, advertising, distribution, wages, overheads, and, forlorn hope it must have seemed, profit.

Longman's soon realised the possible consequences of their rashness, and on 20 February 1818, before a single issue had been published, they were already seeking ways of recouping their investment:

Dear Sir,
Have you any one in view as likely to purchase Turners view[s] of Yorkshire, as a gentleman has made applications to us respecting them, & we have offered them to him at prime cost, & to allow him £10 for every subject we engrave, but he will not take them on these terms; we therefore think of offering them to him at £5 each below cost, What say you to this? The docter [sic] is in town & I had a long interview with him to day. He is very anxious to have an answer whether we will proceed with the remainder of the Counties but we decline any answer on that head till we have tried the Richmondshire. He says that the remainder of the counties will not exceed in quanterty [sic] the Craven, Richmondshire, Linsdale [i.e. Lonsdale] and the additions [i.e. editions] of the Leeds. As we shall not have one of Turners subjects done before April we positively decline putting a sheet to press till them [i.e. then] or in fact till we have a finished plate. The Docter [sic] is very dry with us for being so very strict with him

Yours very truly

P N Row Feb 20 1818 *(Owen Rees)*
Mr O J Robinson
Booksr.
Leeds

It seems from this that Longmans had already decided that they might not be engraving all 120 of Turner's watercolours. The twenty watercolours they bought are recorded in their ledgers for 12 April 1817, 'Turner for 12 drawings of Richmond & district 315£ [i.e. 25 gns each]', and 31 December 1818, 'J.M.W. Turner for 8 drawings 25 Gns 210£-'. By 22 February 1819, however, it must have become quite obvious that there was no point in even buying the 120 watercolours from Turner, for on that day Longmans paid 13s. 4d. 'Law expenses in consulting Sharon Turner [no relation] respecting J M W Turners Agreement'. Since no further payments to the artist appear under the account for *Whitaker's Yorkshire* it seems that the lawyer succeeded in finding Longmans a convenient escape clause.

Such caution was sensible. Subscribers were proving difficult to find, perhaps not surprisingly in view of the price (2 guineas per part on small paper and four guineas on large) and the apparently never-ending nature of the commitment. Longmans printed 125 large and 550 small copies of the first part, but despite the efforts of Edwards of Halifax who delivered it personally, at least to Miss Lister of Shibden Hall, who remembered that he 'brought the first part of Dr Whitaker's Yorkshire—the history of that division called Richmondshire' on 22 April 1819, the subscription failed to hold up. Longmans in fact sold only 85 large copies and 310 small and were forced to cut the numbers of small copies printed to 400 for subsequent parts. Despite further advertising the sales settled down to between 71 and 77 large copies and 241-273 small, and Longman's attempted to stall publication for as long as they could. Part 3, which was supposed to appear in February 1820, according to a slip included in Part 2, did not actually appear until September, and by October 1821, five years after the prospectus was issued and the first subscription received, they were only up to part five.

Lack of subscribers was not the only problem the projects faced. In 1820 Whitaker suffered a paralysis, followed by asthma and then dropsy. He died at Blackburn Vicarage on 18 December 1821 and was buried at Holme. He had prepared *Richmondshire* and *Lonsdale* for the press, together with a few pages dealing with Rievaulx Abbey. The remaining parts were issued in quick succession, Parts 6 and 7 in November and December 1821, and the remaining parts to Part 12, which contained title pages, labels, an index, and directions to the binder, was issued in June 1823.

Between July 1815 and September 1823 Longmans spent £9,627 0s.1d.on the project and recouped only £7,791 10s.6d. from sales. After they sold six of Turner's watercolours themselves, and the remaining fourteen to Hurst, Robinson & Co. at cost, the books showed a loss of £1,193 18s.5d., which was shared 75%/25% between themselves and Hurst, Robinson. After the remaining stock, copper plates and Buckler's drawings were sold to Robinson and Hernaman in November for £1,500, and some few outstanding debts were settled the partners had £1,433 3s.6d. to share between them. Set against the loss shown by the books earlier, Longmans could declare a final profit on the project as a whole of £251 11s.3½d.

The fact that Longmans declined to put even a single sheet of Whitaker's text to the press before seeing the first finished Turner engraving indicates the importance that the publishers attached to the illustrations. They were, in fact the principal attraction of the book, for while in 1801 Whitaker's elaborate prose and elegant history might have been saleable, by 1816 it must have seemed distinctly old-fashioned. The taste in topography was for guidebooks with vivid descriptions, pictures and poetry, an emotional rather than a cerebral response to place. The armchair tourist wanted to be moved and inspired, above all to feel that he was actually there, responding powerfully and positively. Whitaker's history was hardly the stuff of which experience such as this was made, but Turner's visions were the essence, pure and undiluted, particularly as he took so much care to ensure that the engravings transmitted his ideas exactly. This is not to say that Whitaker's text is totally without interest, far from it, but the only subsequent editions of the *Richmondshire* were *A Series of Views of the most Picturesque Scenes in Richmondshire from drawings by J.M.W. Turner, Esq R.A. and John Buckler, Esq, F.S.A., in thirty-two plates, Executed in the best style of Art by the most eminent engravers, with Descriptions by the Rev. Thomas Dunham Whitaker, LL.D. Extracted from his 'History of Richmondshire'*, published by Nichols in 1843, where the badly-worn plates were published with odd bits of Whitaker's text used merely as commentary, and *Richmondshire Illustrated by Twenty Line Engravings after drawings by J.M.W. Turner, R.A. with Descriptions by Mrs Alfred Hunt, and an introduction by Marcus B. Huish*, issued in 1891 with the plates reworked, and Whitaker's text banished altogether.

It is said that Longmans commissioned a committee of four gentlemen, the Rev. James Raine of Crook Hall, Durham, Dr William Turner (no relation), Mr William Whitaker, and Canon Tate, the headmaster of Richmond Grammar School, to select the viewpoints for Turner, but despite this apparent cramping of the artist's freedom of choice, his watercolours were some of the most successful he ever produced. It was a particularly fortunate coincidence that the area of Yorkshire was also Turner's favourite part of the world, and it must have been particularly galling to the artist when the opportunity to pay tribute to it in so many pictures was suddenly strangled when Longman's cancelled their agreement. On 3 June 1819 Turner described 'Longman's conduct...as bad as could be' and he seems to have been left with a number of finished and unfinished watercolours left on his hands. Perhaps even more frustratingly, he was left with an unrivalled collection of sketches, and memories of some of the finest scenery in the country and no opportunity to make use of them. He found an opportunity to use some of the subjects in the *Picturesque Views in England and Wales* series published from 1827, and it is significant that of the first nine plates issued, with the whole of England and Wales to choose from, six were north of England subjects sketched in 1816, and a further three followed within the following two years. These subjects, together with other finished works based on sketches made in 1816, and originally intended for the *County of York* but never engraved, can give only an approximate idea of what the full complement of 120 subjects would have been like. On the evidence of the twenty that were actually published in the *History of Richmondshire*, Ruskin thought the Yorkshire drawings one of the culminating points of Turner's career. They are the most affirmative, affectionate, personally vivid, of all his watercolours, symphonies of the sky and the weather, fresh, and alive. The collection of the surviving pictures here published gives an indication of what might have been if the economics of the time had not prevailed.

THE SKETCHBOOKS AND THE TOUR

Turner dedicated himself to exploring the more rewarding possibilities of life. He climbed among snow-capped peaks and glaciers, watched the sea from barques and packet-boats, observed storms and showers, gales and breezes, lightning and stars, dawns and sunsets, the particular steeliness of a cloud, or the light sparkling on a mountain stream, with a strength and depth of feeling uncommon in its intensity and constancy. It is not so much Turner's subject-matter which is extraordinary as the importance he attached to it. Few care for such things so much, or derive more satisfaction from their contemplation.

The collection of sketchbooks that Turner left to the nation when he died is a remarkable record of a life of travel, an odd-bin of fish-hooks, fish-wives, recipes, cures, songs, poems, boats, coaches, birds, fish, cows, horses, plants, oil cans, baskets, quaysides, roadsides, bonnets, bodices and bodies, foreign words and phrases, directions, addresses, sums and lists of bank-notes, besides being a detailed and beautiful record of the landscape and architecture of England, Scotland, Wales, France, Belgium, Holland, Germany, Austria, Switzerland and Italy as it was during the sixty years before 1851.

Turner's finished pictures are the considered reports of his exploration of landscape and imagination, but this does not mean that the sketches can be discounted as so many rough jottings, worth considering only for the light they shed on the finished works. Turner's sketches were created at the point of contact between artist and reality, and no-one valued this contact more than he did. His sketches may lack, in comparison with others, expressionistic calligraphy, although some are as excited and wild as can be, they may lack self-conscious style and flourishes, tone and 'colour' of pencil, but they have a freshness of personality, which makes the artist seem closer in his sketches than in any other of his works. To leaf through one of Turner's sketchbooks is to share with him those experiences that constitute some of the most vivid moments of his life. Through Turner's sketches we can see through his eyes; trace, select, compose and check off what every mark stands for in fact. To compare the real landscape with what Turner sketched offers a remarkable insight into the workings of his mind, and a journey in Turner's footsteps becomes as much a journey through his imagination as a journey through the landscape that inspired it.

Turner thought in pictures more articulately than he did in words, kept no journals, wrote sometimes incomprehensible letters, and, since he usually travelled alone, offered few opportunities for others to record his activities on the road. His sketchbooks, however, are perhaps the most vivid journals of any traveller. He sketched constantly, often linking one sketch to another by looking from one viewpoint to another, surveying his route both forward and back. From early in his career many of his finished pictures seem to recall the exact time of day, weather conditions and activities that he had witnessed when making his sketch. By the time he arrived in the north of England in 1816 he had developed his sketching practice to a peak of economy and precision. The pressure of the pencil on the side of a tree trunk could indicate the direction of the light; a few lines of cloud, a reflection or a weather-vane, the direction of the wind. Sometimes he used written notes, 'sky light', 'Refn v. dark' to remind him of some particularly striking effect, and, having stared at the subject for perhaps an hour while engraving it on his memory with his pencil-point, he could recall and reconstruct the whole event, often months or several years afterwards. It is impossible to understand Turner's landscapes without knowing the landscape they record. From the various pieces of surviving documentation — a few letters, Mrs Fawkes's Diary, Turner's sketchbooks and the finished watercolours—it is possible to reconstruct the exact itinerary of his first tour through the north of England in 1816, and build up a vivid picture of the artist at work in one of his favourite landscapes.

The primary sources of documentation for this tour are sketchbooks preserved in Turner's bequest to the nation. There are three of these, labelled by Turner 'Yorkshire' and numbered '2', '4' and '5' (TB CXLV, CXLVII, CXLVIII). From these an itinerary can be identified from Skipton, through North Lancashire, Gordale, Swaledale, Wensleydale, Teesdale, Westmorland, and Lonsdale back to Skipton. There are two more sketchbooks which relate to a second tour in 1816 through Central Yorkshire via York, Ripon, Middleham, Richmond and Knaresborough, which can also be connected with Whitaker's *County of York* (TB CXLIV, CXLVI), although they do not relate to the twenty watercolours supplied to Longmans before they cancelled the contract, and therefore are not included here.

Considerable care is required in the interpretation of these sketchbooks. Even after individual subjects have been identified, formidable problems remain in establishing the chronological sequence in which the sketches were made. These problems are further complicated by the fact that some of these sketchbooks were broken up during Turner's lifetime, others while they were in the Turner Bequest, with in some cases no surviving record of the original order of the pages. Some are therefore now bound with their pages in the wrong order, some completely arbitrarily. To compound the problem, Turner occasionally entered sketches out of sequence, though he was usually systematic, working from front cover to back and any departure from the normal pattern can usually be detected and explained. Turner occasionally used sketchbooks on separate occasions, sometimes several years apart, but this is not usually such a cause for despair as it might seem. These problems, however, together with the sheer weight of numbers, have meant that most writers on Turner have tended to avoid his sketches, and the great wealth of information that they reveal about the man and his work. This book is an attempt to see just how much detail the sketchbooks can be made to yield when subjected to as close an analysis as possible.

A pocket-book bound in marbled boards, with brown leather spine and corners, inscribed 'Yorkshire 2' on the back cover (TB CXLV), provides the itinerary of the tour, for despite the fact that the covers had been broken off by 1909, the 187 pages appear to have survived stitched together in their original order. We know from Mrs Fawkes's diary that Turner started from Farnley on 17 July and travelled to Skipton, thence to Browsholme Hall, the Trough of Bowland, Malham and Gordale, and exactly this itinerary is to be found in this book. Unfortunately the sketchbook contains sketches of Skipton at both ends, and completely ignoring the main piece of evidence, which is the bookseller's label stuck inside the front cover, the executors decided for some reason to number this book from the back. The page numbers are stamped indelibly on each page. To facilitate easy location of individual drawings these numbers are retained here but in the catalogue which appears below the numbering appears reversed. Turner bought the sketchbook at 'Mills & Son, Booksellers, Stationers & Binders, No. 368 Oxford Street, near the Pantheon' according to the label, which itself is an object of some historical interest. The price was 3s.6d. according to a note pencilled inside the back cover. This particular book was more a pocket-book than a sketchbook, Turner always seems to have carried one of this size stuffed in his waistcoat pocket, and a very grubby pocket it was, to judge by the dirt that has accumulated inside the covers. Nevertheless the book is a lively, day-to-day record book, full of quick notes, jottings, scribbles of virtually everything that required less than patient study, and it remains the basis from which the whole tour can be reconstructed.

The second sketchbook of the group (TB CXLVII) is one of the standard, medium-sized landscape-format sketchbooks, each measuring about 5 x 8 in, which Turner used throughout his career. This particular example is bound in mottled boards with red leather spine, cloth and corners, inscribed on the back, on the spine-cloth 'Yorkshire 4'. It would have been particularly attractive to Turner, for from the price marked inside the cover, it had been reduced from 4s. to 3s.. It was broken up by Ruskin for distribution but, fortunately, the executors had already numbered the individual pages and it was possible to rebind the book with the original sequence, even if many of the pages had been badly discoloured by exhibition in too strong a light. Turner used this size of sketchbook for subjects that required some careful study, and many of his finished compositions were drawn from it.

The final member of the group is a sketchbook of 42 pages measuring approximately 7 x 10 in, bound in reddish board with black leather spine and corners, inscribed 'Yorkshire 5' on the back cover (TB CXLVIII). This was reserved for the best subjects, those requiring a large format and a particularly detailed treatment, subjects which were often decided upon only after a series of exploratory sketches in the smaller books. The pages were again distributed for exhibition by Ruskin, except on this occasion not only were many of the leaves damaged and discoloured, but to make matters worse, no record was kept of their original order, nor, apparently, was any explanation left as to what condition the book was in before distribution. Finberg found it 'impossible to reconstitute the book with any pretensions to accuracy' and the order in which he listed the leaves in the inventory was largely fortuitous. Since then the book has been rebound, so that the present order of the pages no longer even follows that of the *Inventory*. On the basis of new identifications of sketches it is now possible to offer a more rational ordering for the book, following the line of the known itinerary, and allowing for any obvious clues given by the book itself, such as drawings continued across pages and marks duplicated on fronts and backs of different sheets. It seems in this case that the right-handed Turner found it easier to start at the back of the book, and draw mostly from the left-hand page to the right. This would have had a number of practical benefits such as keeping the large pages under control in a wind, and providing him with something to rest his hand on when drawing on the left-hand page, where most of the detail is confined in two-page panoramas. The catalogue of this sketchbook below presents the drawings in the order they were made, as a proposal for the order in which they ought to be rebound, starting at the back cover.

Having identified most of the subjects of the sketches, many for the first time, it has proved possible to reconstruct the probable daily itinerary of the artist, taking into account the various secure parts of the documentation—Mrs Fawkes's Diary and a letter written at Richmond on 31 July—and times of day indicated by the light in various sketches and the finished watercolours. The locations of overnight stops after Malham, except for Richmond, are conjectural, and though most seem fairly certain from the evidence, some, e.g. that at Staveley, are merely likely. On average, it appears that Turner covered about 25 miles per day and made about the same number of sketches, though the exact figure varies, undoubtedly depending on the weather and road conditions, and the requirement to make sketches or distance.

It is often possible to be quite precise about what Turner would have known of the various places he visited. We know, for example, that he subscribed to Edward Dayes's *Works* in 1805, which contained an account of Dayes's excursion to Yorkshire in 1803, covering many of the places visited by Turner in 1816. On that basis alone, it would seem very likely that Turner stayed in the *King's Arms* at Askrigg, for Dayes recommends it by name. We may also be sure that Turner read Whitaker's already published *Craven* (second edition 1812) for many of the drawings he had to make, such as Kilnsey, Gordale, Malham, Skipton, were intended to illustrate that text when it was published in series with the other parts of the *County of York*. For the rest we may only speculate, and bear in mind that he had a reputation for being well-informed about his subjects. For navigation it seems probable that he would have used an up-to-date edition of Cary's *Roads*, or something similar, and an up-to-date map, for how else could he have known, for example, which mountain was Helvellyn when he was at the top of High Cup Nick.

One of the most exciting aspects of following in Turner's footsteps, searching for the views that he drew, was the moment when the subject of a sketch could be confirmed by standing on the exact spot from which it was made, and being able to understand for the first time exactly what the pencil marks mean. There were a number of surprises. At Askrigg, for example, there is a water trough which only became visible in the sketch after actually seeing it. One of the most thought-provoking aspects of comparing the sketches to the landscape, however, came in attempting to photograph the sites today. Turner's sketches are sometimes quite unlike the photographs of exactly the same scene, yet it does not follow that the sketches are unlike the place. In fact the reverse is usually true. Turner's sketches are much more like the places than the photographs. The impression that one forms in the mind of a site is a cumulative one, the sum total of one's knowledge of the place, built up by walking about it, and taking into account one's particular interest in the light on the water, or the rocks, or the trees, or the place one ate one's sandwiches, or dived from the moss-covered rocks for a swim. A camera cannot discriminate, nor can it in any way reproduce the way in which the eye can seize upon and selectively pick out details. All this an artist can do, every element of the scene is under his control. So while, in relation to a photograph, Turner might exaggerate the profile of a hill, or enlarge the background in relation to the foreground, or emphasise a building or a road, these are the same activities that the eye and mind engage in. It becomes unsatisfactory to say that simply because a photograph is mechanical it is more true, for the only standard of truth can be the way that a place is perceived by a living human mind. Turner's sketches in the end seem much more like the places than the photographs.

The most important aspect, however, of following in Turner's footsteps is not the landscape but Turner's response to it. However varied the sights and weather, Turner is constantly moved by them. Though many now have the ability to enjoy the landscapes of northern England, and agree that they are among the world's finest, this has not always been the case. Though many today will feel some excitement at visiting the sites enjoyed by Turner, few will feel with his care, inspiration, or intensity. Still fewer will realise that they perhaps owe their response to Turner in the first place, for the engravings of his Yorkshire watercolours were some of the first pictures to mould the taste of the public in its appreciation of wild landscape.

'Yorkshire 2' Sketchbook

TB CXLV, 1816

Small pocket-book, bound in marbled boards with brown leather spine and corners. Inscr. on back cover, 'Yorkshire 2'.

187 leaves, mostly drawn on both sides, 152 x 95 mm. Watermarked: 'I & E Smith 1812'.

This sketchbook covers the whole itinerary of Turner's *Richmondshire* tour of 1816 and includes notes of his expenses from London to Leeds (f.186), and of bills cashed on the tour (f.186a).

Unfortunately Turner's executors numbered the pages back to front and this sequence was followed by Finberg. The following catalogue reverses the page numbering so that the correct itinerary can be followed.

Inside cover: Three slight sketches: 'Crook of Lune Quarry'; 'Inglboro & Heysham'; and a range of hills inscr. 'L Dull ...'(?). Plus the trade label of 'Mills & Son, Booksellers, Stationers & Binders, No. 368 Oxford Street, near the Pantheon. Stationary Wares Wholesale & Retail on low terms; for ready Money. Account Books bound & ruled in an improved manner. No Charge for Ruling. The greatest variety of Bath, Note & Letter Papers, so much esteemed for their cheapness & good qualities. Engraving & Printing.'

187 Now bound between ff.134a & 135.

186a A note of bills taken on the tour, their dates and values, and places of encashment:

''' ' =	2022	25 May	1816	20
	2021			20
	8376	8 June	1816	10
	8375			10
	6890	17 May	1816	10
	6890	17 May	1816	5
	7923	17 May	Greta Bridge	5
	16135	11 May		5
	[cf TB CXLIV 105]			
	18032	11 May		5
	1718	6 April	Lancaster	5
	14971	8 May	Chapman	10
	2			10
	34788	13 May	Sup at Askrigg	1
	34789	Richmond		1
	17917	13 April	Chapman	2
	45520	11 April	Chapman	1''

186. A note of expenses on the road to London to Leeds:

''Porterage	2	8
Fare to Leeds	2 2	
1 Coachman	1	
Dinner at Eaton	5	6*
2 Coachman —Scrooby —	1	6
3 Ditto	1	
Breakfast Doncaster	2	3
Brandy & Water Grantham	1	6
4 Coachman and Guard	4	6
	3 2 11'' †	

*[i.e. Eaton Socon, near St. Neots, Hunts.]

†[i.e. £3.1.11]

185a. Road beside a river with two one-arched bridges, probably the canal near Skipton.

185 Skipton Castle: detail of the roofline, cf. 184a, top right.

184a. Skipton Castle: North front from Eller Beck. cf. 183a, 181a.

184-183a Skipton Castle from Eller Beck, continued to right above, cf. 184a, 181a **Ill.7.**

183-182a Skipton Castle and church from the north west, with the 'water' of Eller Beck below.

182-181a Skipton Castle: North front and Eller Beck, in two parts, cf.184a, 183a.

181 Blank

180a Skipton Castle and church from the north west, a distant view, cf.183-182a.

180 Blank

179a Two-arched bridge, with distant hills. Probably between Skipton and Clitheroe.

179-178a A two-part panorama of the Ribble valley from Great Mitton: the Great Mitton church and bridge, the 'River' Ribble, and a detail of the church, above, and Mitton Hall, a view of Clitheroe Castle and Pendle Hill below, **Ill.4.**

178 A 16th(?)-century house in the Great Mitton/Browsholme area. Inscr: 'Mr. Cross Ri[-?]'.

(178-)177a Distant views of the hills of 'Bolun' (i.e. Bowland); 'L. ridge' (i.e. Longridge; and around 'Ribchester').

177. As 176a: a more distant view.

176a. A view from high ground: Longridge?

176 As 175a: a more distant view.

175a. A prospect of the sea: Morecambe Bay from Longridge?

175. 'Bolland' [i.e. Bowland]' from 'Longridge', two drawings.

174a. Near the Trough of Bowland?

174. The Trough of Bowland, inscr. (left) 'G Brow'; (right) 'Road'.

173a Two views of the Trough of Bowland, with colour notes &c: 'Br G'; 'G'; 'R'(oad?)

173 Blank

172a. Trough of Bowland: Langden Beck, looking towards Hodder Bank Fell.?

172 Hareden, near the Trough of Bowland, cf. TB CXLVIII - 2a.

171a. Clitheroe Castle and town.

171. 'Skipton' Castle from the north, cf.170. (out of sequence). This and f.170 taken from the east bank of Eller Beck, and therefore probably made on return journey.

170a. Sawley Abbey on the Ribble cf.169a.

170. Skipton Castle from the north, a nearer view, cf.171, 27a ff.

169a. Sawley abbey and bridge, cf. 170a, & TB CXLVIII 21a-22.

169-168a. Gordale Scar, inscr: 'Gill'.

168-167a. Gordale Scar, inscr: 'Grass'; 'G'; continued on f.116a, **Ill.13.**

167. Blank

166a. Gordale Scar: continuation of 168-167a. to right. **Ill.13.**

166. Blank.

165a. Malham village with Cove beyond, inscr: (right) 'Pigs'; 'Poultry'(?)

65-164a. Blank.

164-163a. Entrance to Gordale, with Janet's Foss lower right **Ill.15.**

163. Entrance to Gordale Scar.

162a. Blank.

162-161a. Gordale Scar, cf.TB CLIV - O **Ill.6.**

161-160a Gordale Scar, the waterfall, cf. TB CXLVIII 30a. **Ill.17.**

160 Blank

159a Malham Tarn and Tarn House, from near Water Sinks, inscr: 'water'.

159-158a Four sketches:
i. Tarn House
ii. Malham Tarn and Tarn House from near Tarn Foot.
iii. Malham Tarn from the West
iv. Limestone valley, probably between Malham Tarn and Kettlewell.

158-157a The entrance to Dow Cave, near Kettlewell, cf. 155a, & TB CXLVII 1,2.

157 Interior of (Dow?) Cave, inscr: 'L.D.'

156a As 157, a quick sketch.

156 Interior of (Dow?) Cave, looking back towards the entrance.

155a 'Dow' Cave

155 The same(?) looking down.

154a A figure in limestone country

154 Interior of a cave, cf. 158-155

153a Three sketches:
i. Kilnsey Crag and Wharfedale from the north.
ii. Kilnsey Crag from the south, cf. 152, 151a, TB CXLVIII 18a.
iii. Kilnsey Crag from the north.

153 Kilnsey Crag and Conistone Bridge, from Conistone, cf.TB CXLVIII 19a-20

152a 'Peneghent' (i.e. Buckden Pike from Kilnsey).

152 Kilnsey village and crag from the south, cf. 153a(ii), 151a,TB CXLVIII 18a.

151a Kilnsey Crag from south, Inscr: Illegible cf.153a(ii), 152, TB CXLVIII 18a.

151 Blank.

150a Wharfedale and Kilnsey Crag from above Kettlewell.

150 Blank

149a Hubberholme Bridge and church, upper Wharfedale.

149 Blank

148a 'Craig', i.e. Cray, upper Wharfedale, the waterfall, inscr: 'Rock'; 'Grass'.

148 Blank

147a Semer Water from the east.

147 View near Semer Water (?).

146a Semer Water from the noth, cf.TB CXLVII 3a-4. Inscr: 'Simm[er Lake]'.

146-145a Mill Gill Falls, near Askrigg, cf.TB CXLVIII 17a-18

145 Blank

144a Askrigg village and church, with a view of Semer Water, cf. 143a. Inscr: 'Sheep'.**Ill.29.**

144 Blank

143a Askrigg and Wensleydale, with a view of Semer Water, a higher viewpoint that 144a. Inscr: 'Addleborough'.

143-142a 'Colton Hall Fall', i.e. Colby Fall, near Askrigg.

142-141a As 143-142a, see from the left. Inscr: 'L Lime'.

141 'Askrigg' from the river 'Ure', looking north.

140a 'Ure Bridge', i.e. Yorebridge, from the east.

140 'Whernside' from the south, looking over 'Chapel Vale' i.e. Chapel le Dale (with 139 out of sequence, see 39).

139a 'Askrigg' (altered from 'Grinton'), from the north-east. Inscr: 'Ure', 'Grass'.

139 Ingleborough from near Ingleton (out of sequence).

138a Waterfall at West 'Burton', cf. TB CXLVIII 9

138-137a Mill and falls at West Burton. Inscr: 'Elder' (?).

137 Blank

136a Bishopdale and Wensleydale from above West 'Burton.'

136 Blank

135a Aysgarth, middle falls, cf.TB CXLVII 13,14,15

135 Wensleydale, looking east from near Aysgarth, cf. 187, TB CXLVII 12,16

187 (Now bound here). As 135; a more distant view

187a Blank : a piece torn off

134a Bolton Castle from near Aysgarth, cf.TB CXLVII 16

134 Bear Park, Aysgarth, from the east.

133a Aysgarth with Addlebrough beyond, the river 'Ure' in the foreground; continuing 134 to the left. Cf. 129a for a more distant view.

133 Blank

132a Aysgarth bridge, mill and church, looking down the upper falls.

132 Blank

131a Aysgarth bridge, mill and church from downstream, cf. TB CXLVII 13

131 Aysgarth upper falls from the bridge

130a Three sketches:
i. Near Aysgarth,
ii. Wensleydale from Aysgarth, with Bolton Castle
iii. As ii, continuing to the right.

130 Blank

129a Aysgarth and Wensleydale from the east, Addlebrough in the distance, cf. 133a.

129 Blank

128a Aysgarth and Wensleydale from the west, Bolton Castle in the distance, cf.TB CXLVII 16. Inscr: 'Cattle'.

128 Blank

127a Blank

127 Bolton Castle from Low Bolton, with figures 'washing wool'. Also inscr: 'Corn'and 'Green'.

126a Bolton Castle from the south-west.

126 Bolton Castle from the north, cf. 125a

125a Bolton Castle from the north, a closer view than 126

125 Bolton Castle from the south-east.

124a Bolton Castle from the west. cf.TB CXLVII 17

124 Bolton Castle from the south

123 Bolton Castle from the east

123 Wensleydale, looking east from the Castle Bolton – Grinton Road.

122a Bolton Castle and Wensleydale from the Grinton road, cf. 122, with the detail of Addlebrough above.

122 As 122a, a more distant view

121a Swaledale from the Grinton road.

121 Three sketches:
i. Swaledale from the Grinton road.
ii. As i. continuing to the right.
iii. Grinton in Swaledale, Reeth bridge beyond.

120a 'Grinton', looking west.

120 Swaledale, near Grinton (?)

119a Marrick Priory, Swaledale, from the east, cf.TB CXLVII 18a-19, and watercolour, 1818, (W.569).

119 Ellerton Priory from the west, cf. 118a, 117a,TB CXLVII 20]

118a Ellerton Priory from the west, a nearer view, cf. 117a.

118 Blank

117a As 118a, a more distant view.

117 Swaledale from near Downholme, looking towards Ellerton, cf. TB CXLVII 20

116a (?) Swaledale from near Downholme.

116 Blank

115a Richmond from Swaledale, with the Hambledon hills in the distance, cf.TB CXLVIII 11a-12, and watercolour, *c.*1819, (W.808).

115 Blank

114a Richmond Castle and bridge from the west

114 'Wycliffe' Hall, inscr: 'wall', (out of sequence). cf. 104a and TB CXLVII 26/27

113a Richmond castle and river from the bridge: inscr: 'Stones'; 'Dead ale[?]'.

113-112a Five sketches,
i. 'St. Agatha' from the west, cf.TB CXLVII22,TB CXLVIII 14a.
ii. 'St. Agatha' with the 'River'.
iii. St. Agatha's from the north-east.
iv. 'St. Martins' priory, near Richmond.
v. St. Agatha from the west.

112 St Agatha's abbey, Easby, cf. watercolour, 1818, (W.561); TBXIV 25 (1797); and watercolour,*c.*1798, (W.273).

111a Blank

111 Four sketches at Aske Hall,
i. The house, cf. watercolour, 1818, (W.562).
ii. The bridge.

	iii. The chapel. iv. Rotunda by the lake.
110a	Aske Hall from the south, cf.TB CXLVII 23 and watercolour, 1818 (W.562)
110	'Ken Pool', i.e. Kentmere, near Staveley (out of sequence).
109a	Ravensworth Castle, near Rokeby, with 'Cattle'.
109	Distant hills—the Lake District?
108a	Ravensworth Castle, with Kirby Hill church
108	Greta banks and steps at 'Rokeby'.
107a	Ravensworth Castle, with Kirby Hill church, and 'Children at Play'. Inscr: 'Wool,' 'Corn', 'val'.
107	Three sketches: i.'Cotherstone Castle', near Barnard Castle. ii. 'Middleton' in Teesdale, the bridge and village. iii. As Barnard Castle from the road to Rokeby.
106	Brignall church on the banks of the Greta, cf.TB CXLVII 29, 29a, and watercolour, 1818. (W.567).
105a	Mortham Tower, near Rokeby.
105	Three sketches: i. Bowes castle and village from the south-east. ii. 'Bowes' bridge and castle. iii. 'Middleton' bridge, Teesdale.
104a	View towards Whorlton from Wycliffe Hall, inscr: 'Worton near Wycliffe' and (by Ruskin?) 'With page 105, interesting', cf.TB CXLVII 28a.
104	Two sketches: i.Rokeby Hall from the Abbey bridge, Egglestone. ii. Egglestone Abbey from near the abbey bride
103a	Barnard Castle from the north-east, cf.TB CXLVII 32.
103	Four sketches: i. Barnard Castle and bridge from the north-east, cf. 103a. ii. Bowes Castle, inscr: 'Road Rush [illegible] S'. iii. Bowes Castle. iv. River Tees(?) with a mill.
102a	Wynch Bridge over the Tees
102	Wynch Bridge and Salmon Leap
101a	High Force
101	High Force: Rocks at the foot of the fells. Inscr: 'Cold G and B[?]
100a	High Force, cf.TB CXLVII 34,TB CXLVIII 9a and watercolours,*c*.1817-18 (W.563,564). Inscr: 'G&B', 'DG', 'Do Fissur [?]
100	The fells of upper Teesdale
99a	Upper Teesdale, inscr: 'Pool'.
99	Blank
98a	Cauldron Snout with a bridge over the Tees, cf.TB CXLVIII 6a and watercolour *c*.1826, (W.878).
98	High Cup Nick, near Appleby. **Ill.78.**
97a	High Cup Nick: 'Helevelyn' in the distance, a 'fall & arch[?]' in the foreground. **Ill.78.**
97	Witherslack church with Castle Head in the distance, a detail of Castle Head above, inscr: 'Black Cattle', 'Birch', (ff. 97- 93a out of sequence).
96a	Village and church in Morecambe Bay area
96	Morecambe Bay from near Grange, continued to right above, inscr 'Mile' i.e. Milnthorpe, and continued to right on f.95a. cf.TB CXLVII 38
95a	Three sketches; i. Continuation to right of f.96, inscr: 'water', 'Medcup', and 'this belongs to the Castle Head and W[itherslack] Chapel'. ii. 'Wither[slack] Chaple' details of the north side. iii. Witherslack church, inscr. 'Birch', 'Wolne[?]'
95	Levens Hall and bridge, with notes of window lights. **Ill.85.**
94a	Orton and the Lune valley from Orton Scar, inscr: 'Road'. **Ill.79.**
94	Whitbarrow Scar, with Morecambe Bay beyond, continued to right above.
93a	Whitbarrow Scar.
93	Mountains and clouds
92a	Bargate Mill at 'Appleby', cf. 92
92	As 92a, a more distant view, including the castle, upper left.
91a	River running between hills, with town in distance, Appleby(?)
91	Appleby, the bridge and castle, cf. 90a.
90a	'Apple'[by], as 91, a more distant view.
90	Appleby, the castle, town and church.
89a	Bridge, castle and town, Appleby(?)
89	Panorama of the Lake District (?) mountains.
88a	Kentmere from Millriggs.
88	Blank
87a	Kent Head.
87	Kentmere.
86a	Blank
86	Panorama in three parts: (?) Conishead Priory and Furness hills.
85a	'Conishead' Priory and Cartmel Sands.
85	Cartmel Sands from near Ulverston.
84a	Lake District Mountains from Cartmel Sands.
84	'Rayham the Tower', i.e. Wraysholme Tower, near Flookburgh.
83a	Coniston Old Man from Cartmel Sands.
83	View from Grange Fell(?), 'Med' i.e. Meathop, to right.
82a	'Lancaster' from above the Aqueduct, cf.TB CXLVIII 36-35.
82	Blank
81a	Blank
81	Detail of the Aqueduct, Lancaster, cf.TB CXLVIII 36-35, and watercolour,*c*.1825, (W.786). Inscr: '11 Mod[ilions]', 'This band Returns thro Arch'.
80a	Heysham Head with shrimpers in the foreground. Inscr: 'Red Scar', 'Sand', 'Black rocks' &c.
80	Blank
79a	Whitbarrow Scar (out of sequence).
79-78a	'Heysham' head and village, in two parts, cf.TB CXLVII 40a-41 and watercolour, 1818, (W.579). A detail of a 'Porch' above.
78	Blank.
77a	Heysham from the north. Inscr: 'Loose stones', 'Wall,' 'Grass', 'Red' &c.
77	Lancaster from the west, with Aqueduct in the distance, 'In[gl]brgh' to right.
76a	As 77, detail of church and castle.
76	Lancaster, the old and new bridges
75a	Lancaster from the north, with a detail of Williamson Park House, inscr: '4 Ionco' i.e. Ionic columns of customs house, cf.TB CXLVIII 38a-36a.
75	As 75a, from further to the east.
74a	Lancaster bridge and castle from the north-east, cf.TB CXLVIII37a-38.
74	Lancaster from the east, inscr: 'Ship Building'; 'Linnen'; 'Float of timber', details of St. John's church and old town hall (from 73a) to left.
73a	Lancaster from the south-east.
73-72a	Lancaster from the south, a panorama in two parts. **Ill.98.**
72	From the Crook of Lune, looking north, inscr: 'Corn'.
71a	From the Crook of Lune, looking north, bride in the foreground, cf.TB CXLVII 34a.
71	From the Crook of Lune, looking north-east, Hornby Castle and Ingleborough in the distance.
70a	Crook of Lune from the south-east, bride to right, inscr: 'Furze'.
70	Crook of Lune from the south-east, a more distant view than 69a.
69a	'Crook of Lune' bridge from the south-east, inscr: 'Gold'.
69	From 'Crook [of Lune] looking down [stream]' with 'Girl driving cows to Milk'.
68a	'Ingleborough over the Scar + in continuation', from the south-west, with a deep river valley (Crina Bottoms?) in the foreground, in two parts (out of sequence cf.2a).
68-66a	Blank.
66	Lune valley near Hornby Castle(?) inscr: 'Corn'.
65a-65	Blank, a piece torn off.
64a	Hornby Castle from Tatham Bridge Inn, cf. TB CXLVII 41a-42, and watercolour,1818, (W.577), inscr: 'Road', 'Riv[er]', 'Stone'.
64	Hornby Castle and Village fromthe west, with a detail of the church tower. **Ill.101.**
63a	Hornby Castle from the north-east.
63-62a	Inglebrough from 'Hornby Terr[aces]', in three parts, with a detail of 'Inglebrough fr[om] H[ornby]', cf. TB CXLVIII 4a, and watercolour, 1818, (W.576).
62-61a	Blank
61	Thurland Castle, Tunstall, from the south, with a view of the Lune valley and a detail of the house to the left of the bridge. Inscr: 'stone'.
60a	Blank
60-59a	Kirkby Lonsdale bridge, continued to the left above, cf. TB CXLVII 37a,TB CXLVIII 5,4c
59	Kirkby Lonsdale bridge, with the river 'Loon' i.e. Lune
58a	From Kirkby Lonsdale churchyard, with 'Ingleborough'—'The Continuation of K.L.Cyd View' (i.e.TB CXLVIII 5a-3) to the right. Inscr: 'L Stone'.
58	Ingleton, with Ingleborough beyond and details of the church and Ingleborough Hall. Inscr: 'L Lime R', cf.TB CXLVII 16a, 19a
57a	Blank.
57	'Hurtlepot', near Chapel-Le-Dale.
56a	'Ginglepot looking towards the Chapel [Le Dale], i.e., Jingle Pot.
56-55a	Inside 'Yordas' Cave, Kingsdale, inscr: 'Roof', 'Light Gr', 'Loose Stones'.
55-54a	As 56-55a.
54-53a	Inside 'Yordas'[Cave], with 'Day Light', 'Light', 'Loose [stones?]' **Ill.117.**
53-52a	As 54-53a, with 'Day Light', 'Water', 'Running [water?]'.
52-51a	As 53-52a
51-50a	'Entr.[ance] of Yordas'.
50-49a	As 51-50a, a more distant view. Inscr: 'Mullins[?]'.
49-48a	Near Yordas Cave.
48-42a	Blank.
42	Thurland castle, cf.61,41a.
41a	As 42, a more distant view.
41-39a	Blank.
39	Chapel-Le-Dale and Ingleborough 'from the E of Wortle Pot' i.e. Hurtle Pot, cf. 140.
38a-36a	Blank.
36	Distant view of Thurland Castle, cf. 61,42,41a.
35a	Blank, a piece torn off.
35 (As 35a)-34a	Kendal from the south, in two parts, cf. TB CXLVII 44.
34	Kirkby Lonsdale from the south, with another, more distant view of the same, probably made while travelling from Kendal to Farnley.
33a	Kirkby Lonsdale church and village from Millgate, cf.TB CXLVIII 3a-4, inscr: 'Kendale G[reen]'.
33	Distant view of Thurland Castle? from near Kirkby Lonsdale.
32a	Blank.
32	Giggleswick.
31a	'Pennegent' from near Settle, cf. 21a.
31-28	Blank.
27a	'Skipton' castle; north gate, cf. 171, 170.
27	Blank.
26a	Skipton Castle, a nearer view than 27a.
26-23a	Blank.
23	Skipton Castle: Inscr: 'Ivy', '2 4 [i.e. the numbers of window lights]'.
22a	Skipton Castle: the main gateway with Rombald's Moor beyond.
22	Blank.
21a	'Ingleboro' and 'Penne[ghent] from Settle', in two parts, cf. 31a.
21-15a	Blank.
15-14a	'Skipton' Castle from the north, in two parts, inscr: 'Rock', 'ash', cf.TB CXLVII 7a.
14	Kendal Church and castle from the south, with a detail of a building, cf. 34a-35 (out of sequence).
13a	'Kendal C[hurch]'.
13-12a	'Weathercote Cave'—inside the cave looking out to 'Day L[ight]'.
12	Blank.
11a	'Skipton' castle from the north, a more distant view than 14a.
11-9	Blank.
8a	Skipton castle from the north, cf. 14a-15,TB CXLVII 7a.
8-5	Blank.
4a	'Skipton' castle from the north, with 'trees', 'Wall', 'Girls'.
4-3	Blank.
2a	'Ingleboro' from the south-west, cf. 68a.
2-1a	A panorama of the Kent estuary in six parts, with 'Mith' i.e. Milnthorpe, 'Whitbarrow Scar', 'Medcup Marsh' i.e. Meathop Marsh, 'Sand', 'Wood' &c. out of sequence, cf. Inside back cover,TB CXLVII 35a-36.
1	Architectural detail, possibly Skipton castle, with executors' endorsement: 'No 275 157 leaves with pencil sketches. [signed] *H.S. Trimmer*' [and initialled] 'W.K.' [i.e. William Kingsley], 'C.L.E.'[i.e. Charles Lock Eastlake], and a note in Turner's hand 'Robert Thompson Castilly [there is a castley near Pool in Wharfedale, about two miles from Farnley Hall]. Sunday July 24 [Sundays in July 1816 fell on the 21st and 28th, as Finberg points out in his note, if the reading of 24 is correct then the year could be either 1814 or 1825] at ½ past eight in the morning was from home no fire, or either Hay or Corn in the House for Horse.' Plus a note by A.J. Finberg: '(Either 1814 or 1825 A.J.F.)'
Inside Cover	Inside Slight sketch of the Kent estuary at 'Miln thorpe'. Plus the price, '3/0'.

'Yorkshire 4' Sketchbook

TB CXLVII, 1816

Sketchbook, bound in mottled boards with red leather spine and corners. Inscr. on back spine cloth: 'Yorkshire 4'.
44 leaves, many drawn on both sides, 122 x 203 mm. Watermarked 'J. Whatman 1814'.

Inside Cover	Executor's endorsement: 'No 279 Containing 44 Leaves Pencil Sketches on both Sides—[signed] *H.S.Trimmer, C Turner,* [and initialled] *C.L.E.* [i.e. Charles Lock Eastlake], *W.K.* [i.e. William Kingsley]'. Also stamped with the Turner Bequest number CXLVII (twice) and inscribed with the price '4/' reduced to '3/0'.
Inside cover-1a	A figure at the entrance to 'Dove Cove' i.e. Dow Cave, near Kettlewell, cf.TB CXLV 158-157a ff.
1	'Thornton force', near Ingleton, out of sequence.
2	'Dove Cove', i.e. Dow Cave, near Kettlewell. **Ill.24.**
2a-3	'Simmer Water' i.e. Semer Water, near Askrigg, c.f. watercolour, 1817–18, (W.571). **Ill.25.**
3a-4	'Sim[mer] Water' from the north, Addleborough to the left, cf. TB CXLV 146a.
4a-5	Whitfield Gill Fall, inscr: 'Whitfield [Gill] fall Mill beck or Mill Gill. Askrigg'. Two drawings, near and distant views.
6	'Askrigg at the lower fall [i.e. Mill Gill Fall]'. Inscr: 'G.B.'. 'L.L.', 'Firs'.
7	Mill Gill, Askrigg, the mill and bridge, Addleborough to the right, 'cows' seen in the centre, a figure stood under the water-trough.
7a	Skipton Castle from the north, cf.TB CXLV 15-14a, 26a &c. **Ill.120.**
8	Cotter Force, near Hawes, with 'Children looking over', and 'dark Pool'.
9	'Fall at [West] Burton', cf.TB CXLV 138-137a. **Ill.34.**
10	'Upper Wednesly dale' from above West Burton. **Ill.40.**
11	'Asgarth Force' cf. watercolour, 1818, (W.570). **Ill.42.**
12	Aysgarth Force, 'looking down the Fall', cf.TB CXLV 135, 187. Inscr: 'Dark W[ater]'.
12a-13	Middle Asgarth fall', with the bridge, mill and church, cf. 14,15,TB CXLV 135a. **Ill.43.**
13a	'Asgarth Sd fall'.
14	'Ditto' i.e. Aysgarth, middle falls, cf. 12a-13.
15	'Sd fall', i.e. middle falls, cows to left, cf. 14.
16	Aysgarth church from the 'Church Path', looking west, Bolton Castle in the distance to left, cf. TB CXLV 134a.
16a	Ingleton and Ingleborough from the west, cf. 19a, TB CXLV 58 (out of sequence).
17	Bolton Castle from the west, cf.TB CXLV 124a.
18	Bolton Castle from the north-east, cf. TB CXLV 126, 125a. **Ill.45.**
18a-19	Marrick Priory, Swaledale, from the east, cf. watercolour, 1818, (W.569), and TB CXLV 119a. **Ill.47.**
19a	Ingleborough and Ingleton from the west, as 16a, a nearer view, cf. TB CXLV 58. Inscr: 'yellow' &c. **Ill.114.**
20	Ellerton Priory, Swaledale, from the Downholme road, cf.TB CXLV 119.
21	St. Agatha's Abbey, easby, from the south-east, Richmond in the distance, cf. Colour-beginning,TB CCLXIII 31.
22	St. Agatha's Abbey, Easby, from the west, cf.TB CXLV 112a, TB CXLVIII 14a.
23	Aske Hall, Near Richmond, cf. watercolour, 1816-17, (W.562), and TB CXLV 111,110a. **Ill.61.**
24	'Steps' and a 'Cave at Rokeby', with 'River [Greta] v Light', the 'Sky' seen through trees &c.
	Lune Bridge and Farm, near Tebay, with the 'Road to Orton' and 'Stone R', (out of sequence). **Ill.82.**
25	Mortham Tower and the river 'Tees', cf. watercolour, *c.* 1831, (W.1086).
25a	Mortham Tower, as 25, from further to the left.
26-27	'Wycliff', near Rokeby, cf. watercolour, 1817, (W.568). Inscr: 'Calm', 'Ston[es]'.
26a	'Wy[cliffe]', as 26/27, a more distant view. **Ill.66.**
27	'Wycliffe', the continuation of 26 to the right with a passing cart. **Ill.67.**
28	The Tees from 'Wycliffe', continued to right on 29.
28a	On the Greta, looking downstream near 'B[r]ignall' church, cf.TB CXLVIII 26a.
29	Two sketches: i. 'B[r]ignall Church', as 29a, a nearer view. ii. 'Wycliffe House', the continuation of 28 to right.
29a	'B[r]ignall' church on the banks of the Greta, cf. watercolour, 1818, (W.567) 29, and TB CXLV 106.
30	'B[r]ignall Hall'.
30a	Egglestone Abbey, bridge and mill, inscr: 'Road'.
31.	'Egg[lestone]' Abbey, nearer view.
31a	Egglestone Abbey from the east, inscr: 'Rock', 'olo this', cf. watercolour, 1818, (W.565).
32	Barnard castle and bridge from the north-east, cf. TB CXLV 103, 103a and watercolour, *c.* 1825 (W.793).
33	'B[arnard] C[astle from] Tollar Hill' [i.e. Towler Hill].
33a	'Weather Cote [Cave] when full' cf. watercolour, 18181 (W.580). (out of sequence). **Ill.116.**
34	High Force, Teesdale, with an artist sketching, cf. TB CXLV 100, 100a, TB CXLVIII 9a, watecolours, 1817, (W.563, 564), and watercolour, *c.* 1825, (W.790). **Ill.73.**
34a-35	'Ken[t] Head', above Kentmere. **Ill. 84.**
35a	The crook of Lune, cf. TB CXLV 71a-72 &c, and watercolour, 1818, (W.575). Inscr: 'Road with walls', 'Corn', 'G'. cf. Colour-beginning TB CXCVII- I, and TB CXLV inside cover. **Ill.99.**
(35a-) 36	A panorama in two parts, i. 'Milnthorpe S[outh]', and ii 'Minthorpe North', cf.TB CXLV 2-1a.
36a-37	Castle Head, near Lindale, cf. TB CXLV 97 &c, TB CXLVIII 34a. Inscr: 'sand', 'corn', 'Gold', 'w[ater]'. **Ill.86.**
37a	Kirkby Lonsdale bridge, cf.TB CXLV 60-59a, TB CXLVIII 5, 4c. Inscr: 'yello[w]', 'Dark', 'v d', 's' &c. out of sequence.
38	Whitbarrow Scar and Witherslack church from near Lindale, continued to right above, cf. TB CXLV 96-95a. Inscr. 'Corn', 'P Bog', 'B'.
38a-39	Castle Head and Whitbarrow Scar from above Whitbarrow Lodge. Inscr: 'Bog', 'Birch', 'G'.
39a-(40)	Whitbarrow Scar, looking east, with 'Loose stones', 'Bog', plus a few lines 'in continuation' to right.
40	'Haysham Hall, continuation of 40a-41 to left.
40a-41	Heysham and Cumberland mountains, cf. TB CXLV 79-78a, and watercolour, 1818, (W.579). Inscr: 'Black Combe', 'Old man [of Coniston]', 'Holker [Hall]', 'Floo[kburgh]', 'Castle H[ead]', continued to right, above, with 'Arnside' and 'Corn'. **Ill.95.**
41a-42	Hornby Castle and Tatham Church from Tatham Bridge Inn, cf.TB CXLV 64a, and watercolour, 1818, (W.577). Inscr: 'Alders', 'River sparkling among the trees', 'Meadow', and illegibly on road to left. **Ill.104.**
42a	Thurland castle, Tunstall, with architectural details inscr: '5 B[attlements]', with a detail of Ingleborough above.
43a	Inside Yordas Cave?, cf.TB CXLV 56 ff.
44	Kendal from the south, with a 'Wall and Bank' in the foreground, cf. TB CXLV 35-34a. **Ill.119.**
44a-Inside Cover	Kendal bridge and church, with two details of the castle.

'Yorkshire 5' sketchbook

TB CXLVIII, 1816

Sketchbook, bound in reddish-brown boards, with black leather spine and corners. Inscribed on back cover, 'Yorkshire 5'. 42 leaves, many drawn on both sides, 173 x 260 mm. Watermarked 'J.Whatman 1815'.

This sketchbook was broken up for exhibition in the nineteenth century. Unfortunately no record was kept of the original sequence of pages, and when A.J. Finberg came to compile the Inventory in 1909 he found it 'impossible to reconstitute the book with any pretensions to accuracy'. The sketchbook is the largest of the three used by Turner on his tour of the north of England in 1816, and since the itinerary of the tour can be established clearly from the other two books, TB CXLV and CXLVII, it has now proved possible to suggest the original order of the pages. The references below give Finberg's numbering, since this is stamped on the pages themselves, but arranges them according to the itinerary. Turner worked through the book from the back to the front.

24-23a	Hurst green on the river Ribble.
23-22a	Harden, near the trough of Bowland, cf.TB CXLV172. Inscr. 'B.G.', 'G' &c. **Ill.8.**
22-21a	Sawley Abbey, near Clitheroe, cf. TB CXLV 170a, 169a.
21	Blank.
30a	Gordale Scar, the waterfalls, cf. TB CXLV 161-160 &c. Inscr: 'Grey'.
30	Blank.
20a	Blank.
20-19a	Kilnsey Crag and Conistone, upper Wharfedale, with a detail of Conistone chapel, cf. TB CXLV 153, Colour-beginning, TB CXCVII - 0, inscr: 'Stones', 'Hay', 'C Cope 29 Park Square by the 31st of Decr' cf. 25. **Ill.26.**
19	Blank.
18a	Kilnsey Village and Crag, Wharfedale, cf.TB CXLV 151a. Inscr: 'Grass Br', 'Wall', 'Willow', 'Large L [...?]'.
18-17a	Mill Gill fall, near Askrigg, cf.TB CXLV 146-145a, and colour-beginning,TB CCLXIII 133, Inscr: (erroneously) 'Whitfield Gill force' (cf. TB CXLVII 4a,5).
17-16	Mossdale Fall, Wensleydale, cf. watercolour, 1816–17, (W.572). Inscr: 'Yell', 'Yello[w]', 'G', 'M' &c. '176'. With (p.17) two architectural designs for gate lodges?, inscr: 'Pantry Room', '2 35'. **Ill.31.**
16a	Blank.
31a	Mossdale, lower fall, with upper falls (17-16) to left.
31	The continuation of a drawing (?)
25a	Mossdale Head, with lower falls (31a) to right.
25	Inscr: 'C Cope 29 Park Square Leeds by the 31 of decr 1825' (cf. 20-19a).
27a	Mossdale head, upper Wharfedale, with upper falls, (17-16) above centre, and lower falls (31a), left of centre.
27	Blank.
15	Hardrow Force, inscr: 'Dark Wa'.
15a-28a	Hardrow Force, a more distant view, cf. Colour-beginning,TB CCLXIII 369, and watercolour, 1816-17 (W.574). Inscr: 'Sun', 'Grey Stone', 'Grass', &c.
28	Blank.
14a	St. Agatha's Abbey Easby, from the West, cf. TB CXLV 113-112a, TB CXLVII 22.
14-13a	Richmond from the south-east, cf. watercolour *c.* 1824–5, (W.791). **Ill.59.**
13-41a	Richmond castle and Mill.
41-12a	Richmond from the South, cf. watercolour, 1816–17, (W.560),TB CXLV 114a,TB CXLVI 27, Inscr: 'Bank', 'Road'.
12-11a	Richmond from the west, cf. watercolour *c.* 1818–19? (W.808),TB CXLV 115a.
11-10a	Richmond from the north-east, cf. watercolour, 1816–17, (W.559).
10	Inscr: '182'.
29a	Junction of the Greta and Tees at Rokeby, cf. watercolour, 1816–17, (W.566) Inscr: 'G'.
29	On the Greta, near Brignall church, inscr: 'Dark', 'L', 'D B' &c.
26a	On the Greta, near Brignall, cf.TB CXLVII 28a.
26	Blank.
9a	High Force on the Tees, cf. watercolours, 1816–17, (W.563, 564), TB CXLV 100, 100a, TB CXLVII 34. Inscr: 'D G', 'Color RBY Brown'.Ill. 71.
9	Blank.
8a	High Force, a figure seated at the top of the falls.
8	Blank.
7a	High Force, distant view, cf. watercolour, *c.* 1825 (W.790). **Ill.71.**
7	Blank.
6a	Cauldron Snout, upper Teesdale, cf.TB CXLV 98a, and watecolour, *c.* 1825, (W.878). **Ill.75.**
6-42	Dallam Tower, near Milnthorpe, Levens estuary and the Lake District fells beyond. Inscr: 'Deer'.
42a	Blank.
34a	Castle Head from Lindale, looking over the Kent estuary and Morecambe Bay, cf. Colour-Beginning, TB CCLXIII 350.
34-33a	Levens estuary and Coniston Old Man from Canal Foot, Ulverston.
33-32a	Ulverston and Coniston Old Man from Conishead Park. Inscr: 'wood', 'corn'. **Ill.90.**
32	Blank.
35a	Lancaster from the Aqueduct cf. watercolour, *c.* 1825 (W.786).
35-36	Lancaster, with the Aqueduct, a more distant view than 35a. cf. TB CXLV 82a. **Ill.96.**
36a-38a	Lancaster castle, church and town, from the north, cf. TB CXLV 75a. Inscr: '177'.
38-37a	Lancaster bridge and castle from the north-east, cf. TB CXLV 74a.
37	Blank.
4a	Ingleborough from Hornby castle Terrace, cf. watercolour, 1818 (W.580), TB CXLV 63-62a. Inscr: 'Rush of W[ater]'.
4-3a	Kirkby Lonsdale from the north, 'Inglebro' to the left. Inscr: 'P W', 'R'. **Ill.108.**
3-5a	Lune valley from Kirkby Lonsdale churchyard, cf. watercolour, 1818, (W.578), Colour-Beginnings, TB CXCVI V,W and TB CXLV 58, 58a for continuation of this view to right. Inscr: 'Stone', 'D W' and 'for Rich[mondshire]'.
5	Kirkby Lonsdale bridge, with a 'Path' and 'Cattle', cf. TB CXLV 60-59a, TBCXLVIII 37a.
4c	Kirkby Lonsdale Bridge, Inscr: 'Sky Light', 'V D', 'bot G' &c. **Ill.110.**
4b-2a	A fertile valley with houses and churches and distant hills Kendal?
2	Blank.
39-40a	Blank.
1a	Blank.
1	Inscr: 'No 263 40 pencil sketches sgd H.S. Trimmer, initialled C.L.E. W.K.
Inside Cover	Song: 'Here's a health to Honest John Bull ' (six verses in Turner's hand).

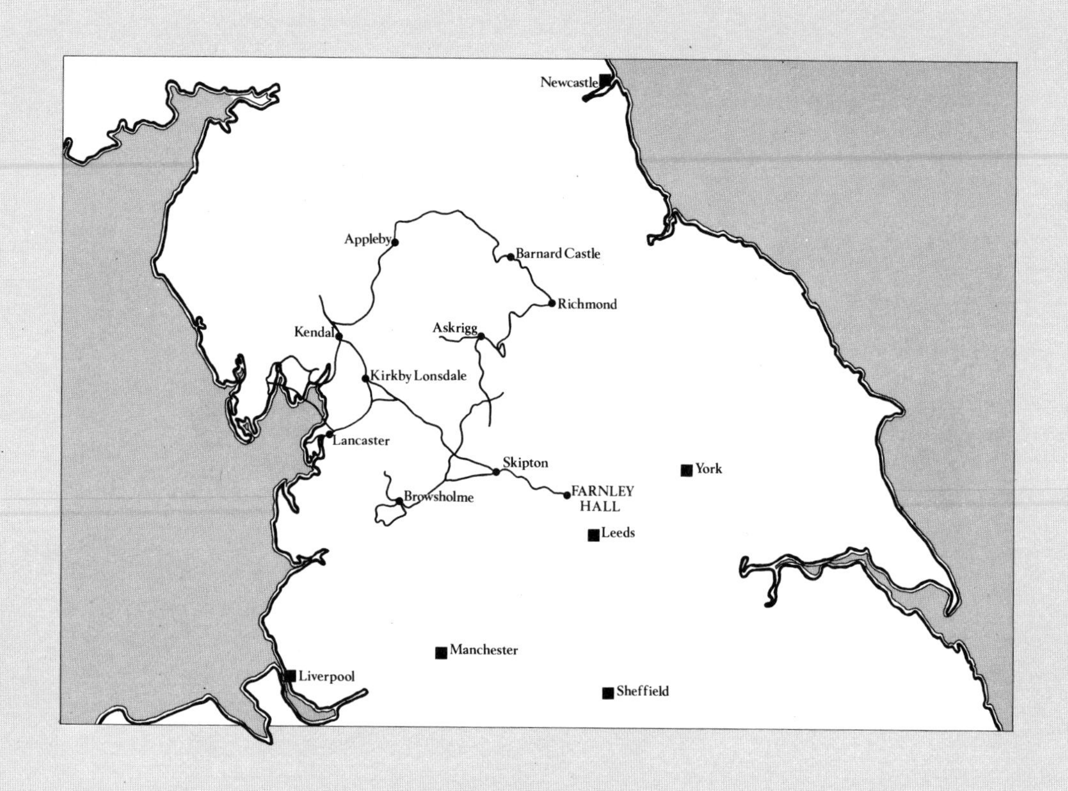
Newcastle
Appleby
Barnard Castle
Richmond
Askrigg
Kendal
Kirkby Lonsdale
Lancaster
Skipton
York
FARNLEY
HALL
Browsholme
Leeds
Manchester
Liverpool
Sheffield

–THE– TOUR

LONDON TO GRANTHAM

On Friday 12 July 1816, at an hour when most artists were still in their beds one of their number was already up and about. J.M.W. Turner, Professor of Perspective at the Royal Academy, was on board the Leeds coach as it clattered through the streets of north London, setting off on one of the most important tours of his career. He had been commissioned by Longmans to make 120 watercolours as illustrations to a grand seven-volume *General History of the County of York*. He was to be paid 3000 guineas for the drawings — the most valuable commission he had ever received. His fellow travellers would hardly have guessed his profession from his appearance. Habitually huddled up in a dark greatcoat and hat; somewhat heavy in his features; side-whiskered; his complexion 'as red as the skin of a boiled lobster'; looking 'more like an old man o' war boatswain' than the greatest landscape painter of the day, and sounding like one too, when he spoke with a thick, Covent Garden accent. He was among the two-guinea passengers, and sat outside at the back. It was a style of travelling to which he had long become accustomed for he made annual trips to the north on the *True Briton, Highflyer or Lord Nelson*. It was also a manner that he evidently enjoyed, and one which accounted for the colour of his complexion. From the roof he could watch the showers drift across the Cambridgeshire plains, or survey the cloudscape that towered all around him. He could observe the particularities of each village and town, the comedy and incident of the wayside, as the coach lurched up the Great North Road towards Yorkshire.

Turner was prepared for an expedition of considerable length. His baggage cost him 2s.8d. already in 'porterage' to the coach, and his pocket-book reveals that he was carrying £110 in bank notes. That was as much as the coach driver might have earned in a year, and considering that Turner cashed only £25 during the whole tour, he had enough to insure himself against almost any mishap that might occur. The coach kept up a good pace, on average about ten miles per hour, and they would have made the fifty-five miles to 'Eaton' Socon by mid-day in time for 'dinner' for which Turner paid 5s.6d. The passengers parted company with their first driver here, and Turner contributed towards his living with a tip of 1s. Dinner on the road in 1816 was, as now, often a less than satisfactory affair. Wines, on the whole, were disgusting, and one victim of the 'poison' served at the *Cock* in Eaton Socon in 1794 resolved in future to 'send decent liquor to these inns, else when I am tired, and faint, I am forced to drink British spirits call'd brandy—a medicated sloe called port—till I am overwhelmed by bile'.

Pressed to resume their seats as quickly as possible after dinner, the invigorated travellers made the remaining fifty-six miles to Grantham before nightfall. There was little time for observing, but, as they sped through Stamford (not without hindrance, for it was market day), Turner must have spared a glance for the *Bull and Swan*. He had sketched this inn on his very first trip to the north of England in 1797 and was to pay tribute to it and to his coaching days on the Great North Road some ten years later in a watercolour (Ill. 1) which shows the northbound coach parked opposite the inn. The picture gives a vivid sense of the bustle of such a scene. The guard sorts out passengers' luggage. The driver collects his tips as travellers dismount — although he appears to have an argument to deal with first. It was perhaps seven or eight o'clock in the evening when the coach arrived at Grantham for the overnight stop. Turner seems to have been well pleased with their progress, for his 1s.6d. tip was larger than usual.

Even by 1724, Grantham was 'famous as well as Stamford for the abundance of very good inns, some of them fit to entertain persons of the greatest quality and their retinues'. The two principal inns were the medieval *Angel*, notable for its 'venerable front, with an angel, cround,

1

in stone on the top', and its 'large ranges of buildings and of stabling behind', and the modern *George* in the market square, 'a great staring new inn', whose service and accommodation were in the 'grand style', intended to appeal to those in search more of comfort than of history.

Porterage		2	8
Fare to Leeds	2	2	
1 Coachman		1	
Dinner at Eaton		5	6
2 Coachman. Porterage		1	6
3. Ditto		1	
Breakfast Doncaster		2	3
Brandy & Water Grantham		1	6
4 Coachman and Guard		4	6
	3	2	11

2

Inns in Turner's day made no charge for board, though he was charged 1s.6d. for 'brandy and water'. The former was frequently intended more for ablution than for consumption, though its sedative qualities could be useful, as conditions of board were often more sociable than today. A traveller might well find himself sharing a bedroom—even a bed—with a stranger. Such were the standards of hygiene, too, that he might also find his bed occupied by abundant strangers of smaller species.

If Turner needed to stretch his legs before retiring, he no doubt renewed his acquaintance with Grantham's famous church with its spire nearly 275 feet high. Popular opinion had it, and has it still, that the steeple leans. A local jingle explains it as a trick of perspective: 'Tis height makes Grantham steeple stand awry.' Turner had investigated this phenomenon on his tour of the Midlands in 1794, at the beginning of his career. His watercolour had contributed to Grantham's fame, for it was engraved

1. Stamford, *Lincolnshire, c. 1825–8. Turner's tribute to his coaching days on the Great North Road, showing passengers dismounting from the northbound coach opposite the* Bull and Swan *Inn.*

2. Note of travelling expenses on the journey from London to Leeds on the first page of the pocket-book. The fare of £2 2s.0d. shows that Turner travelled outside. The correct total should be £3 1s.11d.

All works of art reproduced are by Turner unless stated otherwise.

GRANTHAM TO OTLEY

and published in Benjamin Howlett's *Selection of Views in the County of Lincoln* of 1797. It had also contributed to Turner's growing reputation as one of the most promising young architectural draughtsmen of the day. Now, however, at forty-one, he was renowned as one of the greatest landscape painters in the country. Those twenty-two years had seen far greater changes in the artist and in his work than had been wrought in the meantime on his subject. This tour of 1816 was to be for Turner as much an exploration of his own past as of the landscape.

Saturday 13 July

The party made an early start, and the coach covered the fifty-two miles to Doncaster in time for 'breakfast'. Viscount Torrington, who had also breakfasted at the old *Angel* in 1792, recorded, 'I expected to find everything comfortable. I found [it] to be nasty, insolent and with dirty stabling ..., could not get a waiter near me. I longed to be able to kick the landlord.' Turner had made this journey at least ten times before 1816, however, and knew where the best service and hospitality were to be found. It was nonetheless a relief to move on through Leeds and to reach Otley by early evening on the second day. His spirits rose as he journeyed northward, and his final tip to 'Coachman and Guard' was an exuberant 4s.6d. The whole journey had cost him £3 1s.11d., including the two guinea fare, meals, tips and porterage en route. This is one of the few accounts (Ill. 2) that Turner ever kept of his travelling expenses, and he was probably intending to claim them back from his publishers. As is not unusual with expense accounts the addition was a trifle slack, and he conjured up an extra shilling, no doubt by mistake.

FARNLEY HALL TO SKIPTON

3

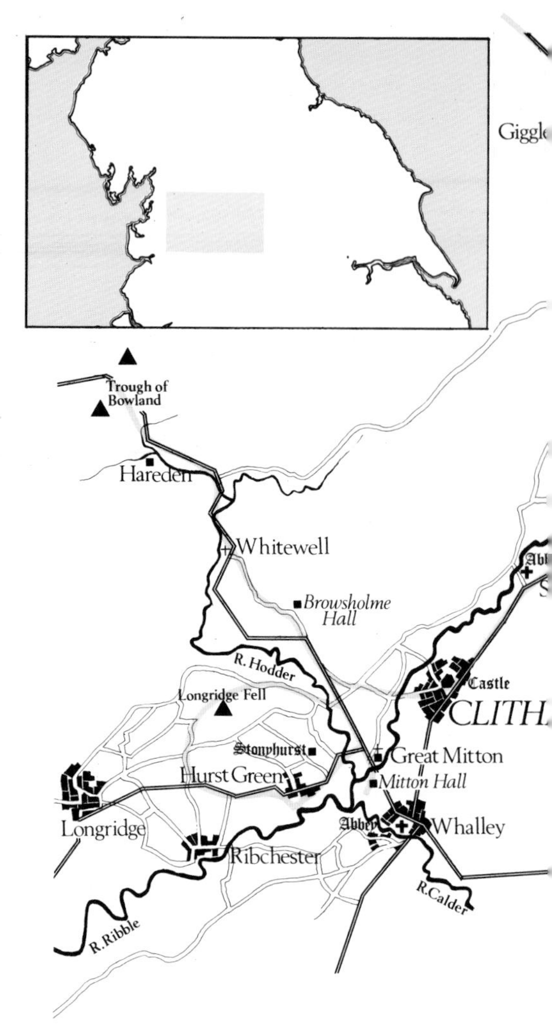

Turner arrived at Farnley Hall to find the whole household busy with preparations for a holiday. Fawkes had decided to take his new wife to see an old friend, Thomas Lister Parker at Browsholme Hall, near Clitheroe, on Yorkshire's western border. Lister Parker was a long-standing admirer and patron of Turner, but the fact that the artist was to be included in what was essentially a private party is testimony to the way he was almost counted as one of the family.

Wednesday 17 July

The new Mrs. Fawkes kept a diary in which she noted the comings and goings of visitors. Today, she duly recorded the family's departure for Browsholme: 'Left Farnley with Walter, Maria, Amelia, Ayscough, Richard and Mr. Turner. Met John Parker at Skipton, where we slept and saw Skipton castle.' The four children were now aged between twenty (Maria) and seven (Richard). The carriage was occupied by them and their new step-mother, while their father and his artist-friend rode along outside where they could talk in peace. Turner was certainly not allowed to drive. His inability with the reins was legendary at Farnley where he was known as 'Over-Turner'.

Their route took them out of the west gates at Farnley past Newhall, over Otley Bridge and along the main road, through Ilkley and Addingham, leaving Rombalds Moor on their left. A few years earlier, Turner had painted a watercolour of Addingham Mill. Fawkes wrote of it in a letter of thanks, that he 'sat a long time before it every day'. Over the valley beyond Addingham they could see Beamsley Beacon, the site of Fawkes's shooting expeditions and the subject of many Turner sketches and watercolours. Fawkes planned to hold his usual shooting party at the start of the grouse-shooting season on 12 August. The two men's conversation probably included of the coming shooting season, Turner's business in the north or any of the many interests that they shared: poetry, history, sport, politics and art. Whatever the topic of conversation, the seventeen miles between Otley and Skipton passed with Turner sufficiently engrossed by his companion not to make a single sketch.

Before the arrival of the great spinning mills, Skipton consisted 'chiefly of one very spacious street, which serves for a market place, and some straggling lanes', and appears to have enjoyed its own brand of picturesque disarray with pigs, dogs, cattle and sheep at large amongst the market stalls and traders, crowded with traffic making its way between the dales and the commercial centres of the West Riding. Its main street offered a wide choice of public houses and hotels, amongst them the still flourishing *Black Horse* at the top of the street nearest to the great castle and the church of Holy Trinity. According to an advertisement in the *Leeds Intelligencer* of 1817, this had 'lately been fitted up in an elegant stile for the Accommodation of Gentlemen, Travellers and others; the Posting Business at the same is carried on to a very considerable Extent.' It would have offered to the Fawkes party the sort of comfort to which they were accustomed when travelling.

Turner installed himself in his new quarters and set out to explore the town.

Edward Dayes described Skipton in his *Excursion through Yorkshire* in 1803 (to which Turner had subscribed when it was published in 1805). 'The Castle at Skipton is the great object which

4

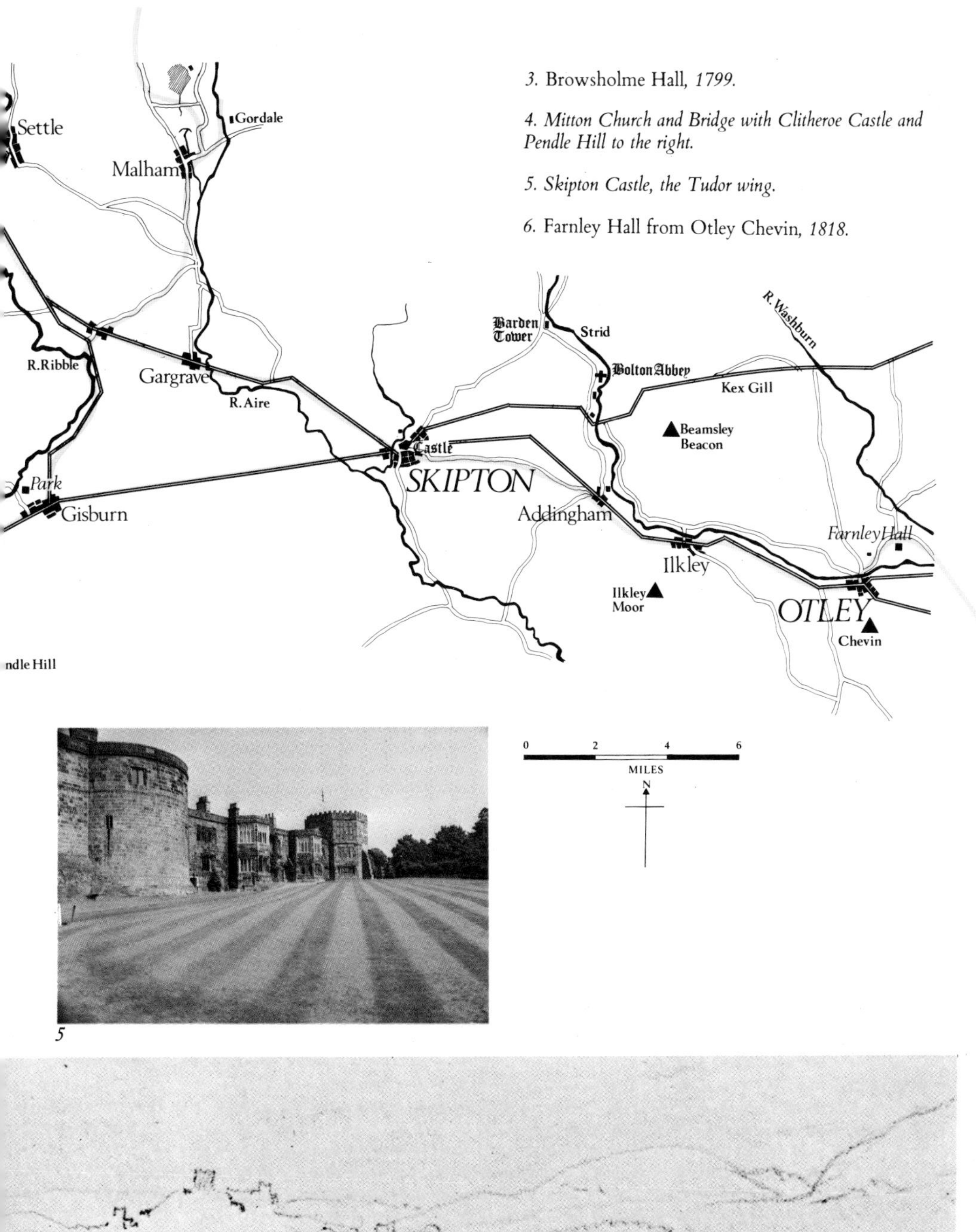

3. Browsholme Hall, *1799.*

4. *Mitton Church and Bridge with Clitheroe Castle and Pendle Hill to the right.*

5. *Skipton Castle, the Tudor wing.*

6. Farnley Hall from Otley Chevin, *1818.*

6

attracts the attention of strangers. It stands on an eminence, that commands the town, and also a good prospect of the surrounding country. The Castle itself is by no means a picturesque object: its outward appearance is heavy, and ugly; its form being composed of several round towers with long sweeping apartments, and heavy stone window frames.'

Skipton Castle bears eloquent witness to the warlike nature of the Cliffords, whose first scion to live there, Robert Clifford, only chose it as his seat in order that he should never miss an opportunity to fight the Scots. He entertained Edward I there, fought the Scots ceaselessly, and died, still engaged in his favourite sport, at Bannockburn. Although fragments of the old Norman castle remain, most of the fortifications date from Robert's time. Walls ranging from nine to twelve feet thick have served their turn countless times. Generation after generation of Cliffords carried on Robert's bellicose family tradition until 'Butcher' Clifford fell at Ferrybridge during the Wars of the Roses and Edward IV swore vengeance on his defeated foes. The name Clifford was high on his blacklist, but Henry Clifford, the heir, then only seven years old, was hidden and brought up by peasants. His noble childhood was nothing but a distant memory when at last Richard III died at Bosworth and he turned up at the House of Lords, still in his shepherd's rags, unable to read or write, to claim Skipton Castle and the Barony of Westmoreland. Wordsworth wrote his story in *The Shepherd Lord*.

Skipton Castle was unsuccessfully besieged in the Pilgrimage of Grace and held out for three years against Cromwell's troops during the Civil War, though the ceaseless bombardments did terrible damage to the fabric of the building. Then came the Sailor Earl, the Elizabethan courtier whose feelings towards Spaniards in galleons was roughly the same as those of his ancestor towards Scots in general. He fought with Raleigh, commanded the strongest ship in the Armada, and is said to have told Queen Elizabeth of the Spaniards' defeat. She dropped her glove in excitement and told Clifford to keep it as a souvenir. The portrait of Clifford with this diamond-studded glove in his hat is in the National Portrait Gallery.

Last of the Cliffords of Skipton was Lady Anne, Countess of Pembroke, who devoted many years to the restoration of the castle, the tombs of her ancestors and the church. All this Turner must have known, but, as Walter Fawkes and his family explored the castle for evidence of Civil War damage, the sketches indicate that

SKIPTON TO BROWSHOLME HALL

Turner, no longer historian nor architecture enthusiast but single-minded landscape-painter, made his way past the church down to the mill on Eller Beck and up the side of the canal where he made drawings of the north front of the castle and its natural cliff defences. Whitaker had already described this view. 'The northern wall of Skipton Castle stands on the bank of a perpendicular rock, washed by a torrent, to the bed of which from the battlements is a depth of 200 feet. In the glen beneath was the pleasure-ground of the Cliffords consisting of fish-ponds, walks, and 'topiary' works, such as appear to have been introduced in the reign of Henry VIII. Forty years ago a little improvement would have rendered this a very beautiful spot, as the depth of the glen gives a consequence to the castle, which it assumes from no other point, and the rest of the scene would have been proportionately solemn and exclusive. But now ...

Turner evidently thought this aspect of the castle still had potential. He took a sequence of views in a small pocket-book as he walked up the valley bottom, with the fish-ponds and Eller Beck to the left and the castle with a new canal at its foot on the right. This pocket-book, measuring a mere 5½ x 3 ins and bound in patterned boards with a tanned calf leather spine, was his principal means of exploring different views. He worked standing up, holding the book in his left hand and blocking in the details of the scene with his right. In one of the sketches we can see where his unsupported hand trembled slightly as he sketched in the path at the bottom and where the side of his palm rested on the right side of the page.

As he returned along the valley on the road higher up, he continued taking views, including both the castle and the church, and then made another looking back up the valley. His aim was

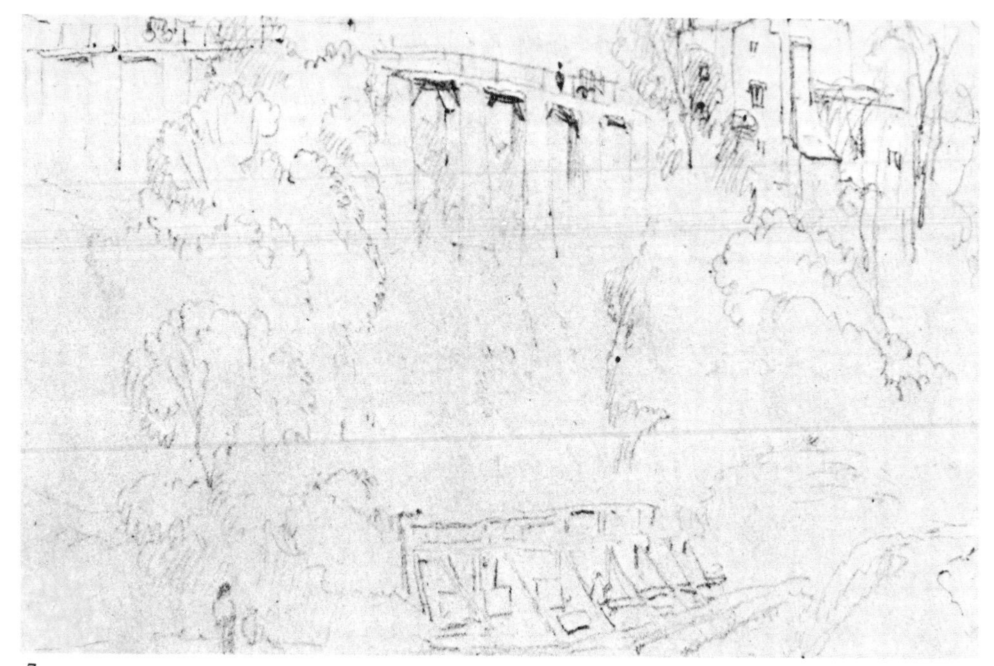

7

to emphasise precisely those features which the text extolled; the fish-ponds, streams, walks and woods, and the way that the 'depth of the glen gives consequence to the castle'. The constraints of the rather overgrown site, however, made it difficult to unite all this in a single composition, and to do justice to the buildings of the castle itself. The principal feature in Turner's sketches is the buttress wall that carries the road into the north entrance to the castle. The second sketch (Ill. 7) in his sequence elaborates on its details to include the small trucks that carried stone from a quarry along a railway into the castle, with two figures in the foreground, who may even have been Fawkes's children waiting by the brook while he made his sketch.

Returning along the road on the north side of the valley he tried an alternative composition, looking across the valley to the castle with the church at the right. The buildings, however, seem to have been too obscured by foliage for him to make much of it and the sketch was abandoned at an early stage. Instead, he sketched an alternative view looking again up the buttress wall from a vantage point further to the south. Turner continued his explorations by walking up into the fields above the northern side of the valley. There he could look out over the castle and the town and take in the surrounding fells.

The sketch he made ingeniously compresses a great sweep of landscape into a tiny page, taking in an angle of vision of about 90 degrees. He was looking for one view which would unite the castle and the church and at the same time give a sense of its location in the surrounding countryside. This view had to be from the same northern viewpoint mentioned in the text. He used his small pocket- book to note down his explorations rather than for finished compositions, and he evidently had not yet found a view which was worth setting down in either of his larger sketchbooks.

It was now dusk and his search for the solution had to be postponed until he returned at the end of his tour, nearly four weeks and 550 miles later.

Thursday 18 July

The next day Mrs. Fawkes records simply 'Arrived at Browsholme. Heavy rain.' The downpour was evidently heavy enough to prevent Turner sketching, for he made only one slight drawing on the whole journey via Gisburne, Sawley and Clitheroe.

Browsholme was interesting both to Turner and to Fawkes. Its history had recently been published in an illustrated volume. Like Fawkes, Parker had brought architectural features from his ancestral homes, including a gateway and arch from Ingleton Hall, and developed 'the earliest and arguably the finest surviving antiquarian interior in England' to which Fawkes himself contributed with a seventeenth-century oak table for the Hall. The interiors at Browsholme had been illustrated by Buckler, and since the same artist was already engaged by Longmans to make the architectural subjects for the *County of York*, Turner was free to concentrate on his landscapes, and to attend to more immediate social pleasures.

Friday 19 July

'Rained all day,' recorded Mrs. Fawke's diary, but Turner braved the elements to make an excursion to Great Mitton, four or five miles to the south west. This was another of the sites he had visited in 1799 in order to make the illustration of the Sherburne Chapel, Mitton Church, engraved and published in Whitaker's *History of Whalley*. The Sherburne Chapel was built in the late sixteenth century to house the magnificent monuments to the Sherburnes of Stonyhurst, now a famous Jesuit school just over the border in Lancashire. It is unlikely that Turner could have resisted the temptation to look again on the three Richard Sherburnes carved in effigy by William Stanton, but once again he concentrated on landscape rather than architecture or sculpture. He made a sketch (Ill. 4) of the church and the village from below the Ribble bridge, looking up the Ribble valley, and continuing to the right on the page below to take in Clitheroe town and castle, Mitton Hall and Pendle Hill.

The Ribble starts its long journey seaward high up on Cam Fell in the Yorkshire Pennines. It runs in a stubborn straight line through its own dale, through the many famous potholes about Whernside and Ingleborough, past countless limestone quarries which have scarred its banks

7. Skipton Castle from Eller Beck, looking up at the northern defences and showing at the top the railway built to carry stone from nearby quarries, and two figures, perhaps the Fawkes children, in the foreground.

8. Hareden, near the Trough of Bowland. On Monday 22 July Mrs. Fawkes 'went with the girls to the Trough to see them fish'. Turner was a keen fisherman himself and his sketch may record this excursion. Beyond the bridge a gig and figures can just be made out beside the river.

8

and down into the lowlands. Where it swerves around Settle, it is already a considerable size. Now the river abandons its resolute course and meanders through Rathmell and down to Sawley. At Mitton, where Turner now stood, it leaves Yorkshire to pass on through Lancaster and at last emerges into the Irish sea just below Blackpool.

Whitaker described the river as Turner saw it in terms of unqualified enthusiasm. 'The remaining course of the Ribble is wholly in Yorkshire. Of this six miles every step has its beauties. The broad and rapid channel of the river, hung on either side with luxuriant woods, the half-monastic and half-castellated form of Stonyhurst, the insulated rock and castle of Clitheroe, the vast bulk of Pendle to the east, the fells of Bowland to the west, and the more distant but more majestic mountains of Pen-y-ghent and Ingleborough to the north, combine almost every feature which is required to constitute a picture on the grandest most extensive scale.'

By the river near Hurst Green Turner took out his largest sketchbook for the first time. He drew in everything Whitaker had described: the luxuriant woods, the bulk of Pendle to the east, the great sweeping bends in the river near Hurst Green, and in the distance the Ribble valley towards Clitheroe. Turner had already sketched Stonyhurst in detail before, so he continued down the Ribble valley to Ribchester, taking a quick sketch above the town looking north to Pendle, before riding up over Longridge Fell back to Browsholme, then views looking west to the mouth of the Ribble at Preston, and north over Bowland from very near the summit.

The weather lifted on his return to the house and in the evening he went for a short walk with Mrs. Fawkes, and John Parker.

Saturday 20 July and Sunday 21 July

How Turner spent the weekend is a mystery. There is a note scrawled inside the cover of the pocket-book, 'Robert Thompson Carlilly Sunday July 21st[?] at ½ past eight in the morning was from home no fire, or either Hay or Corn in the House for Horse.' It is almost indecipherable in parts. We do not know who Robert Thompson was, why Turner went to see him, nor whether Carlilly was the name of a house or village. In the past it has been suggested that Carlilly was Carlisle, but Turner is very unlikely to have ridden the long, high and hard road to Carlisle and back in the space of a weekend—a round trip of 180 miles.

Wherever he went, Turner missed a day's sketching, which must have been infuriating, since the weather at Browsholme had brightened up sufficiently for Walter Fawkes to drive his wife over to the Trough of Bowland on the Saturday.

Monday 22 July

The weather continued to improve. Mrs. Fawkes went over to the Trough of Bowland again, this time with her daughters who wanted to fish. Turner, who was a keen fisherman himself, recorded the excursion with a number of views back down Langden Valley as he made his way up through the Trough, before returning to the fishing-spot at the confluence of the Langden and Hareden Brooks at Hareden.

Having jotted down one view of Hareden looking back up to the Trough from below the bridge, he settled down by the riverside to make a careful, detailed drawing (Ill. 8) in his largest sketchbook. The result shows Turner for the first time on the tour starting to come to terms with the steep hillsides and treeless valleys of the northern Pennines. Human details punctuate and animate the otherwise desolate landscape—the houses at the left are planted round with trees for shelter; the flimsy wooden bridge will surely be swept away in the next spate; travellers on foot climb the rough road snaking up the valley to the Trough; and in the centre there appears to be a gig and figures, perhaps the Fawkes party going fishing. In this drawing, Turner began to develop one of the central themes of his finished *County of York* compositions: the presence of man in remote landscapes.

Tuesday 23 July

Turner made no sketches today. The rain was so heavy that Mr. and Mrs. Fawkes had to take shelter in a farmhouse while out driving.

Wednesday 24 July

No improvement in the weather. The party left Browsholme in torrential rain and slithered and splashed their way to the village of Malham. Nonetheless, Turner managed four sketches on the journey; a quick note of the High Street at Clitheroe, looking up to the castle, and three studies of the village of Sawley with its ruins of a twelfth- century abbey.

It would have been early evening by the time the rain-soaked party arrived at Malham village, a tiny huddle of houses about the River Aire, but Turner rushed off at once to see Gordale in what daylight remained. On their way up to Malham the party had passed by Gisburn Park where James Ward's enormous canvas of Gordale Scar (Ill. 11) had been installed exactly a year earlier. Turner did not call in to see it on this occasion, but he must certainly have seen it at the Royal Academy in 1815, when it was described as 'ostrogothic' by the critic of *The Sporting Magazine*, and as a piece of 'high-wrought tapestry' by *The Times*.

Gordale's towering limestone chasm with its thundering waterfalls and overhanging cliffs was considered one of the most sublime sights in the country, and had been brought to prominence by Thomas Gray whose *Journal in the Lakes, 1769* included a particularly vivid account of the gorge and was read by virtually every tourist in Britain.

Gray saw Gordale in conditions similar to those that Turner must have encountered: 'a gloomy uncomfortable day well suited [to] the savage aspect of the place'. His account became the basis of every subsequent guide: 'The rock on the left rises perpendicular with stubbed yew-trees and shrubs, staring from its side to the height of at least 300 feet; but those are not the things: it is that to the right under which you stand to see the fall, that forms the principal horror of the place. From its very base it begins to slope forwards over you in one black and solid mass without any crevice in its surface and overshadows half the area below with its dreadful canopy ... I stayed here (not without shuddering) a quarter of an hour, and thought my trouble richly paid, for the impression will last for life ...'

9

10

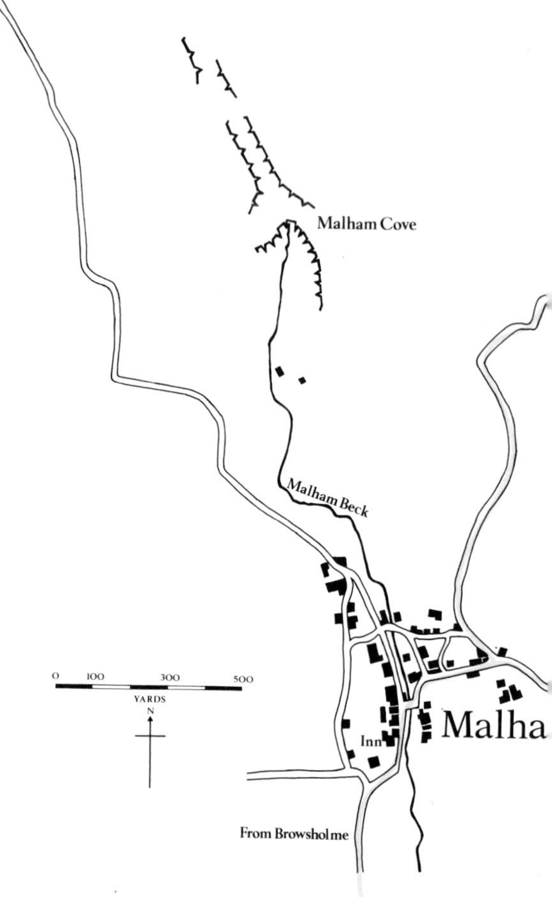

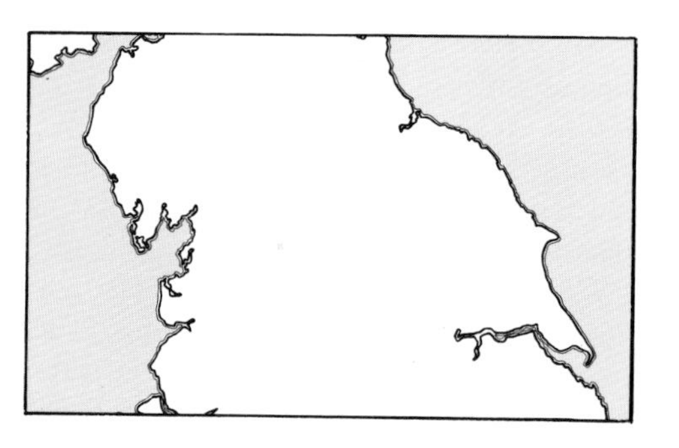

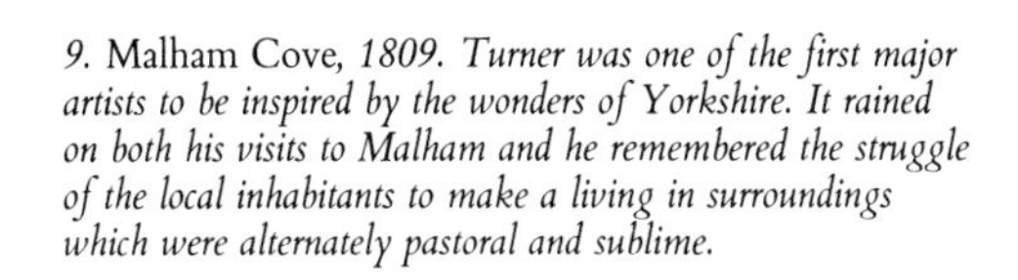

9. Malham Cove, *1809. Turner was one of the first major artists to be inspired by the wonders of Yorkshire. It rained on both his visits to Malham and he remembered the struggle of the local inhabitants to make a living in surroundings which were alternately pastoral and sublime.*

10. Malhamdale from Malham Cove, looking back to the viewpoint of Turner's watercolour of the Cove.

11

11. Gordale Scar *by James Ward, 1814. Although one of the most astonishing sights in the country, the 300-foot gorge of Gordale had never been successfully captured by an artist until 1809 when Turner painted a (now lost) watercolour of it. Ward visited the site in 1811 to make sketches for this huge painting exhibited at the Academy in 1815. It was painted for Lord Ribblesdale and had been hanging at Gisburn Park for almost a year when Turner and the Fawkes party passed by on their way to Gordale in 1816.*

12

12. A colour study of Gordale Scar. Studies such as this one were made in the studio and are known as colour beginnings. Turner, like Ward, responded to the enormity of the subject by working on a large scale, combining a number of different viewpoints in a single composition.

GORDALE SCAR

Turner had visited Gordale before in 1808, and painted a watercolour, now lost, which probably showed the valley leading up to the entrance

He was tremendously excited when he arrived at the jaws of the gorge and rounded the corner to be confronted by the sight of the waterfall. His sketch is wildly animate, dashed off almost as if he feared that the impression might overwhelm him, or disappear before he had a chance to get it all down. His next sketch was that of the waterfall in his largest sketch-book, and is almost as excited as the first. Thomas Girtin, Turner's friend and rival water-colourist (of whom Turner is supposed to have said, 'Had Girtin lived, I should have starved') had visited Gordale in 1799, and it is interesting that he, Ward and now Turner came to terms with the site in exactly the same way. On this overcast July evening the falls were at their grandest as a result of the rain, and, whereas Girtin and Ward had drawn the rocks which divide the channels, Turner's sketch shows the whole of the lower fall as one solid, thundering face. The roar of the waters must have been deafening, echoing from the dark gleaming cliffs all around. Interestingly, when Turner retreated to the entrance of the gorge to make a calmer and wider view, he chose almost exactly the same viewpoint as that of Ward's famous painting and, like Ward, rolled out flat a composition that literally surrounded him. In making the sketch(Ill. 13) he changed his viewpoint at least once in order to record the two separate sides, his drawing spilling over on to the next page as he took in all that he wanted on the right of the scene.

Of the only inn in Malham, the *White House Alehouse*, even the local guidebook writer Thomas Hurtley could only give an equivocal account in 1786: 'There is a comfortable Public House in the Village, and although the traveller must not expect to find here the luxuries of life, he may at least be sure of meeting with attention and rural fare'.

Thursday 25 July

The whole party now 'Went to see Gordale Waterfall', but before they set out, Turner took a sketch of Malham Village, with Malham Cove beyond, where the Aire first springs above ground, with the 'White House' just visible at the left and 'pigs' and 'poultry'—very probably its 'rural fare'—at the right. Turner's sketches at Gordale this morning were more considered than they had been the previous evening. He reflected on one of Whitaker's passages: 'The approach to Gordale on the east side of the village happily remains what nature left it, a stony and desolate valley, without a single object to divert the eye from the scene before it. This is a solid mass of limestone of, perhaps, equal height with the Cove, cleft asunder by some great convulsion of Nature and opening 'its ponderous and marble jaws' on the right and left. The sensation of horror on approaching it is increased by the projection on either side from its base, so that the two connivent rocks, though considerably distant at the bottom, admit only a narrow line of daylight from above. At the very entrance you turn a little to the right, and are struck by a yawning mouth in the face of the opposite crag, whence the torrent, pent up beyond, suddenly forced a passage, within the memory of man, which at every swell continues to spout out one of the boldest and most beautiful cataracts that can be conceived. Wherever a cleft in the rock, or a lodgment of earth appears, the yew-tree, indigenous in such situations, contrasts its deep and glossy green with the pale grey of the limestone; but the goat, the old adventurous inhabitant of situations inaccessible to every other quadruped, had been lately banished from the sides of Gordale.'

13

15

14

13. Gordale Scar. It is impossible to take in Gordale in a single glance.

14. Janet's Foss beside the entrance to Gordale.

15. The entrance to Gordale with Janet's Foss lower right. The first of a sequence of sketches recording different views as the artist approached and entered Gordale Scar.

Turner's sketches lead us up the stony valley in the same way as Whitaker's account. There is the first sight of Gordale from the Malham road, with Gordale House in the centre and Janet's Foss below to the right (Ills.14 and 15). Then we descend into the valley, look up at the 'closed' jaws of the gorge and passing through them under the overhang (Ill. 16), finally arriving at the very foot of the falls (Ills. 17 and 18). But Turner seems to have been defeated by his subject. A large study (Ill. 12) in the Turner Bequest marks the beginning of an attempt to synthesise the different viewpoints in a way very similar to Ward's painting—Turner even includes the cattle sheltering under the cliff as Ward had done but he abandoned the picture. Whitaker had written, 'It must, however, be remembered that the pencil, as well as the pen, has hitherto failed in representing this astonishing scene,' but he wrote these lines before Ward painted his masterpieces and as we know, Turner had seen it. Whatever the reason, no finished picture of this view was ever completed.

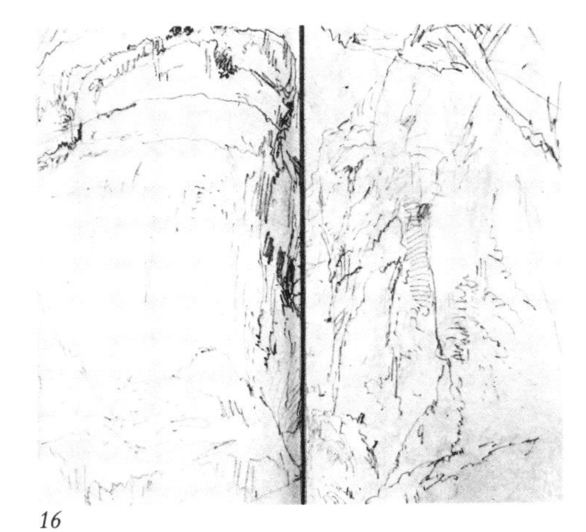

16

16. *Gordale Scar, taken from beneath the overhang beneath whose 'dreadful canopy' the poet Thomas Gray shuddered for a quarter of an hour.*

17. *Gordale Scar, the waterfalls.*

18. *Gordale Scar, the waterfalls. The view sketched by Turner.*

That afternoon Mrs. Fawkes records that the party 'Returned home in heavy rain. Turner went on a sketching tour.' He took his farewell of the Fawkes at Malham and went on alone over the moors towards Littondale and Wharfedale. It is a solitary landscape, high, bare, swept by wind and rain. Turner was for the first time in the tour completely on his own, with the prospect of a 400-mile ride in weather such as this to ponder, while dark clouds swept over the desolate hills all around him. His road took him past Malham Cove to Malham Tarn, 'a small lake on the moors'; according to Edward Dayes (in fact, with an area of 150 acres, 1200 feet up, it is one of our biggest upland lakes) 'but, from being destitute of wood ... by no means an object of interest to the artist. I must own I looked upon it with indifference, notwithstanding it has been called, in the language of poetry, 'A Lake embosomed in the cloud-capt mountains'. Thomas Gray's line seems to have been written with the fondness of memory, for even in summer the reality can be chill and bleak, and in heavy rain such as Turner experienced, positively daunting. These were qualities, however, which Turner found more appealing than repellent. He followed the advice of the local guide, Thomas Hurtley, in finding 'the best situation ... of this delightful place ... towards the South Western Angle', making three panoramic sketches from there looking over the lake to Tarn House, a shooting lodge of Lord Ribblesdale, with High Folds Scar behind and Great Close to the right.

Later in the century, Walter Morrison, millionaire, eccentric, Liberal M.P. and philanthropist, would come to live on the shores of Malham Tarn and, plainly agreeing with Dayes's objections as to the lack of wood, planted one

MALHAM TARN

million trees about the lake. He was to welcome John Ruskin, John Stuart Mill, Charles Darwin, Charles Kingsley and many other friends to his lonely refuge beneath Great Close Scar. Kingsley wrote the first chapters of *The Water Babies* in his house. It was the bells of Malham which Tom heard as he headed down to the river Aire to become a water-baby.

Dayes had been impressed by the surroundings: 'These moors are truly wild and roman-

17

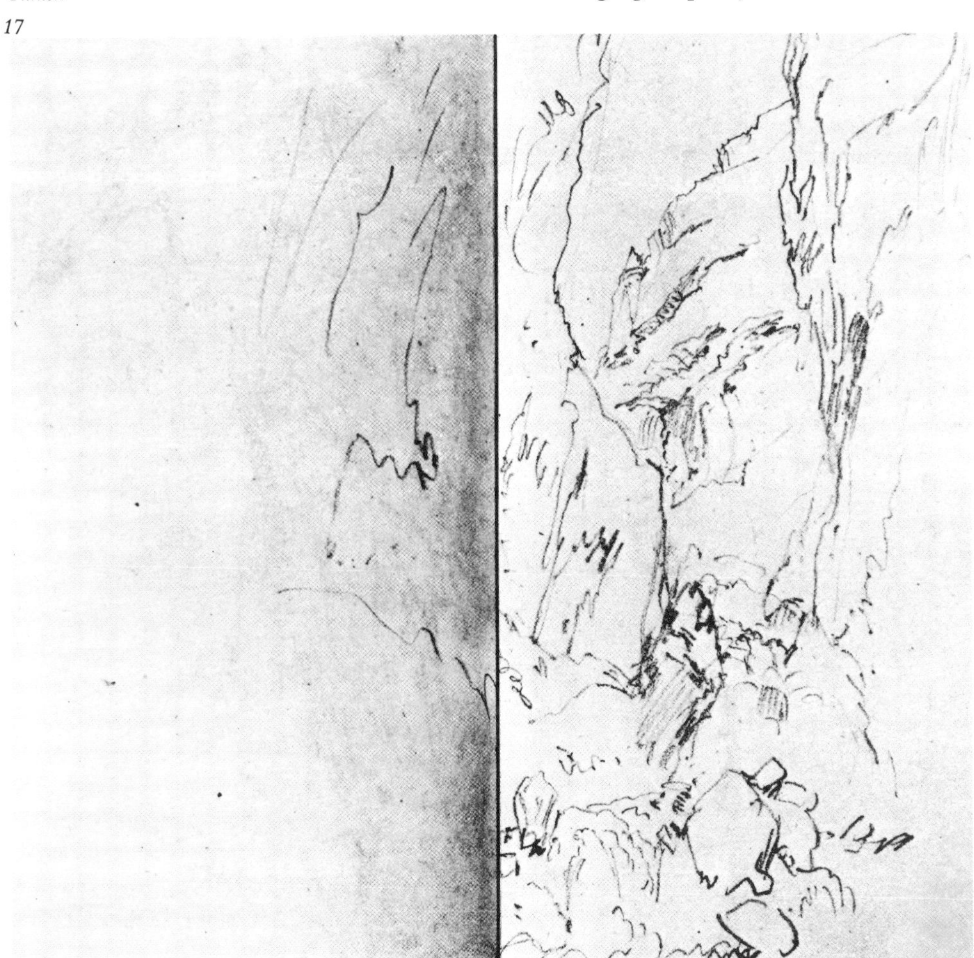

18

KETTLEWELL

19

tic; Nature here sits in solitary grandeur. The hills are lofty and green to their tops, and rise in irregular heaps on all sides, in their primeval state of pasture ... It would be highly imprudent for a stranger to travel these moors without a guide, as he would risk the danger of perishing for want; or the probable chance of breaking his neck down some precipice in the dark, or from being caught in a fog.' Turner will have confined himself to the safety of the road running down Arncliffe Gill to Arncliffe Village and thence over Old Cote Moor to Kettlewell.

It was late afternoon when he rode over the bridge at Kettlewell to put up at one of the two main inns, the *Blue Bell* or the *Racehorses*. Having attended to his horse and his accommodation he made an excursion to Dow Cave, one of the principal local curiosities, about two miles away on the lower slopes of Great Whernside. Whitaker recommends it in the *Craven*: 'Dove Cave' (which was the name that Turner also used) 'is the finest cavern in the district. Its proportions are those of a lofty vaulted Gothic chapel, and the stalactites which adorn the sides and roof prove, I think, beyond controversy, from what source the later enrichments of that order were derived.'

Dow Cave is now famous to potholers as one end of the famous Dowbergill passage, but in Turner's day subterranean tourism was generally more tentative, and more literary. Most tourists thought of Milton or Dante's descent into Hell* 'A Dungeon terrible on all sides—No Light but rather Darkness visible—&c', and no doubt the guides would stimulate these literary apprehensions with tales of human bones and remains. Some fears were more justified than others. The huge slippery rocks at the mouth of the cave have fallen from the roof, and constant drips

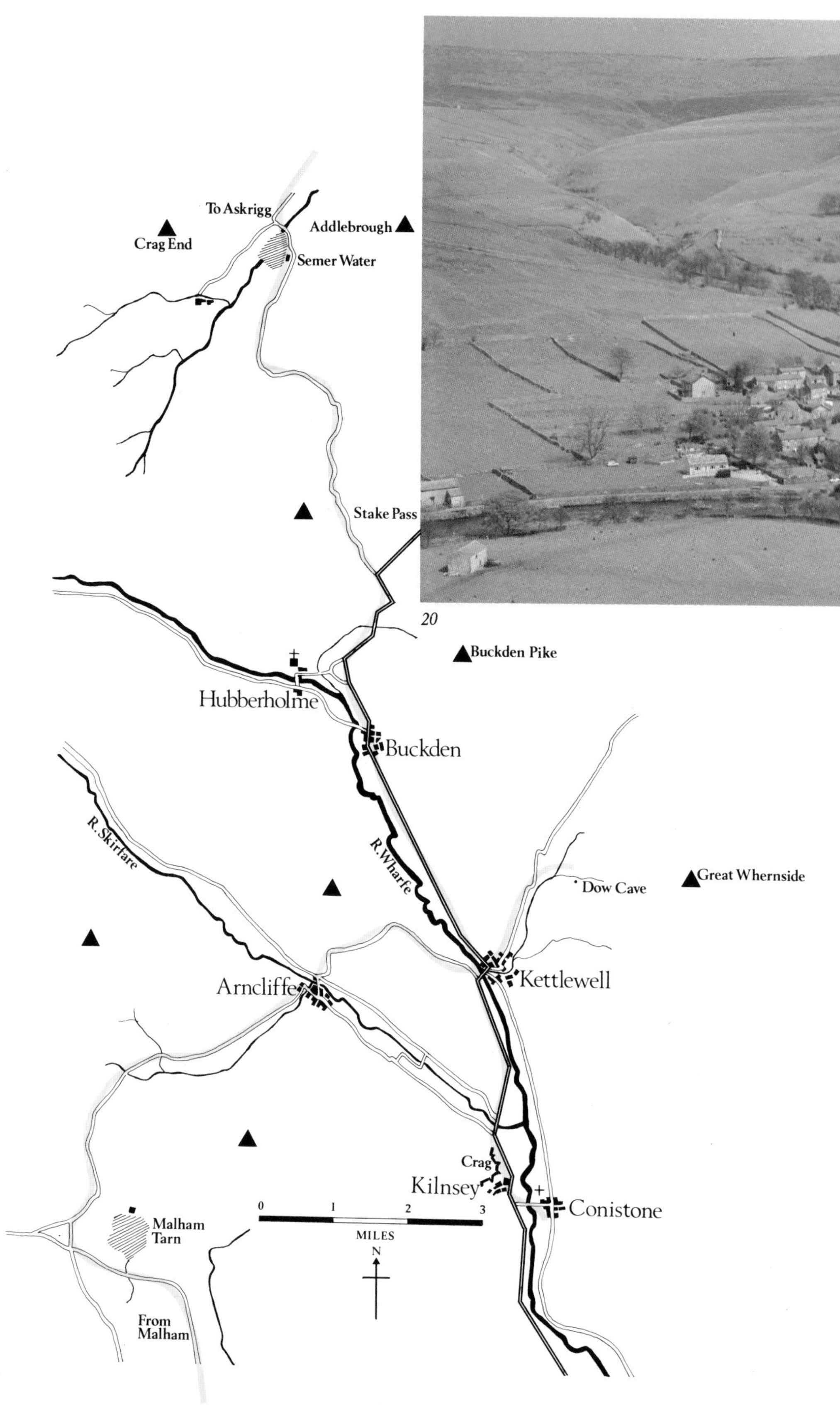

20

21

serve as reminders of this, as one makes the descent away from daylight.

Turner's nerves were on edge even before the descent. Once inside, his sketches in the pocket-book become little more than incoherent scribbles. At the bottom is a large stream passage, followed by walking and scrambling for about 450 feet to sandbanks. Then comes another passage to old mine workings, and a large, dripping chamber. This constant dripping would have been more insistent and menacing than usual after the heavy rains, and the underground rivers must have burbled below in full spate. It is possible then to squeeze and crawl through a narrow tunnel to a series of large chambers ending at a waterfall, but Turner would have seen enough. No one ever loved light more than he, and the darkness

22

19. Malham Tarn.

20. Kettlewell, the view Turner would have seen coming over into Wharfedale from Arncliffe in Littondale.

21. Kilnsey Crag and Conistone, with Turner's viewpoint for one of his sketches (see Ill.24) lower left.

22. Kilnsey Crag and Conistone, Upper Wharfedale, 1816. An unfinished watercolour probably made in the autumn of 1816 after Turner's return to London. It is based on the large sketch (Ill.24) and shows how freely the artist worked when creating effects of light and weather.

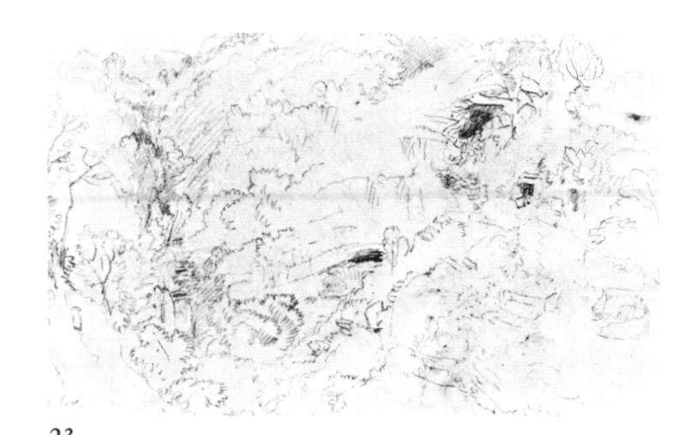

23

seems to have oppressed him. He calmed down again only when safely above ground, where he made a drawing (Ill. 23) of Caseker Gill to the left and the entrance of Dow Cave above to the right.

It was a damp, scuffed and mud-spattered figure that arrived back at the inn that evening, no doubt well pleased with his adventures. Making a smart appearance at supper must have been a problem. He had a choice between clothes that had been stuffed in a rain-soaked saddlebag all day, or dragged underground through a pothole. Not surprisingly, unless he had made arrangements to send fresh outfits on ahead, Turner's appearance would soon deteriorate even further.

Friday 26 July

Turner awoke to the bleating of sheep echoing across the dale. Wool had been the mainstay of the local economy since the Middle Ages, and Turner's preparation for his day's work included reading Whitaker's description of his morning's destination: 'Kilnsey was the place to which the immense flocks of ..[Fountains] ... abbey were driven from the surrounding hills for their annual sheep-shearing; a scene of primitive festivity, to which the imagination delights on recurring.

'The bleatings of the sheep, the echoes of the overhanging rocks, the picturesque habits of the monks, the uncouth dress, long beards and cheerful countenances of the shepherds, the bustle of the morning, and the good cheer of the evening ... even at present a large sheep-shearing is one of the most animating and cheerful scenes with which I am acquainted.'

Turner could have observed various surviving aspects of the pastoral life that Whitaker so fondly recalled on his morning's four-mile ride from Kettlewell down the sunny west side of the valley. Kilnsey, however, offers rather more conspicuous interest to the tourist, in the 'Crag', a towering inland cliff, 165 feet high, overhanging by more than thirty feet, which juts out into Wharfedale. It is an astonishing mass of limestone, which stretches nearly half a mile along the valley, and as dramatic a feature of the local landscape as Gordale.

Turner stopped where the road rounds High Wind Bank towards Littondale to sketch the view that suddenly opens up of Wharfedale dominated by Kilnsey Crag. His main purpose, however, was to take a view of Kilnsey from the village of Conistone across the valley, and he passed under the Crag, pausing only to make a couple of jottings in his pocket-book, going directly to find the viewpoint he required to unite the Crag, the villages of Kilnsey and Conistone, and the bridge between them. Just downstream from the bridge, he tried out a view in his pocket-book that seemed to have all the required elements. It also included a view up the dale to 'Peneghent', or so he thought, and in order to be sure of its details he made an enlarged drawing of its profile. His geography let him down here, however, for the hill shown is in fact Buckden Pike (2302 feet) above Kettlewell. Pen-y-ghent is hidden behind Kilnsey Crag to the left.

He found an even better vantage point on top of a small bluff beyond a stile further downstream, good enough for him to take out his largest sketchbook for the first time since Gordale. Conditions seem to have been fine enough for him to spend some considerable time and care on this drawing (Ill. 24), and there is a sense of evident enjoyment in the detailed pencil work as, like a cameraman, he panned through about ninety degrees from Kilnsey Old Hall over every building in the village, past Kilnsey Crag with Conistone Bridge below, to the entrance to Littondale beyond. Each drystone wall, gate and field is meticulously

24

23. The entrance to Dow Cave, near Kettlewell. Turner made a descent into the cave now famous among potholers as the entrance to the Dowbergill passage.

24. Kilnsey Crag and Conistone, upper Wharfedale. One of the most carefully detailed of all Turner's sketches, looking up Wharfedale towards Buckden Pike. The stile in the wall in the foreground may still be found in a scene changed only by the growth of trees.

THE STAKE PASS

made out—the 'stones' in the river, the Norman chapel at Conistone, Wharfedale closed by Buckden Pike behind and, to the right, Conistone village and a rocky 'Hay' field very nearly ready to cut. Every detail is lovingly set in its proper place,right down to the still-surviving stile in the foreground wall.

Turner had stocked his memory with exceptional care, and the vitality of the watercolour that he later started (Ill. 22) in his studio reflects the quality of the experience that had inspired it. It seems from an inscription on the drawing that 'C [harles] Cope [the engraver and watercolourist] of 29 Park Square [Leeds] had ordered a version of the subject' by the '31 Dec [1825]'. There is now no record of a finished version of this subject but, if Cope ever took charge of one, he must have been the owner of one of Turner's finest watercolours.

As always, Turner made a few more pencil sketches for reference before setting off for Askrigg in the late afternoon. Throughout this tour, he rarely omitted to take notes of any aspect of his valuable experience. There was no need to sketch three-quarters of the views he included in the pocket-book, for they were not large enough nor detailed enough to form the basis of finished paintings. Nonetheless, he hoarded glimpses of details or effects in order to engrave the landscape through which he moved on his mind. In the same way that we may use a diary, a camera or notes on a map to recall moments of a holiday, Turner made pocket-book jottings so that he might unlock memories of the tour at a later date. The detailed scrutiny involved in the very act of sketching reinforces visual memory.

The extraordinary thing about Turner's sketches is the amount of detail they carry. A hillside is not simply drawn to provide an effective mass in the composition, but is covered in squiggles, slanting lines and dots which served as a visual shorthand for specific observations. Turner's memory was legendary among his contemporaries. As we shall see from the way he sketched on this tour, one of the reasons it was so powerful was because he trained himself to remember by sketching. Later he labelled and numbered all his sketchbooks and kept them in his library, so that he could have instant references which would help him to retrieve places he had seen, sometimes years earlier.

After Kilnsey his route lay towards the head of the dale, where, at the junction of the road down to Hubberholme he stopped to make a sketch looking up higher Wharfedale towards a little medieval church tower and bridge, which he enlarged. His road did not lead down to Hubberholme, however, but turned north east past the waterfall at Cray, in spate in Turner's sketch of it, and on past the buildings shown in his drawing, one of them now the *White Lion* pub, leaving the modern road down into Bishopsdale after about a mile to strike off to the left along the green road over the Stake Pass.

The cloud-laden sky of Turner's unfinished *Kilnsey* watercolour shows that his crossing of the Stake Pass was not an altogether dry one. Surrounded by moors, and with an hour and a half of stony riding from Cray, he had ample time to reflect on Edward Dayes's approach to Semer Water thirteen years before.'The rain began to descend in torrents, when I had a considerable part of my day's rambles over the moors to perform, and for twelve miles, I courageously endured 'the pelting of the pitiless storm'. At length, being very wet, I sat down in a most forlorn and uncomfortable mood, to meditate on the objects of my journey, and naturally digressed to the cause which had operated to place me in such a situation. I blamed myself for suffering a propensity to admire the stupendous and beautiful scenery of nature, to prevail so strongly, as to induce me to wander so many miles from a comfortable home, and began to condemn it as mere idle curiosity. Influenced by melancholy, I had painted the evils of life with such strong and deadly colouring, that the mind had become terrified by the gigantic images it had conjured up; nor could it rest satisfied, till they were reduced to their proper size and colour. Under these impressions, I thought of *Park*, and of his Travels in Africa; without even a road to direct him, uncertain but that death might await his approach to the first human habitation, wandering through forests almost impervious to the rays of the sun, where his footsteps might lead to the abode of some deadly reptile, or his safety be endangered by wild beasts; and withal doubtful, from what source he might derive his next meal.. The rain still came down in torrents, the moors looked black and dismal; and Ingleborough, whenever I looked back, presented its grim front; but I had armed myself by reflection, and the

SEMER WATER TO ASKRIGG

storm passed unheeded. In my descent to Askrigg, I passed a lake, called SEMER-MERE; this is about three miles in compass; but it wants wood to give it interest: as it is but a short distance from the above town a walk round its banks might amuse.'

The inhabitants of Wensleydale were about their peaceful business as Turner dismounted to make a sketch (Ill. 25) looking south over Semer Water. The water level today is lower than it was then, for he portrayed it lapping the shore just in front of the Carlow Stone, whereas now there is a pebble beach which is popular with picnickers. Local legend has it that the Carlow Stone landed beside the lake when the devil tried to throw it from Addlebrough all the way to Crag End. Which demonstrates what no Yorkshireman needs telling: that the devil is a moderate cricketer.

There is another legend concerning Semer Water. It tells that once in this valley there stood a village to which an angel disguised as a beggar came, seeking shelter, but the inhabitants merely made fun of him. At last he came to a hovel in which lived a couple still older and poorer than he, who took him in and fed him and gave him a bed. Next morning, the traveller stood high on the hill and called out:

Simmer water rise, Simmer water sink,
And swallow all the town
Save yon little house
Where they gave me food and drink.

At which a huge wind whipped up the lake, drowning the village except for the house of the old couple. Its ruins stand on the edge of the lake in Turner's watercolour (Pl. 1).

Whether because of this legend, or because of the many other tales of ghostly voices singing by the lakeside or on the site of the old ruined church, the vicar holds an annual service from a boat on Semer with his congregation gathered on the banks.

In Turner's picture the mid-afternoon sun is disappearing behind rain which sweeps up from the south—its last bright rays spreading fan-like across the lake. A half-laden boat puts out in search of reeds for the beasts' winter bedding, and the labourers in the foreground would do well to transfer their load quickly to the waiting cart. Turner too would have been wise to make haste towards Askrigg, but he stopped for a few minutes on the road beyond Countersett to make a view looking back to his previous viewpoint by the Carlow Stone.

The road then winds down to Bainbridge —where to this day they blow the forest horn on winter evenings in order to guide lost travellers to safety, and across the river at Yorebridge. The clock showed five as Turner rode into Askrigg. Eight hundred feet above sea-level, and surrounded by moors and fells a full 1000 feet higher, Askrigg was famous for its clockmakers. Today, potholers come here to explore the Mazeholes below Abbotsford Common, and walkers and naturalists walk the same glens through which Turner climbed, in search of rare wild flowers.

Edward Dayes recommended the *King's Arms*, just beyond the church, with its impressive, then very modern, street frontage. It is still one of the best inns in town. 'I put up at the King's Arms Inn ... very wet and tired, and received the kindest attention from the landlord, and his two amiable daughters.' The daughters were thirteen years older by the time Turner arrived, but he was no doubt well satisfied with the other amenities, of which Viscount Torrington had earlier reported that, 'the accommodation, and wine, were tolerably good; and the stables ... excellent [although] there are no gardens here, adjoining to the houses (probably from the coldness of the climate) so garden stuff is a great rarity as coming from a distance.' The chief local industry, according to the same source was the 'knitting of worsted hose, a very idle employ; and that I might *encourage* the manufactory, I purchased

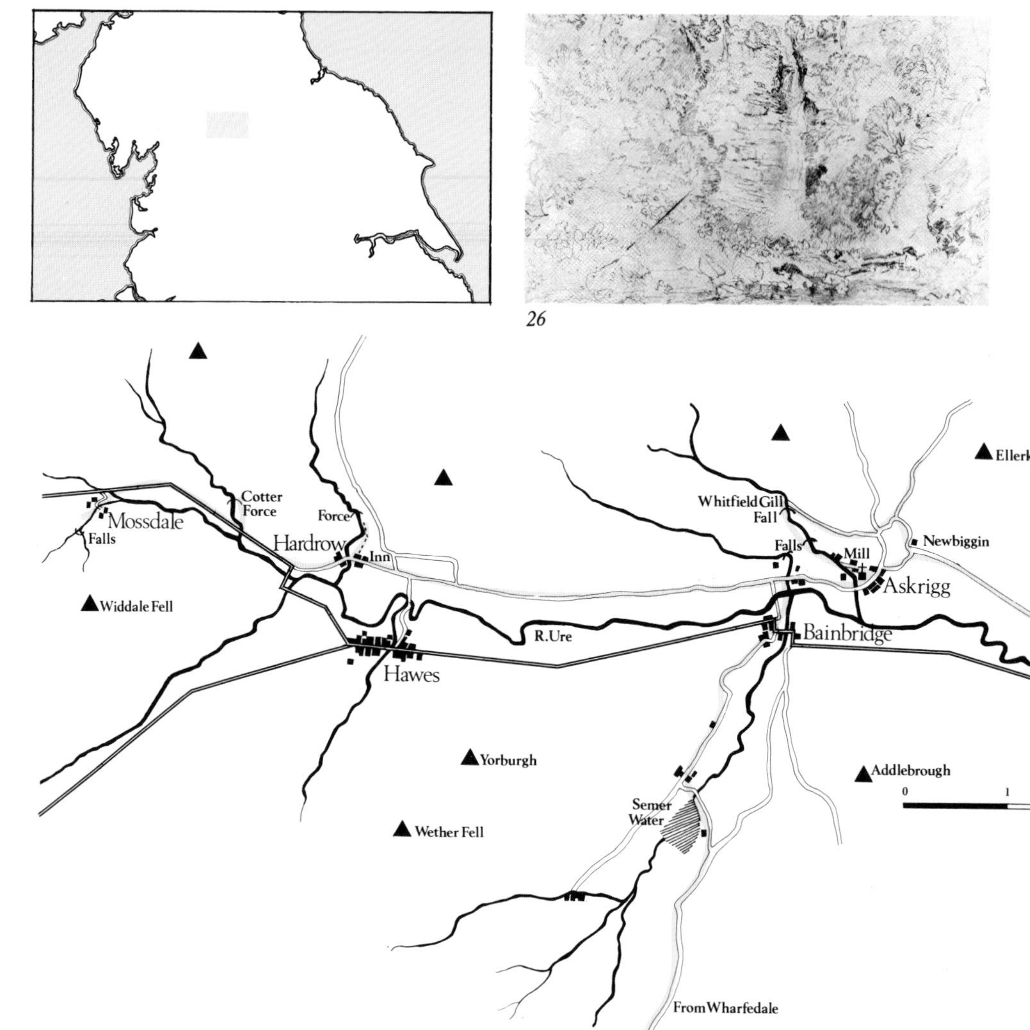

26

25

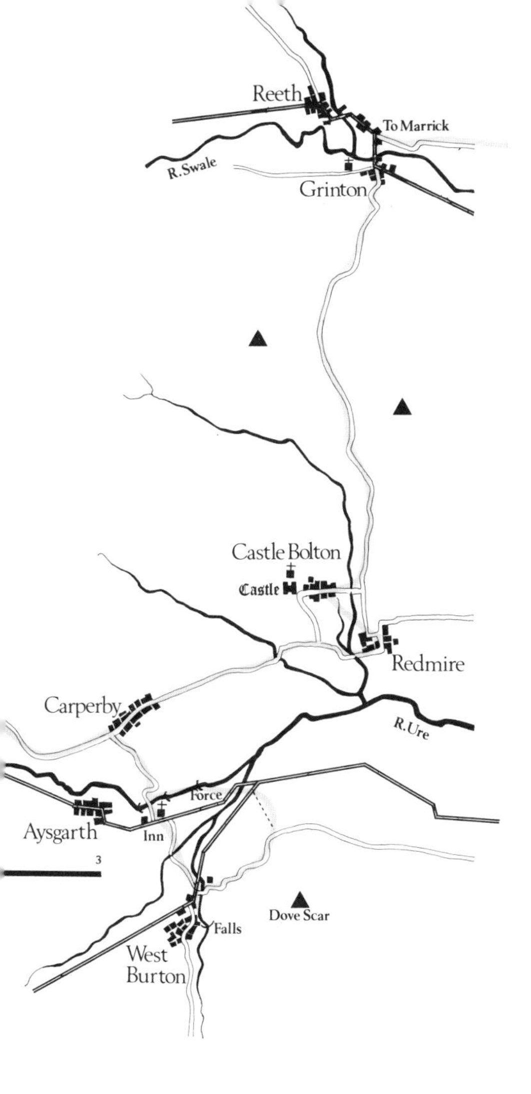

27

a pair for 8½d. to put on if well wetted.'

Dayes's book informed Turner that: 'About half a mile from Askrigg is a water-fall, called MILL-GILL FORCE, which makes one grand vertical fall of about twenty or thirty yards, and then rushes down to the rocky bed of the ravine. This place will afford several interesting studies for the pencil. One mile farther is WHITFIELD'S FORCE, a spectacle highly gratifying to the lover of romantic scenery.' Turner set out with his pencil and sketchbooks to record these sights for himself.

During the nineteenth century many tourists approached Mill Gill by scrambling along the beck, and when the stream was swollen with rain the local stockings would have soon seemed a worthwhile investment. Turner's first impression of the falls was taken from a viewpoint apparently in mid-stream showing the falls full of water and the ravine strewn with 'stones' and debris swept down by the torrent it frequently contains. Today the falls are completely overgrown (Ill. 28), and sunless, even in July, except for about an hour at midday. Turner's sketch shows fewer trees but even so the glen was cast in deep shade and not worth dwelling upon until the light was better. Having made a note of it in his pocket-book he pressed on up the valley to Whitfield Gill Force.

Most tourists stop at Mill Gill Falls, but those who go on are rewarded by a pleasant walk over sheep-grazed pastures, dropping to a pretty bridge over the beck below Leas House, followed by a climb up to Helm, and finally

28

25. Semer Water, near Askrigg. Still one of the most popular views of Yorkshire's largest natural lake, looking towards Raydale, with the Carlow Stone in the foreground and the Stake Pass road winding across the fellside to the left.

26. Mill Gill Fall, near Askrigg, Wensleydale. Turner seems to have been one of the first artists to have portrayed this waterfall. He enjoyed himself, to judge from the sensitivity of his pencil work and the care with which he outlined every bush and tree, rock and crevice.

27. A colour study of Mill Gill Fall, probably made in 1816. An unusually hidden subject in which Turner experimented with the contrast of warm midday sunshine and cool shade. He drew back a little from the viewpoint of his sketch (Ill. 26), to allow the mind's eye to make its own exploration.

28. Mill Gill Fall, now overgrown, from Turner's viewpoint.

29

the descent through native forest to the fifty-feet unbroken fall of Whitfield Force.

Turner's first viewpoint, from an obvious bluff among beech trees to the right of the path, provided him with a magnificent view of the whole gorge, the falls, and the fells above. Today, we look out mainly on thick, choking vegetation, the falls but a murmur in the distance. From here he scrambled down to risk another wetting in the stream bed, taking a slightly closer view looking up at the falls. Today the falls do not reveal themselves until the visitor is virtually beneath them. Turner's sketches are possibly the only records of these lost prospects.

From Whitfield Gill, Turner followed Low Straits Lane towards the scars of Ellerkin where he could enjoy one of the finest views in the area. He was sketching not for business, however, but for pleasure, for he used neither of the two larger sketchbooks in which the commissioned subjects were recorded. It was solely for the sake of his memory, then, that he made two sketches in his pocket-book of the view over Askrigg and Wensleydale to Semer Water glinting between Addlebrough and Wether Fell. In order to see Semer Water at all one has to be so far from Askrigg as to make its individual buildings almost indistinguishable. One of Turner's sketches (Ill. 29) shows every detail of the main street, however, swinging round past the field walls of the back of the *King's Arms* and the church. This exaggeration of buildings and other features within individual sketches occurs frequently in Turner's pocket-book drawings. At Hubberholme which he had sketched earlier it is hard to make out the details of the distant church from the viewpoint he actually used, and the same is true of the church at Mitton. It is tempting to think that Turner was working with a telescope, adding in details which could not be picked out with the naked eye. He appears, however, to have been engaged in a much more subtle and complex exercise, shifting viewpoints so that he could cram as many major features of the landscape as possible into his sketches. If he had used a telescope in the Askrigg sketch, he would have seen more of the roofs of the houses than his sketch shows. In fact, he started the sketch about 500 yards from Askrigg and then continued it while climbing Ellerkin, stopping higher up to add more of the view as it became visible in the distance. At the top he had one of the great views of Wensleydale, downdale to Aysgarth, Penhill, West Burton, Bishopdale and Addlebrough, and updale towards Hawes and Mossdale at the dale's head—a panorama of more than fourteen miles. For the moment, however, he was content to retrace his footsteps over the landscape he had spent the day exploring, through the village of Askrigg, over Yorebridge, up through Bainbridge and Countersett to Semer Water, and from there over the darkening fells back to Wharfedale. He would continue his explorations in the morning.

Saturday 27 July

Whitaker was silent on the subject of Mill Gill or Whitfield Gill falls, but Turner evidently intended finished watercolours of both. He seems to have been satisfied with his sketches of Whitfield Gill, but still needed to return to Mill Gill to sketch it under the proper conditions. With the late morning light shining into the ravine, the falls impressed him enough to use his largest sketchbook for the first time since Kilnsey. Mill Gill was at its best for much more than the light, however, for this was a time at which timber was at such a premium that any mature or fallen wood was promptly removed, and the glen displayed its charms more generously than it does today, framing rather than hiding, offsetting rather than obscuring.

Turner devoted particular care to this drawing (Ill. 26), recording the particulars of rocks and boulders, trees, plants and leaves with the same care that he would have given to the most extensive prospect of town, river or hill. Mill Gill Fall was, however, too large even for Turner's largest sketchbook. The edges of the page seem to diminish it too much, to the point where it can be taken in whole in a single glance. Turner took this into account and his attention to detail increases towards the centre, gradually drawing the eye in, so that it progressively loses sight of

30

the edges of the sheet, into the centre and finally up through the gap at the top of the fall into the valley beyond. The stream carries the eye back down the fall, jumping from step to step, rebounding from one side to the other, plunging down into the shady pool at its base, picking its way between rocks to the foreground.

A magnifying glass would help even more to lose the edges of the paper, especially in a drawing as detailed as this. This is probably something Turner's generation would have taken for granted, but in an age such as ours, where the usual requirement of images is to be immediate, the delights of the glass are often overlooked. It is important to remember that in Turner's day people looked at paintings in a different manner. They allowed their eyes to linger on one area and then another, concentrating on different subjects of interest. This is why topographical engravings, which we often find rather dull to look at, were bought in their thousands and pored over on a table. Turner more than any artist rewards the effort of concentration which is required to enter his world.

We can see the way in which he synthesised the results of such a close study in his unfinished watercolour of Mill Gill (Ill. 27). The main effects of light and colour have been blocked in and already there are suggestions of the engrossing detail that would have followed. Unfortunately he carried it no further, but to judge from the inscription on the sketch he was possibly sketching the wrong fall, anyway. His sketch of Whitfield Gill Fall made the previous evening is inscribed 'Whitfield Fell Mill beck or Mill Gill. Askrigg', and he may well have been under the impression that Mill Gill was Whitfield Gill. Whatever the case, he continued his exploration of Mill Gill by climbing up the left-hand side of the ravine to the top of the fall. Here, in 1799, Wordsworth had observed that, 'The Steeple of Askrigg was not a quarter of a mile distant, but oh, how far we are from it.' Turner was more circumspect in his title for this sketch: 'Askrigg from the lower fall', but the view is clear enough, looking, as Wordsworth would have done, to the church tower, with Penhill beyond, and the scars of Ellerkin, near the viewpoints of the previous evening, above and to the left.

He dropped his sketchbook here. The page is covered with dried mud, but the following one was clean enough for him to conclude his survey of the gill with a sketch of the ancient corn mill from which it had taken its name, with its ramshackle bridge carrying the path up steps and over a stile into a field with a distant glimpse of Addlebrough beyond.

The present public footpath to Mill Gill passes this way and much of the scene is still recognisable. The bridge has been replaced by a new one, but the steps survive, as does the mill and even its water conduit seen crossing the path directly below the church tower. Below it stands one of the very rare figures in Turner's sketches, the miller perhaps, come out to see what this fellow in a black top hat and tails with a notebook was up to.

Sometime after midday, Turner collected his belongings from the inn and saddled up for the next leg of the tour, and with a five-mile ride up to Hardrow it was late afternoon by the time he arrived at the *Green Dragon* in the village. The inn gives entrance to the highest unbroken waterfall in England, Hardrow Force, and Longmans had naturally commissioned a drawing. The falls, however, are best seen before or about midday, after which they become gloomy and dark. Turner therefore decided to press on that evening to Mossdale, three miles further on, where Longmans also required him to make a sketch.

Mossdale Head was the remotest habitation that Turner had so far encountered, a cluster of cottages with a ramshackle bridge near a waterfall, eking out a living among the high fells. Whitaker described it enthusiastically as 'an unfeatured scene of desolation' where 'The junction of the Ure with Mossdale Beck exhibits two waterfalls one in each stream seen from the same point, happily uniting at an oblique angle to the

29. Askrigg village and church, with a view of Semer Water. It is impossible to see Semer Water from a viewpoint so close to the village. Turner must have sketched the village first and then climbed up towards Ellerkin Scars to add a view of the hills beyond to the sketch.

30. Looking over Askrigg towards Semer Water.

MOSSDALE HEAD

eye.' Uncharacteristically, Whitaker identified the streams wrongly, leading one to wonder whether he had actually been there or was working from Turner's drawing and the artist's consistently inaccurate topography.

The remoteness of the location, the lateness of the evening, the rocky stream leading to the falls among the barren hills, impressed Turner deeply. He dispensed with his usual preliminary sketches to work directly in his largest sketchbook.

The first sketch (Ill.31) was of the commissioned view of the twin falls above the farm, where a small stream tumbles down rock steps from Sandy Hill into Great Gill. 'Let it be confessed at once,' remarked a Victorian follower in Turner's footsteps, who had come to see the site of the finished engraving, 'that Mossdale is a very small furrow in a moorland dale, with nothing Alpine about it'. But Turner was determined to give expression to his feelings, while at the same time recording the topography, and his eye gave selective emphasis to the features of the site that particularly impressed him—the deep-scoured valley at the right, the cracked and shattered steps at the left, the bold mass of rock that divides them, the bare fellside beyond, and the stunted trees clinging to scraps of soil for their survival. It is a scene of desolate and primordial violence, and the basis of one of the very few wholly deserted watercolours by Turner (Pl. 2).

As far as we can tell from the shadows in the sketch (they are more explicit in the finished watercolour), the light was shining into Turner's face from the right, making the time about eight o'clock in the evening. Although the light was just beginning to fade, he seems to have wanted to record every aspect of Mossdale, for he embarked on a series of three further sketches which reveal how he worked when he wished to make a permanent *aide-memoire* of a particular landscape .

He followed the beck down to the lower falls by the farm, and, turning round, made a view looking back to the upper falls, in exactly the opposite direction to the first sketch. He then moved further down the hill and sketched Mossdale Head Farm with the old bridge and lower falls to its right—the site of the second sketch. Finally, he made a drawing (Ill. 32) from a vantage point on the Sedbergh-Hawes road which reviewed his whole progress from the upper falls to below Mossdale Head Farm, before riding back to the *Green Dragon*.These four drawings provide a co-ordinated 'image' of Mossdale Head. There was not necessarily anything systematic about the angles at which the different sketches were made, but we find Turner exhibiting here, as elsewhere, a determination to record the different viewpoints from which he sketched. It meant that when he referred back to his notebooks at the end of a tour, he could build a composite picture in his head from any angle.

Sunday 28 July

The Sabbath brought no interruption to Turner's progress, though, for the morning at least, he had no need to venture far from the inn. From the back of the *Green Dragon* it is a short and easy stroll to Hardrow Force. The glen gradually becomes more enclosed, its wooded sides rising up to limestone cliffs, then abruptly, turning to the left, it ends in a dark cliff, or, rather, 'a cave of rocks ... where the stream flows over the top of the rock in one sheet of about seventy yards in height—making a most rumbling noise in falling, with a fierce foam at bottom.'

At most times it is possible to scramble behind the fall and stand under the overhang. Wordsworth described the experience to Coleridge in a letter of 1799: 'We found the rock, which before had appeared like a wall, extending itself over our heads like the ceiling of a huge cave, from the summit of which the water shot directly over our heads into a basin, and among fragments wrinkled over with masses of ice as white as snow, or rather, as Dorothy says, like congealed

32

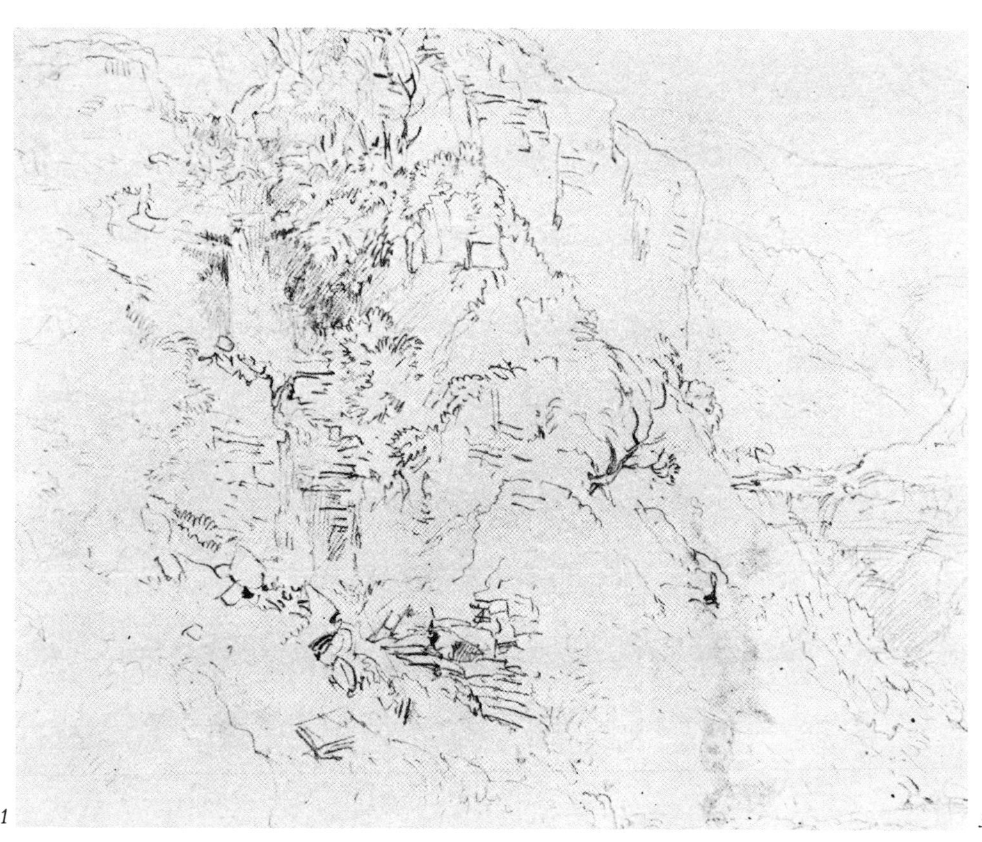

31

33

HARDROW FORCE

34

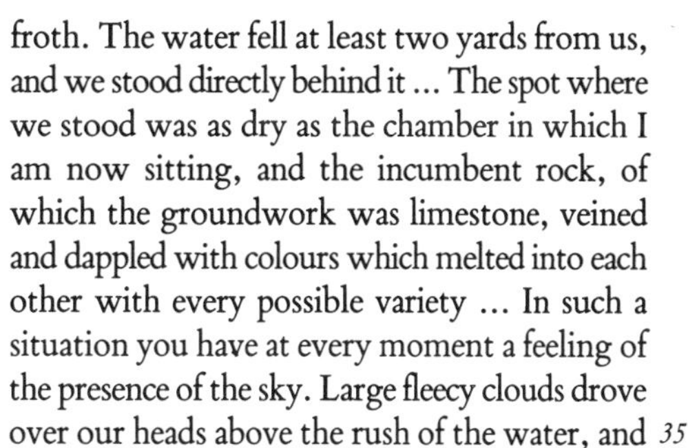

froth. The water fell at least two yards from us, and we stood directly behind it ... The spot where we stood was as dry as the chamber in which I am now sitting, and the incumbent rock, of which the groundwork was limestone, veined and dappled with colours which melted into each other with every possible variety ... In such a situation you have at every moment a feeling of the presence of the sky. Large fleecy clouds drove over our heads above the rush of the water, and

35

36

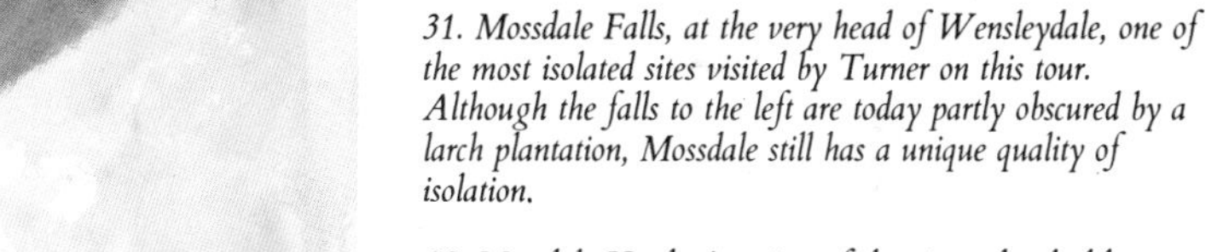

31. Mossdale Falls, at the very head of Wensleydale, one of the most isolated sites visited by Turner on this tour. Although the falls to the left are today partly obscured by a larch plantation, Mossdale still has a unique quality of isolation.

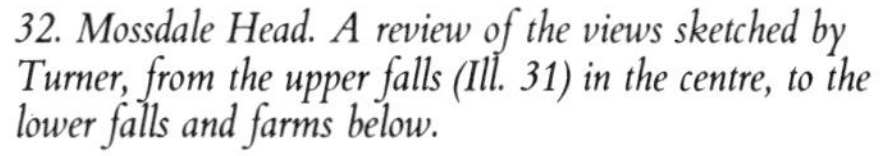

32. Mossdale Head. A review of the views sketched by Turner, from the upper falls (Ill. 31) in the centre, to the lower falls and farms below.

33. Mossdale Head from above the Hawes to Sedbergh road with the plantation obscuring the falls in the middle of the photograph.

34. Three colour studies for Yorkshire subjects, 1816, including Hardrow Force, below, with Barnard Castle upper left, and Kex Gill, upper right.

35. Hardraw Fall. *The engraving, with the old-fashioned spelling for Hardrow, by S. Middiman and John Pye published in 1818.*

36. Hardrow Force, Wensleydale. Claimed to be the highest unbroken fall in England, it is particularly impressive after heavy rains.

HARDROW TO WEST BURTON

37

37. West Burton Falls, Wensleydale. Turner sketched virtually every fall in Wensleydale, his enthusiasm seeming to grow with each one. Here, he delighted particularly in the way that the water fans out to form a veil, allowing the rocks behind to shine through.

the sky appeared to be of a blue more than usually brilliant.' Wordsworth mentioned Turner's 'fine drawing' of Hardrow in his *Guide to the Lakes*, and one can imagine his pleasure at recalling his experiences by retracing his footsteps through the engraving.

Hardrow is a place of extravagant scale that surrounds, overhangs, and completely dominates the spectator, and its din-filled space does not transfer easily to two dimensions, particularly on a page measuring 10 x 7 ins. The first sketch did not work. He was too close to his subject and the waterfall seems mundane—a mere trickle into a basin rather than the highest unbroken fall in the land. The problem that faced him recalls that which he faced at Gordale Scar. There, James Ward had found a solution by painting on a scale grand enough to make the great cliffs of the gorge tower over the spectator. As we have seen, Turner eventually abandoned his painting of Gordale, for Ward's solution would not work on the small scale with which he had to contend. His problem, in fact, was that he had to convey an impression of immense grandeur within the confines of an engraving (Ill. 35).

He found the solution by moving back from the falls to make a distant view. This allowed him to lead the spectator's eye into the glen along the path beneath the cliffs. In the finished watercolour (Pl. 3) he developed the theme even further. It is early morning, and the sun streams from the east, lighting the pasture on the western side of the glen, while the eastern cliffs are still in deep shade. A milkmaid returns from her morning rounds, and is met climbing over a stile in the foreground. Turner's problem was to make the eye lose sight of the edges of the sheet, to lead the viewer right into the gorge and confront him with the enormity of the falls. He diminishes scale gradually so that we make our way along the precipitous path, squeezing past a fellow-tourist in a red waistcoat on the way, until we finally join two tiny figures perched on a bluff (the viewpoint of Turner's first sketch). We are now reduced to a speck, totally surrounded by the cliffs, wetted by the mist drifting up from the basin, and dwarfed by the fall pouring past. At this point the imaginary tourist stands suspended in the middle of the chasm, his imaginary field of view engulfed by the picture.

Before leaving the *Green Dragon*, Turner had to sketch another fall about a mile and a half away west, along a footpath off the Hawes-Sedbergh road. Cotter Force is a rather more intimate subject than Hardrow, with its clear brown beck tumbling down steps into a shaded pool, and Turner chose the more intimate smaller sketchbook in which to record it. The morning sun was shining strongly when he made his sketch, for there are clear shadows on the rocks to the right. The shade would have added lustre to the 'Dark pool', and Turner seems to have been more at peace with this subject than he had been with Hardrow where he did not develop the drawings in any great detail. Here he concentrated on recording all the intricacies of structure and allowed his pencil to trace all the courses and channels of the stream between the rocks and to frame the whole with hanging boughs. His solitude was disturbed, however, by children looking over the bank to the right of the falls, and he noted this on the sketch. We can almost hear them giggling

38

38. West Burton Falls.

and whispering about this peculiar stranger with a drawing pad who had invaded their secret dale.

The road then took him back to Askrigg where he made a farewell sketch from Newbiggin Hill. Here 'the road ascending commands a fine view of a well-wooded country, in a deep vale, with the river Ure meandering through its rich meadows and flowing near the town'. He presumably hoped to be able to remember the stretch of country that he was now leaving, but again his inscription was vague. He wrote 'Grinton', but realised his mistake and changed it to 'Askrigg'. From here the road lead downdale to Carperby, then to the bridge at Aysgarth, and on another mile and a half to West Burton. Allowing for a stop to examine the prospective accommodation at the *Palmer Flatt* inn at the top of the bank at Aysgarth, he must have arrived sometime in the early afternoon.

West Burton is one of the most spacious and attractive villages in Wensleydale, but Turner was concerned solely with the waterfall. Having made a couple of quick sketches in his pocket-book, he decided that there was no good way of marrying the falls with their surroundings, and settled on a close-up viewpoint where he could study the beauties of the fall in isolation (Ill. 37).

West Burton Fall deserves such close scrutiny for it is one of the finest, most delicate falls of water in the dale. There was a lot of water in the stream, but not too much to prevent the rocks shining through the final leap as it fanned it out into a transparent veil. Turner enjoyed this sketch enough to linger for about half an hour, studying not only every detail of the fall itself, but also the particular details of its setting—the rocks scattered around in the foreground, the undercut cave at the left, trees hanging over the pool from the banks and the glimpse of the fellside beyond.

Pressing on he crossed the narrow bridge into the lane at the back of Flanders Hall and climbed quite steeply for about a mile until reaching the junction with the lane from West Witton at the end of the huge limestone escarpment. He celebrated the ascent by recording the way he had come in his pocket-book (Ill. 42). The escarpment provides a grandstand for one of the finest views in the area, from which Turner could

39

40

survey the entire stretch of 'Upper Wednesly-dale' (as he called it) that he had explored in the previous two days. To the right is the tower of Aysgarth Church, clearly visible, with Aysgarth mill to its right, and the river leading down to Aysgarth Force in the bottom right corner.

As well as the falls, Aysgarth now offers to the visitor old houses covered with creepers, a lovely little Tudor bridge, a museum of horse-drawn vehicles and a church more remarkable for its contents even than its structure which, although initially dating from the thirteenth century, is now mostly nineteenth-century reconstruction. Within, however, Aysgarth church contains magnificent woodwork. There is a startling fifteenth-century screen with deep fan-vaulting and a delicate cornice with fruit, birds and grotesques. It so impressed Whitaker that he commissioned an illustration of it for the Richmondshire section of the *County of York*. Two ornate poppyhead bench ends are set in the reading desk. They date from the same period as the screen and show, amongst other symbols, a hazel tree and a tun linked to the letter W. This is the picture name of William de Heslington, Abbot of Jervaulx, and it is reasonable to assume that the screen and the bench-ends were brought to safety here before Jervaulx was destroyed in 1536. Another link with the great Cistercian Abbey can be seen in an oak beam to the north of the chancel. Two hooded men with long ears are carved there, with the date 1536 and the initials of the last abbot of Jervaulx, Adam Sedbergh, who was coerced into joining the Pilgrimage of Grace and, despite the reluctant part that he played in the misconceived mission, was hanged at Tyburn in 1537. Aysgarth's other principal claim to fame is that Garibaldi's red shirts are said to have been made at the mill here.

Dayes had a good deal to say about Aysgarth: 'Here are several *Falls*, both above and below the bridge, the whole range occupying an extent of nearly half a mile. This should be particularly remembered, otherwise a stranger might miss the Force, where the whole body of the river, "collected in one impetuous torrent, down the steep loud thundering shoots, and shakes the country

39. Aysgarth Force.

40. Aysgarth Force. Turner's sketch, by comparison with a photograph, seems to exaggerate the size of the falls in relation to their surroundings. The sketch, however, mimmicks the eye's ability to select the features it finds most interesting and diminishes the less relevant detail. A camera cannot do this. The memory exaggerates this effect still further, and Turner's finished picture (Pl. 4) corresponds more closely to Aysgarth Force as it is remembered than any photograph ever could.

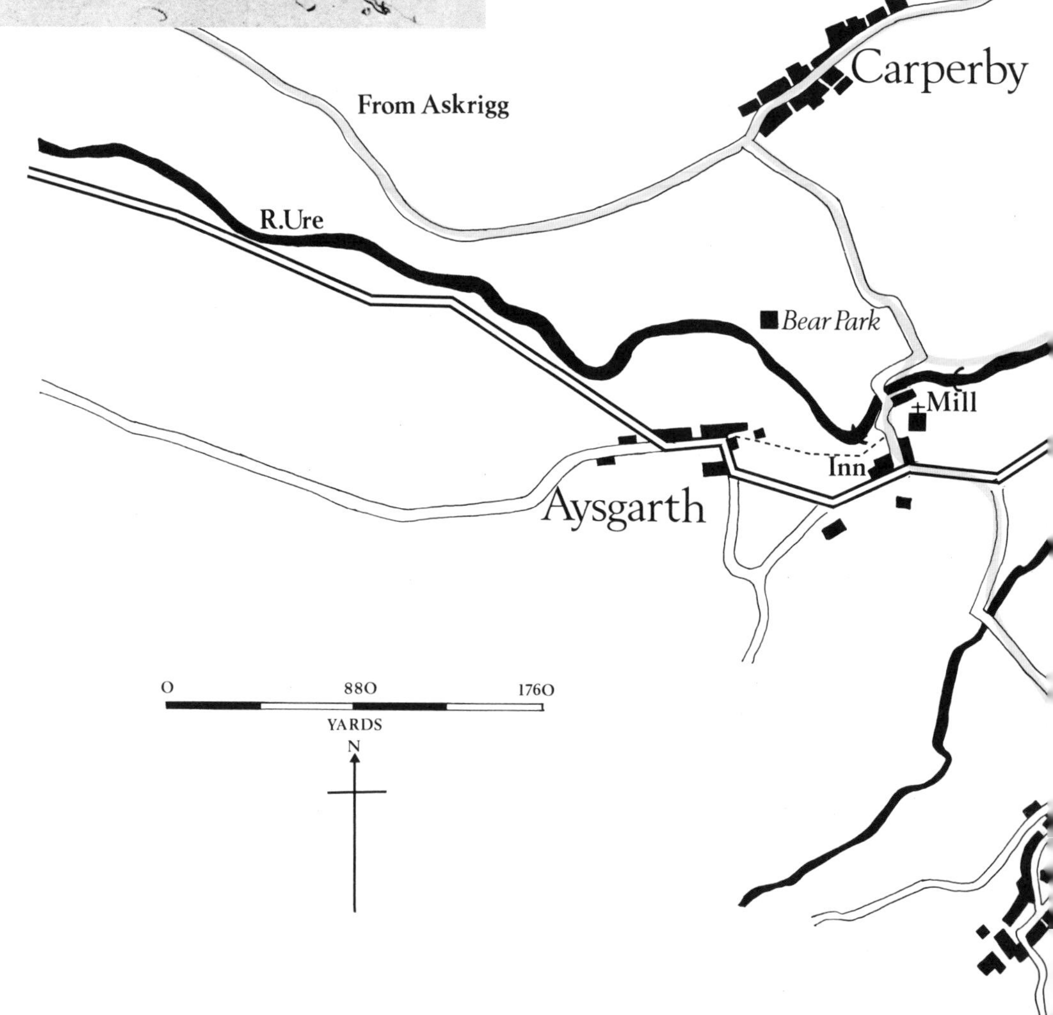

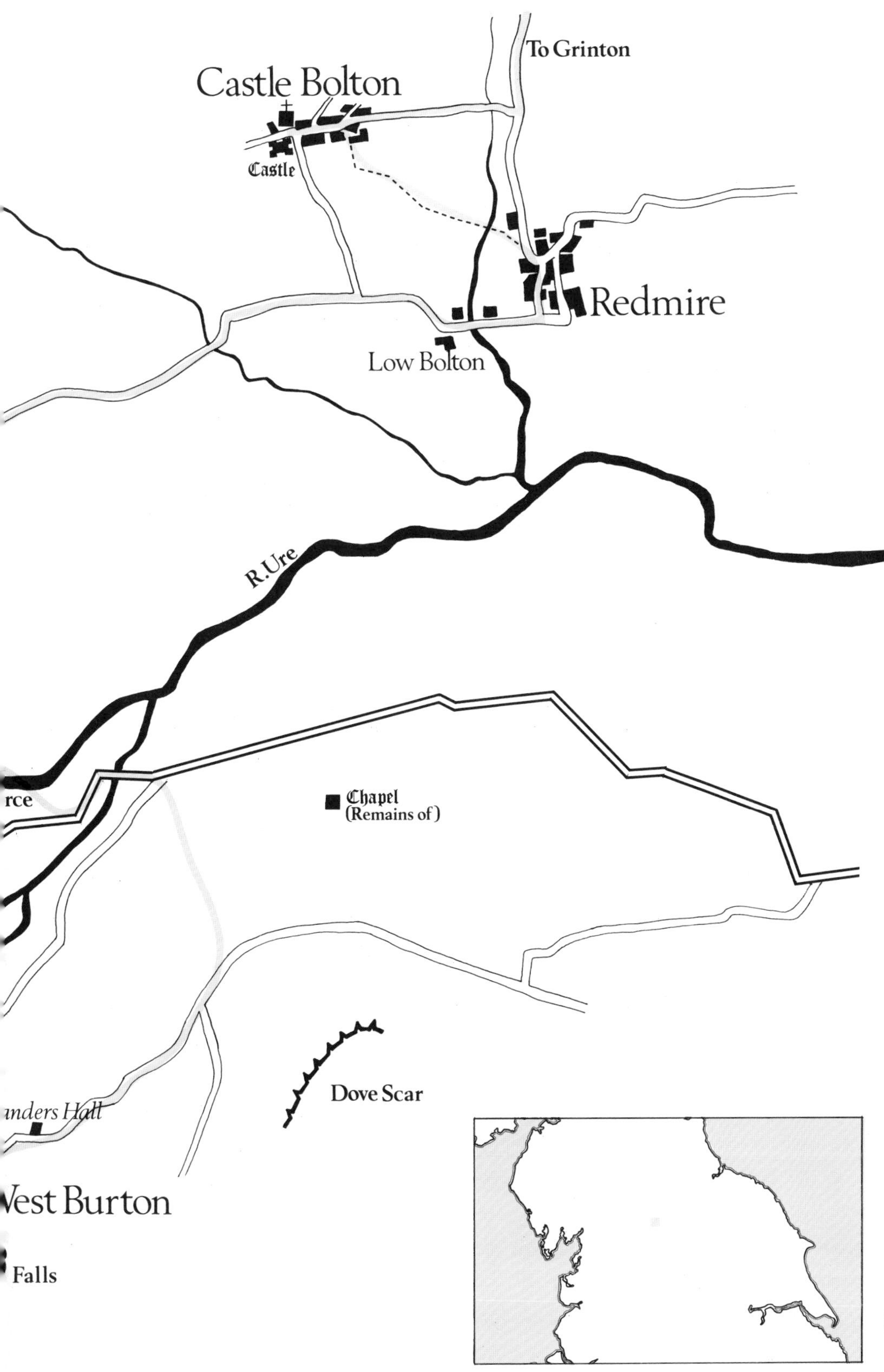

41

42

round.' Above the bridge, the river Ure slides over various ledges of rocks, forming a scene highly delightful. The river here flows through a hollow, enclosed by bold hills, richly decorated with wood, and forming a fine background to the tumultuous cascades. The bridge is composed of one noble arch, of considerable span, through which the water is seen pouring down over various sloping rocks, presenting a view highly picturesque.'

Despite Dayes's warning, Whitaker missed the lower falls, for he only mentioned those either side of the bridge, although Turner's illustration of the lower force made up for the oversight. The descent from above West Burton brought him to Hestholme Farm along the river bank to the falls. He forded the shallows, probably immediately below the falls, to the northern bank. There he made the sketch (Ill. 40) for the finished watercolour (Pl.4). It had recently rained updale, and the erosive effects of the constant deluge were observed by Turner with all the care and precision of a natural scientist. Natural history in the nineteenth century was a basic tool of the tourist's response to place, and Whitaker deals with the geomorphology of Aysgarth in his text at the same time as dealing with its etymology. Turner well understood the processes that had shaped this particular feature, if for no other reason than his personal experience of the rains that were now swelling the river. He

41. Upper Wensleydale from above West Burton. A lane leads up from Flanders Hall in West Burton to one of the finest of all views of Wensleydale. Turner was once again (as at Mossdale, see Ill. 32) tracing his route across the landscape, from Addleborough to the left, to Askrigg in the distance (below the 'x'), down dale to Aysgarth church and mill (right of centre) and Aysgarth Force (lower right). Note Turner's idiosyncratic spelling of 'Wednesly dale'.

42. Upper Wensleydale from above West Burton.

would also have observed that this was the first major obstacle in the river to salmon. Salmon fishing and the rain were to provide the main themes of the finished watercolour.

Turner's exploration of Aysgarth was only just beginning, however. He climbed up to the top of the fall to take a view 'Looking down the Fall', back up to the viewpoint of his sketch of Wensleydale from above West Burton, and then continued up river taking sketches of 'Middle Asgarth force', the first (Ill. 43) from an outcrop on the northern bank, from which it was possible to survey the falls, the church, the mill and the bridge all in one view. Whitaker, unaware of the lower force, probably had this particular view in mind, for in his description of Aysgarth he mentions all these features in relation to the church 'In a charming situation above these falls, whose solemn roar alone interrupts the stillness of the scene'.

It was late afternoon and the stillness of the scene would have been interrupted by the church bells ringing across the dale to call parishioners to evensong. Turner might even have joined them. In any case he devoted himself to contemplating the church, at least from without, with a sketch taken from the 'C[hurch] path' which linked it to the village, looking downdale across the landscape he had just explored, with, at the left, the next day's destination, Castle Bolton.

Monday 29 July

It was now four days since he had left the Fawkes party at Gordale. Although he had made a detailed survey of every site so far, it was becoming apparent that he had covered only a fraction of the required area. He still faced a formidable itinerary of sites which even by the most economical of routes entailed several hundred miles of travel. He had to hurry. He packed away his

43

44

43. Aysgarth Middle Falls, with the church to the left, mill and bridge to the right, 'Stones' by the river to the left, and the 'sky' reflected in the river to the right. This was the view described by Whitaker, who managed to miss seeing the main waterfall lower down the river.

44. Aysgarth Middle Falls.

45

46

largest sketchbook, determined on arriving at Richmond within the day.

His final site in Wensleydale was Bolton Castle. The traveller following in Turner's footsteps will find it remarkably well preserved, although much of it is now in ruins. Richard Scrope, Richard II's Chancellor, spent twenty years and £200,000 in building what was probably, in its time, the strongest house in England. Amongst relics of the past which doubtless gave Turner pause for thought is a dungeon thirteen feet long and nine feet wide, carved out of solid rock. It has no door or window, just a tiny opening at the very top. An arm bone in an iron ring was recently found there. Such sombre sights, and Dayes's gloomy speculations on the ruins—'Thus passes away the glory of man, like a cloud driven before the wind'—no doubt filled Turner's mind once more with those thoughts of futility and transience with which he had been wrestling for years in his long poem, *The Fallacies of Hope*. He would have been fully briefed about the castle's history for Dayes had devoted five pages to it, recounting that Mary, Queen of Scots, had been confined here in 1568, and that 'During the Civil Wars, this castle was gallantly defended by Colonel Scroope, and a party of Richmondshire militia, for the King ...' and how, 'From neglect, and the damage it received during the siege ... the tower on the north-east angle became so injured, that it fell to the ground on the evening of 19th November, 1761.'

He explored every aspect of the building, paying particular attention to the missing tower (Ill. 45), and despite his need to press on made ten sketches in all, from distant as well as close-up viewpoints, relating the castle to the surrounding landscape from west, south and east, including figures 'washing wool' at Redmire, before completing his survey with views from the north west and north east, looking out over the towers into Wensleydale.

The road over to Grinton goes up to about 1500 feet, and from the top he made a note of the sea of fells before him. He had no time to dawdle, however, and made only a quick note of the panorama of Swaledale over to Reeth as he descended, and a hurried sketch of the church

45. Bolton Castle, Wensleydale. Turner made ten sketches of the castle from every possible angle. His final composition, however, typically managed to unite all the main features of the site: the castle, with its collapsed tower, weakened during the Civil War, the tiny church nearby, and the clustering roofs of the village, with the view over Wensleydale beyond to Penhill at the left and towards Aysgarth on the right.

46. Bolton Castle, Wensleydale.

MARRICK PRIORY TO RICHMOND

at Grinton, before crossing the Swale bridge and heading downdale to the priories of Marrick and Ellerton.

The church of St. Andrew at Marrick had been rebuilt only five years before out of the materials of the original twelfth-century Benedictine priory which, like Jervaulx, had been destroyed by the dissolution of the monasteries. Four years before the nuns were forced to abandon their home, however, a rich and very beautiful maid-of-honour named Isabella Beaufort arrived at the gates seeking sanctuary. Henry VIII wished to marry her but she, with commendable foresight, had no desire to be his queen. The prioress admitted Isabella and kept her in hiding, permitting her to correspond with her lover, Edward Herbert. When at last the priory was closed, Herbert rode up to Marrick, bore Isabella back to Somerset and married her.

Turner lost no time in deciding on the best viewpoint, and dashed off only a couple of quick notes before settling down on a bluff immediately downstream to record the view up Swaledale to the fells he had crossed an hour or so before. The priory is set on its own promontory amongst a patchwork of fields, woods, hedges and lanes, and in his drawing (Ill. 47) is punctuated by the new church tower rising from a farmyard, with smoke rising from a hearth fire in the farmhouse kitchen where dinner is being prepared in the late afternoon. As in all the sketches, there is little or no indication of weather. The finished watercolour (Pl. 5) is a magnificent study of billowing clouds and filtered sunlight dropping on different parts of the view.

On the opposite bank of the river Ellerton Priory lies about a mile downstream, and communication between the two convents was established over stepping-stones. Turner forded the river but discovered that little of the old

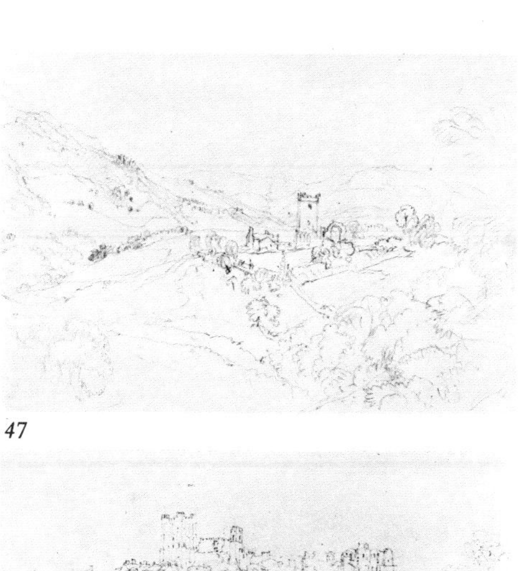

47

48

49

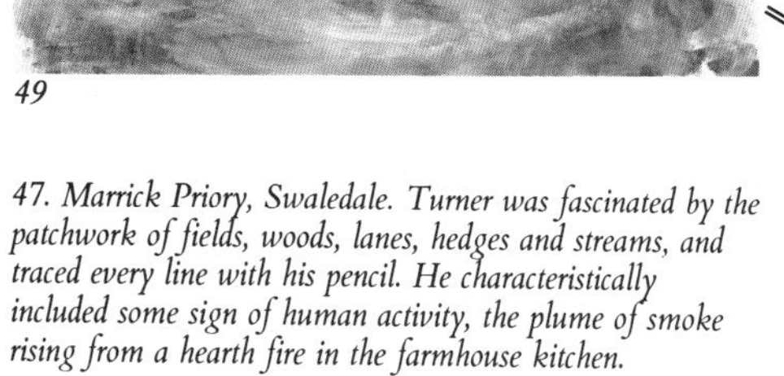

47. Marrick Priory, Swaledale. Turner was fascinated by the patchwork of fields, woods, lanes, hedges and streams, and traced every line with his pencil. He characteristically included some sign of human activity, the plume of smoke rising from a hearth fire in the farmhouse kitchen.

48. Richmond Bridge and Castle with Yorke House to the left. Turner had already visited the site in 1797 and engraved the subject on his memory on that occasion by sketching it and by painting it later in about 1799 (Ill. 50). He was satisfied that it was sufficiently unchanged in 1816 to use the early sketch as the basis of a new watercolour (Ill. 49).

49. Colour study of Richmond Bridge and Castle, made in c.1818.

50. Richmond Bridge and Castle, *1799.*

50

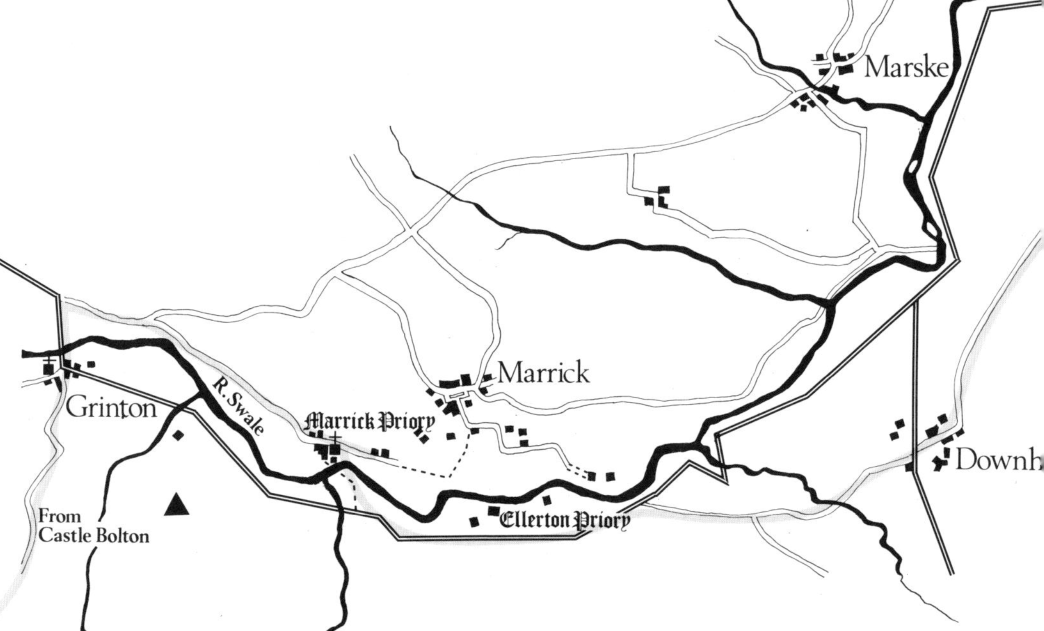

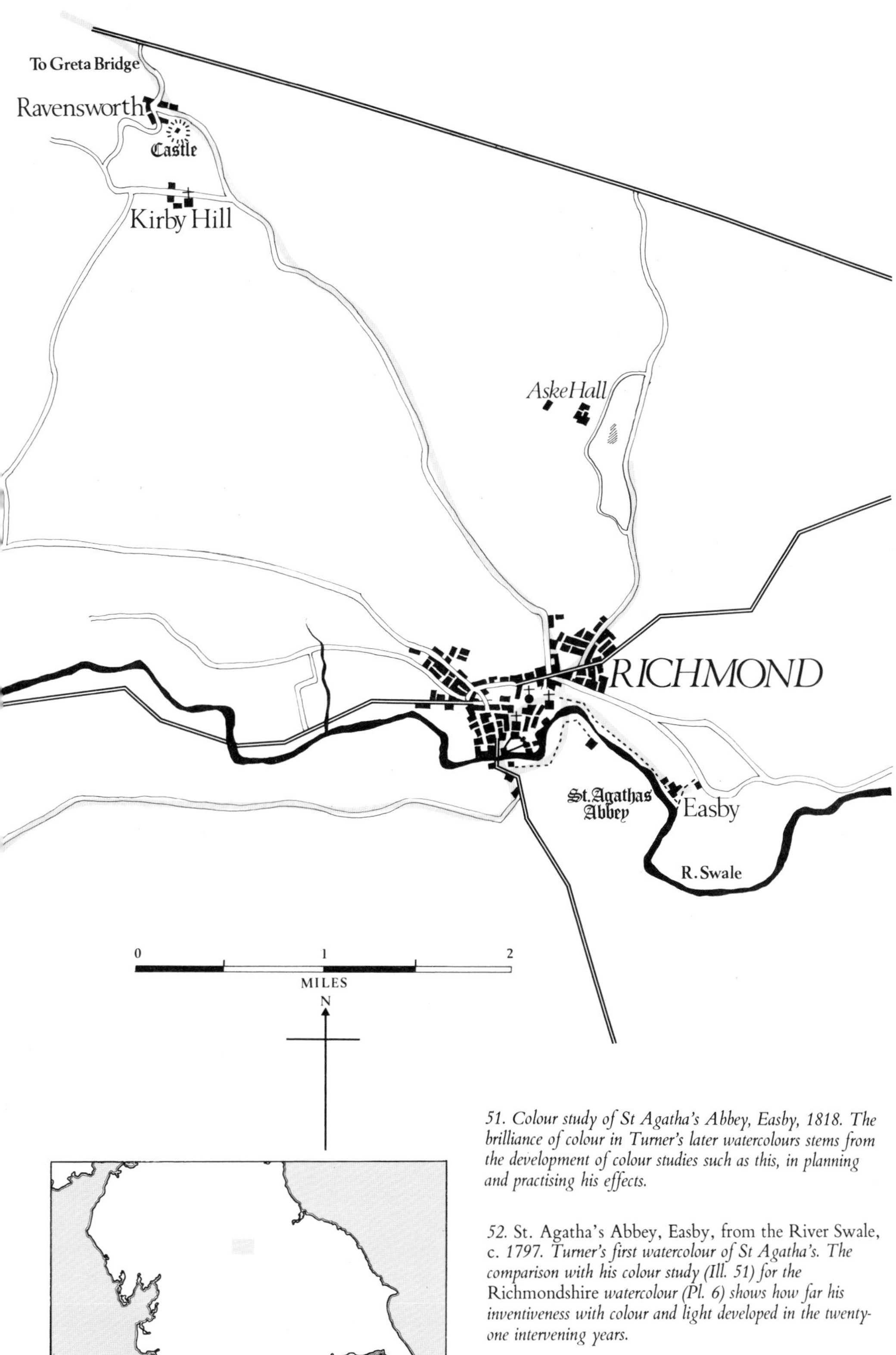

51

52

51. Colour study of St Agatha's Abbey, Easby, 1818. The brilliance of colour in Turner's later watercolours stems from the development of colour studies such as this, in planning and practising his effects.

52. St. Agatha's Abbey, Easby, from the River Swale, c. 1797. *Turner's first watercolour of St Agatha's. The comparison with his colour study (Ill. 51) for the* Richmondshire *watercolour (Pl. 6) shows how far his inventiveness with colour and light developed in the twenty-one intervening years.*

Cistercian nunnery remained worth sketching. Instead, he found a viewpoint further along the valley on the road to Downholme. From here he could record the whole stretch of Swaledale towards Ellerton and Marrick, though the sketch he made covers an angle of about thirty degrees, an unusually small proportion for Turner of the total view available. The priory itself was about a mile and a half away. Its details were barely visible. The angle of view, the foreshortening of distances and the visibility of the priory buildings draw the eye into the composition with an immediacy that demonstrates very vividly the way in which the artist used his eyes, and in which he drew sense and significance out of the raw material of landscape that he encountered.

Turner's first sight of Richmond, capital of Swaledale, was of the great Norman tower of the castle rising above the Swale, with the slate-roofed town clustered around and the whole plain of north Yorkshire spread out beyond. He stopped to commit this to memory, catching the clouds sweeping across the sky and the distant Cleveland Hills in shadow. The subject deserved longer contemplation, but for the moment he was keen to press on to the town. It was nineteen years since he had last sketched at Richmond and his first thought was to revisit the site of one of his early sketches.

The view of the bridge and castle, with Yorke House to the left, taken from a point on the left bank just upstream from the bridge, had formed the basis of a watercolour made about 1799 (Ills. 48 and 50). Although Yorke House was demolished in 1824, the view remains unchanged today except for the growth of trees, and Turner in 1816 found it exactly as he recalled it from 1797. He made a quick sketch in the pocket-book from a slightly higher viewpoint than that of 1797, but although he intended to make a finished watercolour and went so far as to begin one (Ill. 49). It was late afternoon, and both Turner and his horse needed rest and refreshment. After completing his reintroduction to Richmond with a sketch of the castle from the bridge, with some activity on the riverbank by the old dyeworks, he made his way up Cornforth Hill to his inn.

Richmond was the historic centre of the area known as 'Richmondshire'. It was to be the principal subject of the first part of Whitaker's *County of York* and since Longmans seem to have required at least four different views, Turner decided to stay for two nights and take time to make an even more detailed survey than was usual. The most modern and spacious hotel in the town was the *Kings Head* in the market place which continues to offer a civilised environment in which to recover from the exertions of tourism. Nevertheless, after some time spent in attending to his horse, his accommodation and his dinner, he got on with his work the very same evening, and set out for St. Agatha's Abbey at Easby.

Turner had sketched St. Agatha's in 1797 and derived one of his largest early watercolours (Ill. 52) from the results. This time, determined to survey every aspect, he went armed with all three of his sketchbooks for the purpose. Like most tourists coming from Richmond, he approached St. Agatha's on foot along a mile or so of pleasant riverside pathway. He made his initial exploration of the ruins through a series of sketches in the pocket-book,examining first the possibilities of a view of the approaches from Richmond before revisiting his earlier viewpoint downstream.

He was looking for something new, and the hill by Easby Hall provided him with a view worth recording in a larger sketch. Looking over the abbey with the gatehouse and little church of St. Agatha's in the foreground, he could survey the course of the river back up to Richmond, with the castle and church towers rising in the distance. It was now about seven o'clock, and a particularly delightful evening. When he began the watercolour (Ill. 51 and Pl. 6) on his return to London, he recalled the strong evening sun, and the whole scene in light and suffused with a sense of peace and contentment. The ruins, however, were shaded on this side, so on his way back to Richmond he stopped to make a couple of composition sketches of the sunlit side of the ruins seen over the mill weir. One of these is in the largest sketchbook, the first time he had used it since Hardrow.

Walking back to the town he could feel well satisfied with his day's work. Since setting off that morning from Aysgarth he had travelled twenty-five miles, made forty sketches, and obtained enough material for at least seven finished watercolours. The first leg of the tour was now complete, and he could look forward to a 'rest-day' of sorts on the morrow. The day had ended, furthermore, on a high note, with a stroll to St. Agatha's, and even some sunshine.

Richmond was the natural break in most northern tourists' itineraries, a chance to reflect, take stock, and prepare for further trials and tribulations. Viscount Torrington returned from St. Agatha's to the *Kings Head* 'with proper fatigue, to renovate for fresh fatigue and transports: *This is Life; That's your Sort;* fatigue and pleasure, pleasure and fatigue: Thus we struggle thro' life; and a tourist's is a hard life;—but then it is a life of choice.' It may have been a life of choice for a gentleman like Torrington, but for someone with Turner's background—his father had a hairdresser's business in Covent Garden—tourism was not usually an activity within reach. It remained largely the province of the wealthy. To tour at all as Turner did constituted success and fulfilment in its own right. He had earned the opportunity through his art, and repaid the debt with diligent application and hard work.

Tuesday 30 July

Richmond offered Turner a rest from the pressures of travelling. Nonetheless he was up early to begin sketching. Over breakfast he probably read Dayes's description of the town: 'The Castle, which forms the principal feature at Richmond, is most delightfully situated on the banks of the Swale, and near the town; few places being more picturesque. Over the bridge, which forms the fore-ground, rise majestically the bold and rocky banks of the river, agreeably diversified with verdure, which being crowned by the massy battlements of the Castle, form a fine *coup d'oeil*. This Castle and town was built by Alan, Earl of Bretagne, nephew to William the Norman, by whom he was created Earl of Richmond, and had bestowed on him the district called Richmondshire .. The great square tower of Richmond Castle is ninety-nine feet high, and was built by Conan in the twelfth century. It is three stories high, with a massy column in the centre, which supported the floors ... The scenery in the neighbourhood of Richmond will highly engage the picturesque tourist.'

Turner had already painted the view over the bridge, but there are other fine views of the castle, town and river, particularly from the south bank of the Swale, and he appears to have had a particular one in mind, for he went directly to a vantage point below the falls to the south east of the town. The absence of any intermediate sketches suggests that he did not go round by way of the bridge, but forded the river somewhere at the foot of Mill Gate. His sketch (Ill. 56) is a masterpiece of detail and placement, tracking across an angle of about seventy degrees from the bridge at the left, with houses along Bargate Green beyond, up the Castle Bank to Scolland's Hall and Gold Hole Tower with the Cock Pit beneath, across to Robin Hood Tower and the great Norman Keep itself. Further to the right can be seen the top of the great obelisk erected in the market place in 1771, and the tower of Holy Trinity church which faces the *King's Head*, with, below, the houses on Mill Gate with their gardens leading down to the river. At the right stands the fifteenth- century tower of Grey Friars, and below that the houses of Frenchgate, named after the masons who lived there while building the castle. At the head of Frenchgate stands Hill House, which until 1787 was the home of a

53. Richmond Castle and Town. *The engraving by J. Archer published 1820, based on a now untraced watercolour. The view is perfectly preserved today (Ill. 54), but the comparison with the photograph reveals how far Turner compressed the site in his memory. The composition is a labyrinth of pathways for the eye to explore, and despite Turner's complaint at Richmond that the weather was 'miserably wet' and that he would be 'web-footed like a drake', it clearly provided memories of some impressive effects, with evening showers blowing up from the west and the castle keep standing out starkly against the brooding sky.*

54. *Richmond Castle and Town from the South.*

53

54

celebrated beauty, Frances l'Anson. In that year she married an Irish barrister named Leonard McNally, who immortalised her as the 'Sweet Lass of Richmond Hill':

On Richmond Hill there lives a lass
More bright than May-day morn,
Whose charms all other maids surpass
A Rose without a thorn.

Set to music by James Hook, a popular composer of the day, the verses were sung by Inchedon at Vauxhall in 1789 and later at the Covent Garden Theatre. The London audience preferred to believe that the Richmond Hill in question was their own in Surrey and pursued their claim so far as to name an inn there after her. Turner himself lived at Twickenham, only a mile or so from Richmond Hill, Surrey, but he restored the lass to her rightful Yorkshire landscape in every one of his finished watercolours of Richmond. Turner's lass appears to have inspired particular devotion from her dogs, who follow her wherever she goes, quarrelling for her attention on the morning milk round in the watercolour (Ill. 55) based on the present sketch, and in the others following patiently behind her as she carries linen home in the evening, or being instructed in botany, or the latest styles in millinery.

Under the protection of the castle, Richmond had become the centre of the region's milling industry, and the falls beneath its ramparts provided an abundant source of natural energy. Turner was interested in the technological landscape as much as the pastoral, and the various mills act as focal points in his compositions. From the viewpoint to the south east he recorded the flax mill, perhaps with an eye to a passing age, for it had been closed down in 1811 unable to compete with steam-driven mills elsewhere. Turner was fortunate in his date of birth to see industry in a form that had only just begun to contaminate

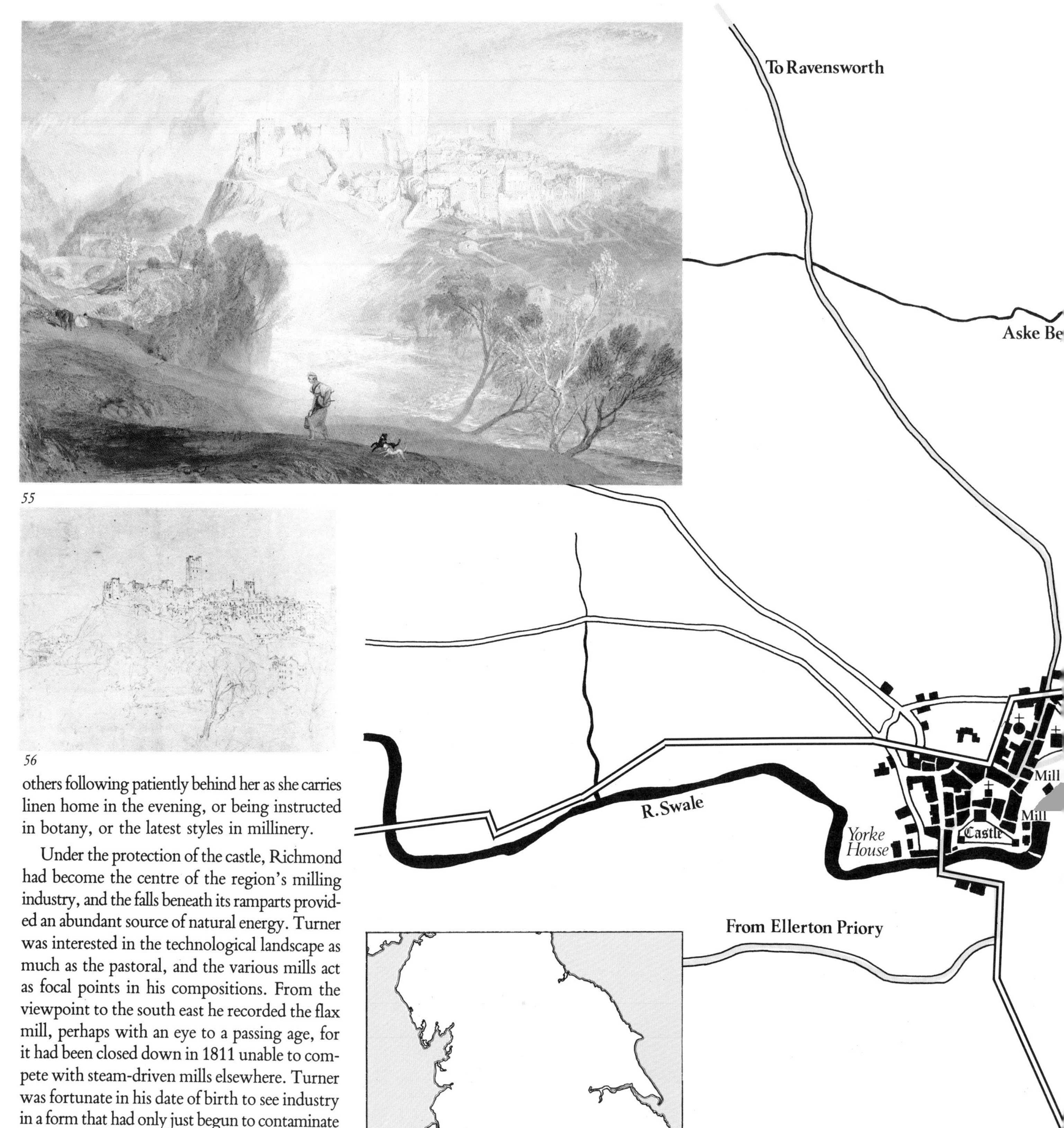

55

56

55. Richmond Castle and Town, Yorkshire, c.*1824. A subject intended to be used in the* County of York *and sketched in 1816 (Ill. 56), but not engraved until 1827, when it was published in* Picturesque Views in England and Wales. *The girl, who appears in all of Turner's post-1816 views of Richmond, was probably inspired by a popular song, 'The Sweet Lass of Richmond Hill'.*

56. Richmond from the south-east, a view of about 70 degrees, with the bridge at the left, houses along Bargate Green beyond and the obelisk in the market-square, Trinity church and Greyfriar's tower to the right, and the same mill as in Ill. 59 below.

RICHMOND

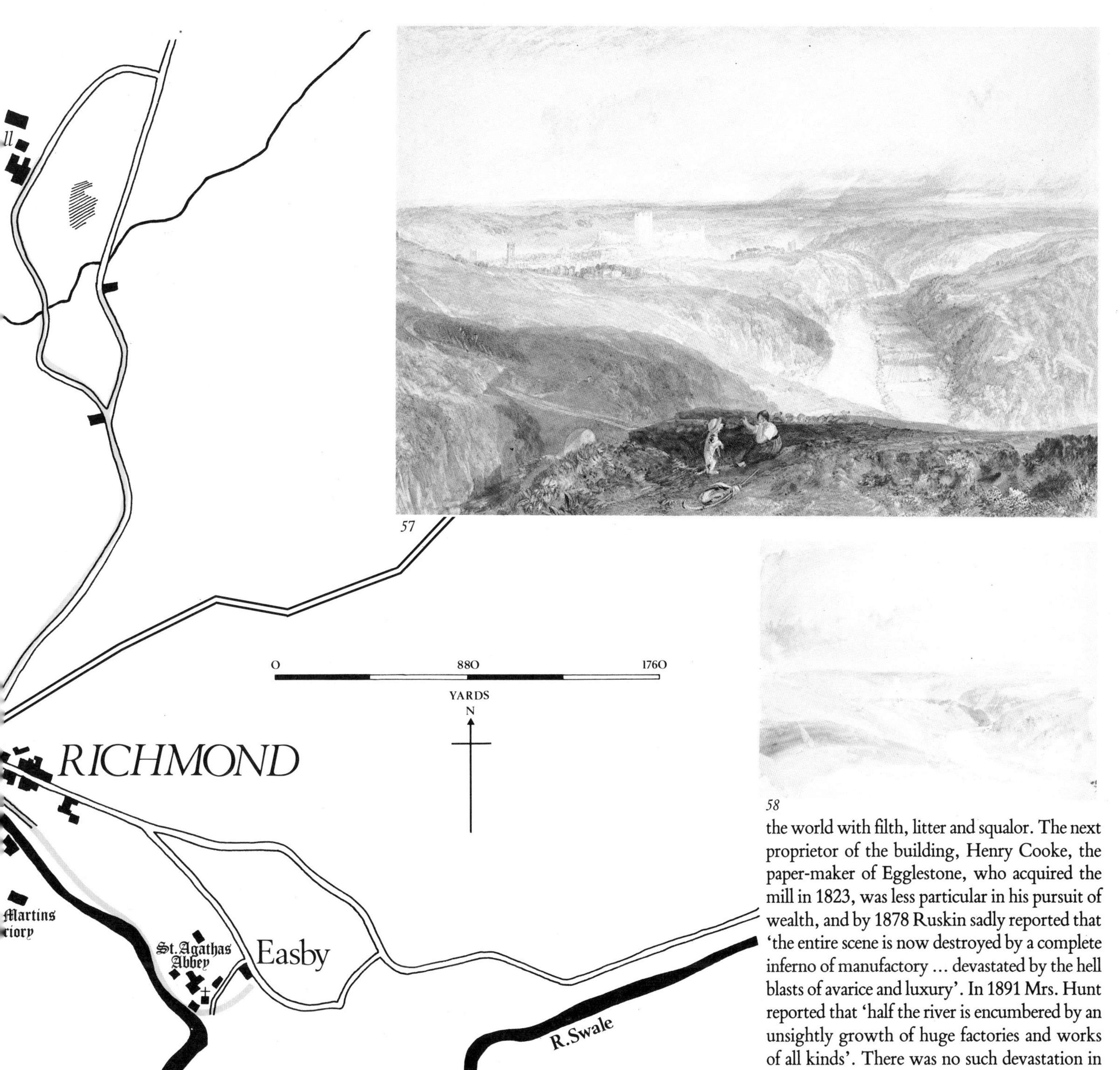

the world with filth, litter and squalor. The next proprietor of the building, Henry Cooke, the paper-maker of Egglestone, who acquired the mill in 1823, was less particular in his pursuit of wealth, and by 1878 Ruskin sadly reported that 'the entire scene is now destroyed by a complete inferno of manufactory ... devastated by the hell blasts of avarice and luxury'. In 1891 Mrs. Hunt reported that 'half the river is encumbered by an unsightly growth of huge factories and works of all kinds'. There was no such devastation in Turner's day, the mills mostly plied a trade that stretched back essentially unchanged over centuries, and his view of the town sparkles with clarity and sweetness.

The mills are thankfully now gone, and Richmond has returned to a condition that is closer to Turner's vision than to Ruskin's, and the modern tourist is well-advised to use this lovely town as Turner and Torrington did—as a place to explore, a place in which to restore energy expended in car-bound sightseeing. The castle, the gigantic keep and St. Mary's in Frenchgate, with its carved stalls from Easby Abbey which warn against such sins as gossiping in the cloister or disorder in the choir, its misericords (on one of which a pig plays the bagpipes to his friends) and the brightly painted monument to Sir Timothy Hutton, his wife and twelve children—all are as they were in Turner's day.

The only surviving Georgian theatre in the country, Samuel Butler's beautiful little building on Friar's Wynd, was a mere twenty-eight years old as Turner passed by. It was to be closed down and used as a corn store, a furniture store, a wine cellar and, in the Second World War, as a salvage store before the imaginative Town Clerk restored and reopened it under the patronage of Sybil Thorndike in 1963.

Turner now made a complete survey of the mills of Richmond. In his next sketch he recorded the corn mill at the bend of the river beneath the

57. Richmond, Yorkshire, c. *1819. The view from the west, looking over the plains of Yorkshire towards the Hambledon Hills. The colouring of this watercolour, eventually also used in* Picturesque Views in England and Wales, *and the colour study (Ill. 58), suggest that it was originally made for the* County of York, *just before Longmans cancelled their agreement for the full complement of 120 watercolours.*

58. The colour study for the finished watercolour Richmond, Yorkshire, c.*1818 – 19 (Ill. 57). Turner made a number of changes in the finished composition, most notably to the line of the river which is used to lead the eye from the girl to the town and beyond.*

RICHMOND TO ASKE HALL

castle, before continuing his stroll upstream to take a view looking across to the castle with the bridge to the left, and the road leading up Bargate to the town. The view provided Turner with a network of pathways for the eye to explore, from the figures crossing the bridge to the sunlit space between the buildings by the Green, and on up Bargate with its solid, prosperous houses to the town.

From the bridge the eye may take a different route, along the waterside, where repair works are being carried out on a house and a figure stands at the top of the river steps, on up a steep stairway and path to the top of the castle bank, and on to the promenade under the castle walls. The eye can also clamber up the ivy-clad walls into the castle green itself, wander on over the sunlit lawns, or climb to the very top of the tower. The whole scene is animated by a shower-laden wind that blows up strongly from the west, carrying dark clouds up behind the tower, which yet stands out brilliantly against them.

Turner's views of Richmond make up a labyrinth, full of incident, interest and vivid contrast. Wind, rain and sunshine, light and dark abound here. Their vitality reflects the painter's simple joy and sense of privilege at being there and the nostalgia with which he looked back on this happy interlude.

Turner still had most of the afternoon in which to take a leisurely ride out to Aske Hall to make his sketches for Whitaker. The late fifteenth-century pele-tower, adapted to a comfortable modern house by succeeding generations, and set in a park landscaped by Capability Brown, was the sort of subject with which Turner had first made his name, but while in 1797 the country house allowed Turner to break significant new ground in landscape painting, as, for example at Harewood, it must now have seemed commonplace and old-fashioned.

It would have seemed even more so had he been aware that exactly the same view of the house from the Gilling Road had been painted some thirty-five years before by Nicholas Dall, whose painting still hangs at Aske today. By 1816 Turner had the business of collecting information for this sort of picture pared down to a simple routine. He needed just three quick notes, one of the first impression of the house from the lane (Ill. 61), framed by trees, which would provide the finished composition; the second of the architectural details of the house, bridge, chapel and lake temple; and third sketch in the composition book of the landscape as a whole, to record all the information that he would need. His watercolour of *Aske* (Pl. 8) shows that he recreated the landscape in his imagination with typical original skill. He re-entered it and re-explored it with characteristic thoroughness.

The worn-down road with the wheel-ruts of some lately passed vehicle is the main subject, over-arched by trees which provide shade for dozing sheep. This is a quiet road, and it is some time since a vehicle passed, for the ruts have lain undisturbed while the road dried out sufficiently for the sheep to lie on it. Heat and idleness are everywhere, and time passes while the world slumbers. Sheep that fell asleep in shade wake to

59

59. Richmond, Yorkshire, from the East. The viewpoint of Ills. 55 and 56 can be seen on the footpath in the first field at the left (looking across to the mill) and that of Ill. 53 above the line of distant cottages.

60. Ravenscroft Castle with Kirby Hill Church beyond.

61. Aske Hall. The basis of the finished watercolour (Pl. 8), to which Turner added a foreground frame of trees based on a note of the first impression of the hall as seen from the Gilling road.

find themselves in sunshine. The shepherd chats to a passing horseman. And the artist, who is content to drift off into reverie, contemplating foxgloves and briars by the roadside, the pattern of bark on trees, or the intricate traceries of the boughs overhead. *Aske* was Turner's record of a day of sunshine and tranquillity.

He returned to Richmond in time to make an excursion to record the view of the town from the west, looking out over the north Yorkshire plains beyond. It was mid-evening when he located the best viewpoint, for the sun was shining on the castle keep from the west. In the finished composition (Ill. 57), showers drift by in the distance from the north, while near to hand it seems predominantly dry, though clouds occasionally obscure the sun. The day's work is virtually finished; hay lies cut in rows in the fields; in the foreground, a girl has already laid aside her scythe and finds amusement with her dog.

She is totally absorbed in her simple pleasures, but the artist's eye roves widely and restlessly out to the horizon. The figures in this landscape show no such restlessness. They are bound to their place without question. Turner had slipped into the rhythm of the country landscape at its summer best at Richmond but the next morning, he knew, he would have to press on. The road to

60

61

the left led him back to Richmond to prepare for the next stage of the journey.

Wednesday 31 July

Turner had one final sketch (Ill. 59) of Richmond to make before leaving, the view from the footpath to Easby. From here he could see every one of the town's principal landmarks, St. Mary's to the right, Greyfriars beyond, Holy Trinity and the obelisk in the centre, the castle to the left and on the river the church and castle mills. He could also see three of the four points from which he had drawn the town, stretched out up the valley on his left, each one providing a different angle to help him memorise its appearance. This final sketch is the master key with which he could unlock his memory and the summary of his explorations of Richmond. The watercolour (Pl. 9) that derived from it was one of the first of the finished views to be completed and with *Hardrow,* the first to be sent to the etcher's.

Back at the inn he had a final task to attend to before leaving. He scribbled a quick note to his friend James Holworthy whom he had planned to meet just south of Doncaster.

Richmond, Yorkshire (not Sandycombe)
July 31, 1816

Dear Holworthy,

I find it impossible to be [sic] meet you at Mr Knight's by the time you wished; therefore have the goodness to make your arrangements without any consideration towards my supposed time of return, for my journey is extended rather than shortened by an excursion into Lancashire [i.e. to Browsholme], which renders it wholly out of my power at present to say when I can be at Llangold. However, I should be very happy to have the honour of hearing from you (by a letter to me at Mr Fawkes's) of your movements in whatever direct they may tend, and believe me to be, your most truly obliged
J.M.W. Turner
P.S. Weather miserably wet; I shall be web-footed like a drake, except the curled feather; but I must proceed northwards. Adieu!

Turner headed north via Ravensworth Castle. It was raining again and after twelve miles and about two hours' riding it would have been a relief to arrive at one of the Greta Bridge inns and have a chance to dry out. Turner's inn may have been the *Morritt Arms*, the same inn that John

ROKEBY AND GRETA BRIDGE

Sell Cotman used eleven years earlier on his visit to Rokeby in 1805. Cotman had stayed with the Morritt family at Rokeby, but after they went away on 23 August, he moved to the inn. He found it difficult to enjoy the scenery alone, writing 'And much should I like to have a house near it [the Greta] that I might have a Study of artist[s] down to see me and do it justice. We might then talk and draw over in a high style. But notwithstanding all this fine scen[er]y I am plaguedly dull. To be cut off from such a party and to remain on the spot in front of the park gates ... I really am quite wretch[e]d.'

Cotman's studies of the Greta are among the first paintings of the subject, and, of all, are probably the finest (Ill. 64). In 1805 the scenery was relatively little known, but after the publication of Sir Walter Scott's poem *Rokeby* in 1813, the landscape between Barnard Castle and Wycliffe had become famous. Scott had stayed at Rokeby in 1809, '11 and '12 and composed his verses in a small cave overlooking the Greta. Turner illustrated a passage from it for an anthology of poems in the Farnley Library (Ill. 65).

62. *Barnard Castle, Co. Durham.*

63. Barnard Castle, Co. Durham, c. *1825. Turner recollected Barnard Castle in sunshine when he came to make this watercolour, although he sketched it in 1816 in the rain, as is shown by the water stains on his pocket-book drawing. The composition, with the bridge in the centre, was a product of his 1816 tour when he needed to show the Yorkshire as well as the Durham side of the river.*

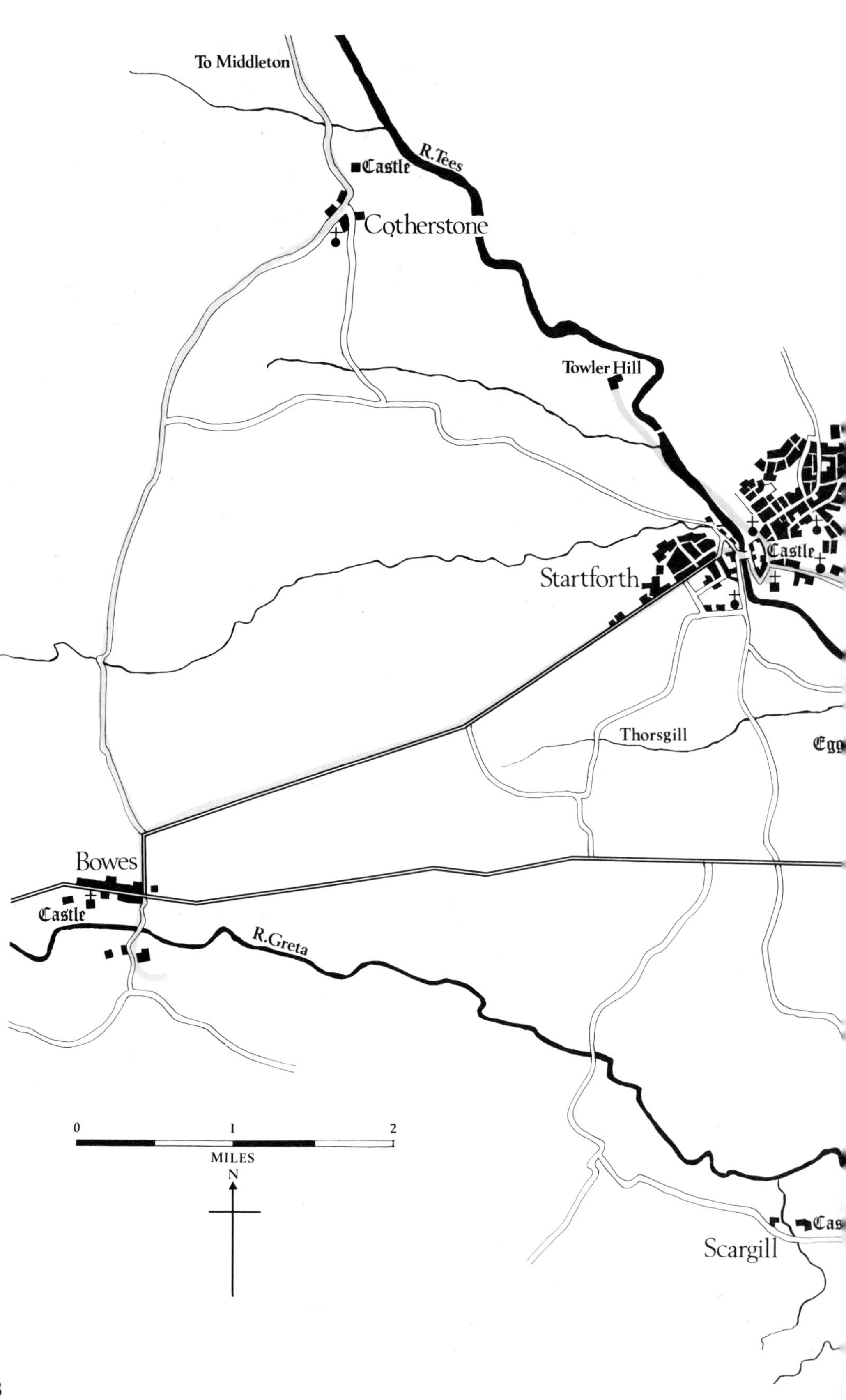

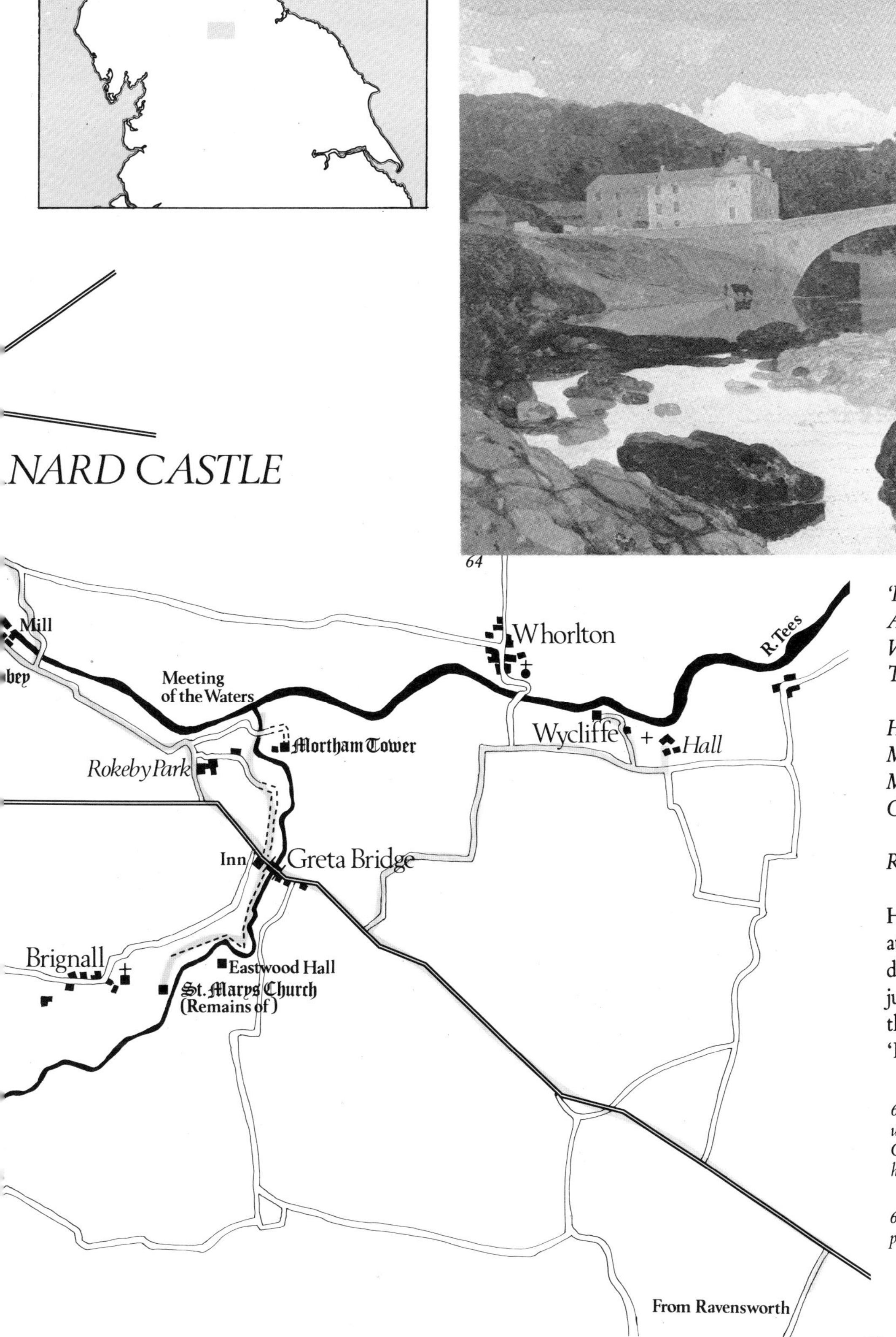

64

65

'Here twixt Rock and River grew
A dismal grove of sable yew
With whose sad tints were mingled seen
The blighted firs sepulchral sic green

He who winds twixt rock and wave
May hear the headlong torrent wave ...
May view her chafe her waves to spray
O'er every rock that bars her way.

Rokeby II, (ix & vii)

His first sketch at Greta Bridge was of the 'Cave at Rokeby'. It was, unfortunately, an unusually desultory effort in his smaller composition book, just a few scrappy indications of tangled trees with the 'sky' shining through and 'Steps' and the 'River v. Light'. It seems to have been raining quite hard, for the sketching quality did not improve even with a commissioned subject—the meeting of the waters of the Greta and Tees.

The next sketch is of the pele-tower of Mortham. For notes such as this he was oblivious of the weather, jotting them on to the tiny pages of the pocket-book with the rain dripping off his hat on to the page, staining the paper and making it cockle. In contrast, he worked in the composition books seated under the shelter of his umbrella and the only stains they show are from where he dropped them in the mud. He owned a particularly ingenious umbrella which converted into a fishing rod, but on this tour at least he seems only to have caught colds.

At the junction of the Greta and the Tees he tried a couple of sketches in the smaller composition book. He was looking for a view that would unite the main features, the rivers, and Rokeby Hall and Mortham Tower, but their disposition simply would not admit of this, so he elected to take a view for the commissioned watercolour (Pl. 10) of the confluence looking across to Rokeby from a rocky platform at the corner of Mortham field. The conditions were beginning to wear Turner down. Normally, this was a subject—the intricate channels of the Greta, the

64. Greta Bridge *by John Sell Cotman, 1805. Cotman was one of the first artists to paint on the banks of the River Greta, several years before Sir Walter Scott popularised it in his poem* Rokeby, *published in 1813.*

65. Rokeby, *1822. The illustration to Sir Walter Scott's poem made for an anthology at Farnley Hall.*

WYCLIFFE HALL AND EGGLESTONE ABBEY

deep, shaded course of the Tees, rocks brought down by torrents, and all overhung by trees—which would have called forth his usual response of patient, loving observation and delighted recording of detail but, although he was working in his largest sketchbook, he dashed down only a few quick notes of the river channels, a few rocks brought down by the Greta, and the suggestion of a few trees. We can imagine Turner now, narrowing his eyes as he peered out under the dripping brim of his hat. It was raining. He had been on his own now for a week, and he had the prospect of another couple of weeks of the same to come. He was cold, wet and depressed. He packed up as soon as possible and beat a retreat to the inn.

Thursday 1 August

The new day brought a new month and restored Turner's spirit. His first destination was Wycliffe Hall, about two miles downstream from the meeting of the waters. He made the required drawing (Ill. 66) straight away while the weather was fair enough for him to note the 'calm' water, and to enjoy the elaboration of details, including riverside cottages and a horse and cart passing by in the lane (Ill. 67). The riverbanks particularly impressed him, and he took a more distant panorama of the house, and some other sketches in which the house is but an afterthought. He concentrated rather on the rocky bluffs and hanging woods and the small meadows trapped in bends of the river.

These sketches of Wycliffe, which took up the first part of the morning, contain no indication of the girls chasing geese who appear in the foreground of the finished watercolour (Pl. 11). Turner may have intended this finished scene to be allegorical. Wycliffe Hall was reputedly the birthplace of John Wycliffe (1324-84) the reformer and translator of the Bible. Many years later, John Pye, who had engraved the watercolour, recalled that when he had remarked to Turner that 'the geese are large'. Turner replied 'They are not geese, but overfed priests.' Turner increased the intensity of light over Wycliffe's house and told Pye that it indicated the symbolic light of the Reformation. Wycliffe's followers are driving away the geese-priests. This might seem fanciful, were it not for the long and serious inscription Turner added to one of the engraving proofs, describing Wycliffe's achievement.

Turner's finished compositions are as much pictures of his mind as literal records of places. 'Always paint your impressions,' he advised, but not the impressions of the eye so much as those of the imagination. The significance of place for Turner was a synthesis of many different elements: literary, historical and artistic associations, allegorical and symbolic details, natural effects, characteristic incidents, and his recollections of actually being there. The associations are a necessary part of the way he worked. As he looked at his sketch he could remember the sounds of cackling geese and girlish cries, a horse-drawn cart trundling down to the river and the sunlight flinting on the 'calm' (written on the sketch) water, but he was searching above all for significance. As he floated the washes over his paper, associations crowded round, and those that surfaced in his picture are those that conveyed to him most vividly the particular spirit of the place.

From Wycliffe Turner returned to Greta Bridge and walked directly from there to his next site, the tiny church of Brignall, about a mile from the inn along the banks of the Greta. 'O Brignall Banks are wild and fair, And Greta woods are green,' Scott had sung in *Rokeby* (III.xvi), and it was particularly these woods and banks that fired Turner's imagination. Brignall church was 'as small in its best days as churches among the North Country mountains and moors are wont to be', though most of it was carried off to help build a new and larger church at the top of the hill in 1834. It stood quite alone in a little meadow by the river Greta enclosed on all sides by hills and woodlands. Turner was delighted by the seclusion.

He began sketching on a hill to the south, looking out over the church. Once again, his first impression proved to be the most compelling, for after exploring the site, he returned to it to make the detailed study for Longmans. The result was one of the most poetical of all the *County of York* series. The watercolour itself was destroyed by fire in the last century but the engraving (Ill. 68) recorded it with special sensitivity. Turner diminished the already tiny church to give special emphasis to the river banks. His studies of rocks and trees prompted, in Brignall Banks,one of the most loving and meticulous of all his pictures of riverbanks, including in the foreground a further sign that he knew the poetic associations of the scene 'where twixt rock and river grew, a dismal grove of sable yew'.

Turner's studies at Brignall took three hours, and it was well into the afternoon by the time he set off for Egglestone Abbey. Little remains of the monastery buildings, though the greater part of the nave and chancel walls of the cruciform church still stand. The north transept has fallen, but was still there in Turner's day. It is the setting above all which makes a visit to this site worthwhile. The stream foams and rattles past the ruins through thick greenery to tumble into a gorge.

Egglestone is only two miles from Greta Bridge and, as Torrington related, 'Makes a grand object from which to see the ... [Rokeby] house, and well brought in is the ruin of Egglestone Abbey; to which (after my full

66

67

66. Wycliffe on the River Tees near Rokeby.

67. A continuation of the sketch illustrated as Ill.66. The pony cart became the main theme of the finished watercolour (Pl. 11) appearing at the centre of the composition about to ford the river.

68. Brignall Church, *engraved by S.Rawle. Described by Ruskin as the perfect image of the painter's mind at this period', this is the only record of the watercolour, which was destroyed by fire about a century ago. It is also one of the few records of the church which was demolished when a new one was built at the top of the hill in 1834. The landscape, however, is largely unchanged with still, silent woods growing up from the banks of the River Greta.*

admiration of the river—and of its banks, and with equal dislike of the new, nasty, tasteless, bridge [a magnificent single arch built in 1773 by J.B.S.Morritt of Rokeby], and my grief, likewise, at the building of a noisy paper mill on such a spot) I bent my course. These ruins are entirely neglected; and choak'd up by weeds and nettles. A mean old house is attach'd to them, and there are some cottages at the back of the orchard.'

Turner's first idea seems to have been to unite all these features in a single drawing, first from outside the 'mean old house' (formerly the Canon's Dorter), and secondly from a viewpoint quite close to one that he he had used on his first visit in 1797, looking up to the abbey ruins over the medieval packhorse bridge spanning Thorsgill, but this time continuing to the left to include the paper mill and abbey bridge. He then went down to the abbey bridge, which he appears to have found neither 'nasty' nor 'tasteless', for he took a view of Rokeby seen over its battlements, seventy-six feet above the River Tees, then crossed to the Durham bank to find another view that he had sketched in 1797, looking over Henry Cooke's paper mill to the great east window of the abbey. He was concerned, however, to record it as it now was. Part of the mill had recently been burned down and workmen were in the process of rebuilding it. The process of paper-making was one which would naturally have interested the artist, and his sympathy with the paper-makers' problems, as they strove to carry on the business—despite having to dry the paper on the riverbanks, is manifest in the finished watercolour (Pl. 13)

Friday 2 August

Turner's next sketches are of Barnard Castle. It seems likely that he stayed there on Thursday night, for the watercolour (Ill. 63) related to these sketches recollects the view at dawn. His first note shows that conditions were less serene than in the finished painting, for it was badly stained by the rain. He persevered, however, and took a second sketch in the smaller composition book, from a viewpoint to the left of the first from which he could see the bridge as well as the castle.

68

BARNARD CASTLE

Turner's perseverance in the conditions at first seems odd, even for him, for he already had an elaborate sketch made on his first visit in 1797. Barnard Castle, however, is in County Durham, and Yorkshire lies on the opposite bank. The original sketch stopped half-way across the bridge, and therefore showed nothing of Yorkshire. Mindful that he was illustrating a history of Yorkshire, Turner accordingly made the bridge the pivotal point of his final composition and included an equal portion of each county in the picture.

He completed his record of the town with a distant view of the castle from 'Tollar [i.e. Towler] Hill', to the north. Scott had described the scene in *Rokeby* (V.i.):

Old Barnard's towers are purple still,
To those that gaze from Toller-Hill.

Above Barnard Castle, Teesdale becomes increasingly bleak, and most tourists made the excursion to High Force, Turner's next important site, in a day and returned to the comfort of their hotel the same evening. Turner had greater ambitions. He intended to continue beyond High Force to the remotest regions of the dale at Cauldron Snout, and thence over the desolate moors to Appleby.

By the time he had finished his sketches at Barnard Castle it was too late to attempt all this in what remained of the day, so he made a detour to see Bowes, once a major Roman settlement, which Scott had mentioned in *Rokeby*. There he made a couple of sketches of the village, church and 'castle'—no more in fact than a Norman keep—from a field beyond the bridge to the south east, before following the moorland road over Deepdale to Cotherstone, making a sketch

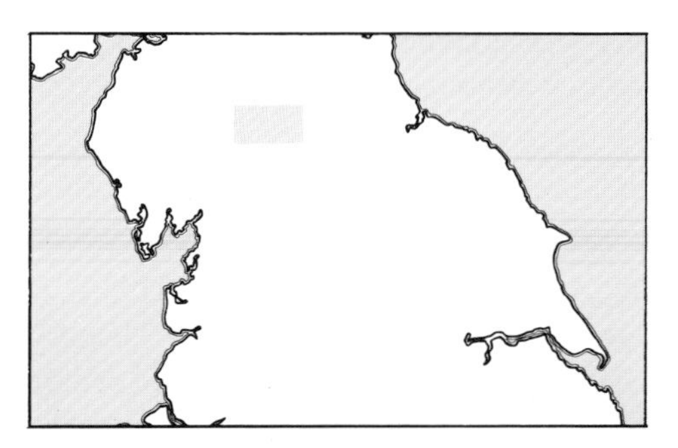

69

69. *High Force on the River Tees.*

in passing of the village and castle remains. He then rode the next six miles to Middleton without making a single sketch.

Middleton lies about ten miles from Barnard Castle and six short of High Force. It was the last refuge for Turner as he travelled towards the head of the dale. He had no choice but to put up there for the night of 2 August. In 1792 the recommended house was 'Mr. Sherlocks' of Bridge End, 'a kind of public house without a sign', where the landlord served 'r[oa]sted fillet of beef and potatoes, with potted trout; (a dish they invented,' and supplied dry woollen socks for wet feet, and half pints of brandy which visitors could either drink or rub into their heads for invigoration. With a long and difficult journey ahead of him, Turner rested himself and his horse, and made only three slight sketches of the village, two of the bridge in the town, a third of that spanning the Tees.

70

70. *High Force. Turner is said to have been so delighted with High Force that on one occasion he all but lost his life there. He stayed so long sketching one evening that he was overtaken by darkness, and got hopelessly lost. The light in the present sketch, reflecting off the spray in a rainbow, seems to come from behind us from the left, suggesting morning rather than evening.*

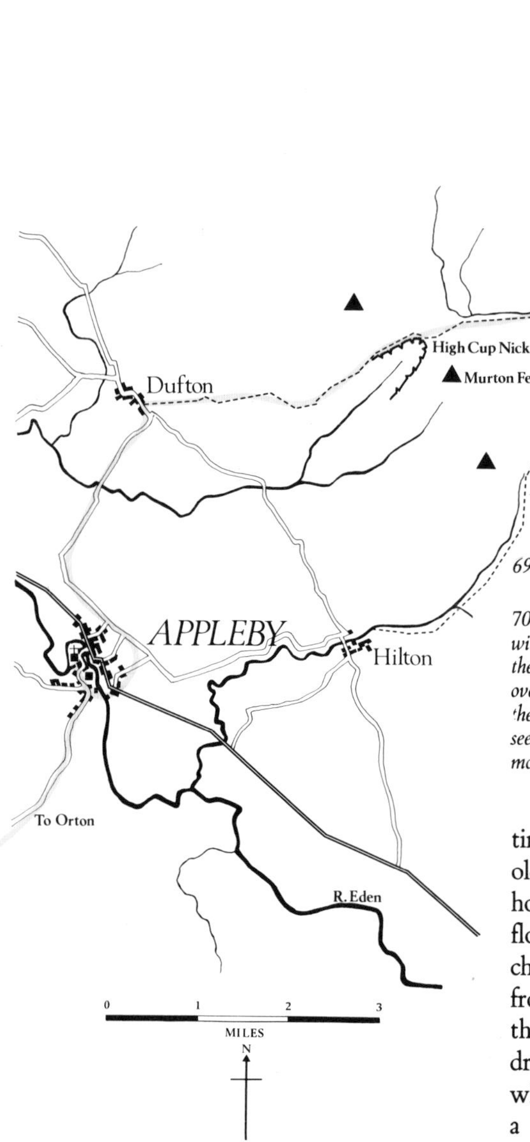

Saturday 3 August

He headed out into the wilds today, and the next civilised resting place was a long way off. He made as early a start as possible and may even have engaged the services of a guide.

His first stop was at Low Force, near Bowlees, where the Tees descends a picturesque step known as the Salmon Leap before running through a polished gorge of grey whinstone crowned by woods of pine and hazel. Turner was particularly interested in the Wynch Bridge spanning the gorge. The original was built some time before 1740 and was reputed to be the oldest suspension bridge in Europe. It was not, however, the most reliable. It suffered severe flood damage in 1771 and, in 1802, one of the chains broke whilst a party of eleven haymakers from Holwick were crossing, and they were thrown into the river below. One was drowned. The old bridge was still standing when Turner was there in 1816, and he made a couple of sketches of it in his notebook, including one looking over the bridge to the Salmon Leap from the Holwick side, so he was evidently bold enough to cross it.

High Force, the greatest of all the waterfalls on Turner's itinerary, lay two miles further on. The approach is now a well-made path and steps, but Turner and his contemporaries had to work harder for their picturesque rewards. In 1792 Torrington's party followed their guide 'thro' many hilly, boggy fields, a mile of walk, till we enter'd a little birch wood; when, being anxious to stand beneath the fall, we endured a most fatiguing descent, and a very dangerous crawl at the river's edge, over great stones, and

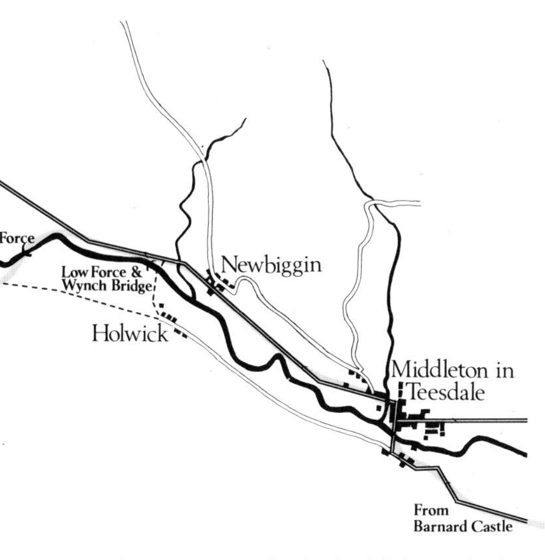

sometimes up to our knees in water, till we arrived at the very bottom of the fall.—The sweat running from my brow, and a flap of my coat, my only coat, nearly torn off by the bushes:...—These are noble falls of water, unequall'd I suppose in this country, of about sixty-nine feet; and must be yet more wonderful after heavy rains, or hard frost ... I recrawled up the wood, and then to the summit of the cascade, as near as possible: the basin at the bottom I should suppose a fine place for fishing, and here the salmon must stop—.'

Turner was almost too excited or agitated on his arrival to draw anything. His first sketch in the pocket-book was simply a half-dozen lines

71. High Force. Having taken his detailed close-up sketches of the Tees pouring over its basalt-topped cliffs, Turner, typically, found a distant viewpoint from which to relate the falls to their surroundings.

72. Fall of the Tees, Yorkshire, c. *1825–6.*

73. High Force with an artist sketching.

71

72

73

HIGH FORCE AND CAULDRON SNOUT

74. Cauldron Snout.

75. Cauldron Snout. The most northerly point on the tour, and the most desolate. Turner would have mixed memories of making this sketch for he recalled the journey from here over the fells to Appleby as the 'most confounded fagg, tho on horseback... the passage out of Teesdale leaves everything far behind for difficulty—bogged most completely Horse and its Rider, and nine hours making 11 miles...'

74

dashed down. He could hardly bring himself to consider sketching the falls at all, and the second sketch recorded just a few rocks at the edge of the basin, and the 'Colo[ours] G[reen] and Brown' of the water.

He eventually settled down sufficiently to make a third sketch, this time of the falls themselves, with notes of the 'Fissures' in the limestone, and 'G&B', 'D.G.' the colours of the rocks. He decided on a viewpoint beneath the falls on the edge of the basin for his first finished sketch, showing the twin falls divided by their basalt-topped bluff, towering over a figure sketching from a large slab on the edge of the pool in the foreground. After the pages of unpeopled landscapes the solitary artist (Ill. 73) comes as a surprise. We do not know who he was, but he appears again in a sketch made at the top of the falls and provides us with a ready symbol of the artist dwarfed by his surroundings.

Now he settled down to consider the views he would take for Longmans, and he found a slightly more distant viewpoint from which to make the first detailed drawing (Ill. 70) of the falls in his largest sketchbook. The sun was shining, for there are indications of a rainbow at the foot of the falls, which appears in the finished watercolour (Pl. 14), and shadows at the top left. He completed his record by clambering up to the top of the falls as Torrington had done, and making a sketch looking down into the basin and the Tees gorge. At the last, he walked round to the cliffs on the left bank, to take an expansive view of the whole setting, looking over the Force to the fells of upper Teesdale beyond (Ill. 71).

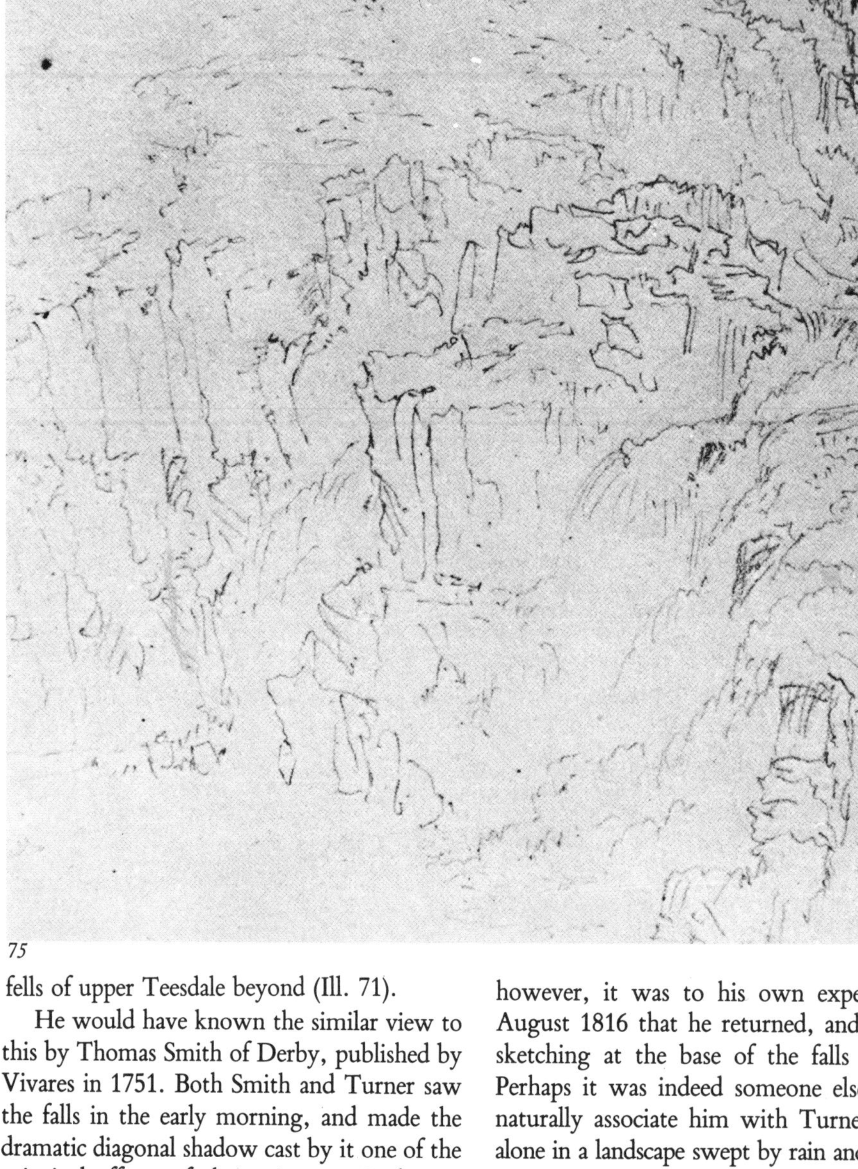

75

He would have known the similar view to this by Thomas Smith of Derby, published by Vivares in 1751. Both Smith and Turner saw the falls in the early morning, and made the dramatic diagonal shadow cast by it one of the principal effects of their pictures. Both saw fishermen at work casting and netting in the pool, and to Turnér the angler this was a characteristic feature. When he came to make his final watercolour (Ill. 72) of this sketch, however, it was to his own experiences in August 1816 that he returned, and the artist sketching at the base of the falls reappears. Perhaps it was indeed someone else, but we naturally associate him with Turner himself, alone in a landscape swept by rain and sunlight.

Turner spent the best part of three hours sketching at High Force and nearly two hours riding from Middleton, and the light in the sketches and watercolours indicates a time of about ten o'clock in the morning. It would

therefore have been at least midday when he arrived at Cauldron Snout having followed the now bare and rocky Tees valley up the route of the modern Pennine Way from High Force.

The Tees falls 200 feet in 150 yards at Cauldron Snout, where the Whin Sill, a formation of igneous rock, creates a great staircase of cataracts. Here the sugar limestone soil and the harsh climate have made the best habitat in Britain for Alpine plants. The meadows of Holmwath, just south of the Snout, are full of violets, primroses and wild pansies, but the visitor will also find there Stone Violets and Bird's Eye Primroses in abundance, Yellow Saxifrage and Shrubby Cinquefoil down by the river banks, and, rarer still, such prizes as the Bog Sandwort and the brilliant Spring Gentian.

The falls which Turner studied have now been regulated by a dam above them. A reservoir stands at the head of the Snout, and some 770 acres of rare tundra vegetation lie under seventy-five feet of water.

This was the northernmost point of Turner's tour, and the furthest from human habitation. Though the falls turn through nearly ninety degrees, Turner contrived to include the whole staircase by skilful manipulation of viewpoints (Ill. 75). It must have epitomised for him the northern wilderness, bare, violent, swept by rain and cold. Nevertheless he introduced signs of life in the finished watercolour (Ill. 76)—a covey of grouse enjoy the protection of overhanging bushes and heather, the warmth of a fleeting patch of sunshine. It was a place in which death came easily, however. The grouse are introduced only as quarry for the gunman who approaches on the opposite bank. The watercolour was one of the last of Turner's Yorkshire subjects to be published, and seems to reflect a darker outlook than most of the others in the series. Immediately after the death of Fawkes in 1825 Turner had written 'Alas! my good Auld lang sine is gone ... and I must follow; indeed I feel as you say, near a million times the brink of eternity.' The chasm at the left is the most dramatic visualisation of what he meant.

The road from Cauldron Snout to Appleby runs over nine miles of the highest uninhabited country in the north of England. Anyone who knows these bleak, dark moors, with their rocky outcrops, sudden bogs and hidden becks, can imagine that Turner urged on his horse with some anxiety. The prospect of being overtaken by dark on the moors was familiar to Turner from one of his favourite poems, James Thomson's *Seasons:*

Drear is the state of the benighted wretch
Who then bewildered wanders through the dark
Full of pale fancies and chimeras huge;
Nor visited by one directive ray
From cottage streaming or from airy hall.
Perhaps, impatient as he stumbles on,
Struck from the root of slimy rushes, blue
The wild-fire scatters round, or gathered, trails
A length of flame deceitful o'er the moss;
Whither decoyed by the fantastic blaze,
Now lost and now renewed, he sinks absorbed,
Rider and horse, amid the miry gulf...

76. Chain Bridge over the River Tees, c. *1825–6. Of all Turner's Yorkshire subjects, this picture is the furthest removed from the actual appearance of the subject. Turner has set the elementary sketch in violent motion, the river leaps down into an apparently bottomless chasm and death creeps up on the unwary in the form of an approaching gunman about to shoot the grouse in the foreground.*

76

When Turner wrote to Holworthy on 11 September he vividly recalled the horrors of the crossing. 'In regard to my present trip which you want to know about, I have but little to say by this post, but a most confounded fagg, tho on horseback. Still, the passage out of Teesdale leaves everything far behind for difficulty—bogged most completely Horse and its Rider, and nine hours making eleven miles ...' This may even have been an understatement, for in 1891, it was related that he was 'so delighted with High Force that on one occasion [1816 seems to have been his only visit] he all but lost his life there. He stayed so long sketching one evening that he was overtaken by darkness, and, when climbing the steep hill, was quite unable to see his way, and soon lost it altogether. After long and fruitless attempts to find it, he became so weary that he sat down in despair, and would never have got home at all if an old shepherd had not chanced to pass by and find him.'

Both the artist and his horse were sodden, muddied and exhausted when at last they came to High Cup Nick and the downward path stretched before them. True to character, Turner stopped to make a couple of rain-soaked sketches (Ill. 78). It is likely now he knew he was safe, and he dismounted to give his horse a breather. He put up at the first roadhouse he found, at Dufton. An inn can never have looked so inviting.

Sunday, 4 August

After his hard slog the day before, Turner had to take it easy, if only for the sake of his horse. A strong horse could manage twenty to twenty-five miles a day regularly, but only over good ground. 'Nine hours making eleven miles' over the highest fells in Yorkshire was enough for any animal and Turner spent Sunday morning quietly. As he rode into Appleby around lunch-time he had to turn over eight pages of the pocket-book, still damp from the rain where he had stopped on High Cup Nick now more than 1500 feet above him.

He took a few sketches of the town and then pressed gently on south over the Maulds Meaburn and Bank Moors to the Lune valley at Tebay. Although the road commands spectacular views of the Lakeland hills to the West, Turner did not pause to record them. Only as he came over Orton Scar did he find himself confronted with a view that was, simply, too good to resist. He made the sketch on one of the now dried four pages in the pocket-book (Ill. 79). Between Tebay Fell on the left and Roundthwaite Common on the right, he could just make out the line of the Kendal Road and the site of his next commissioned drawing, the Lune Gap.

77

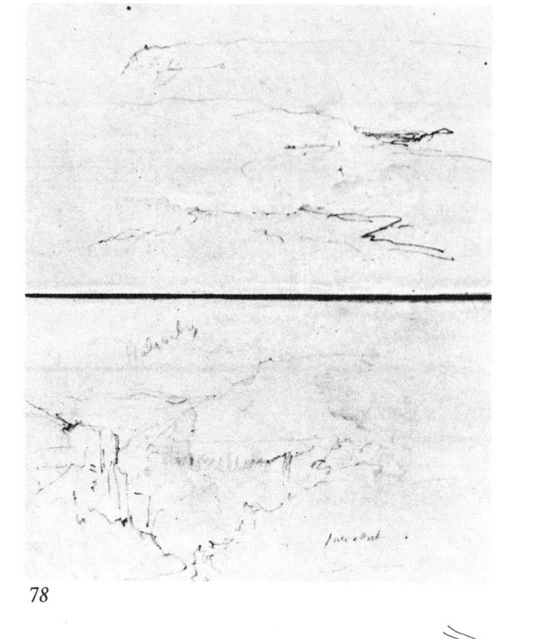

78

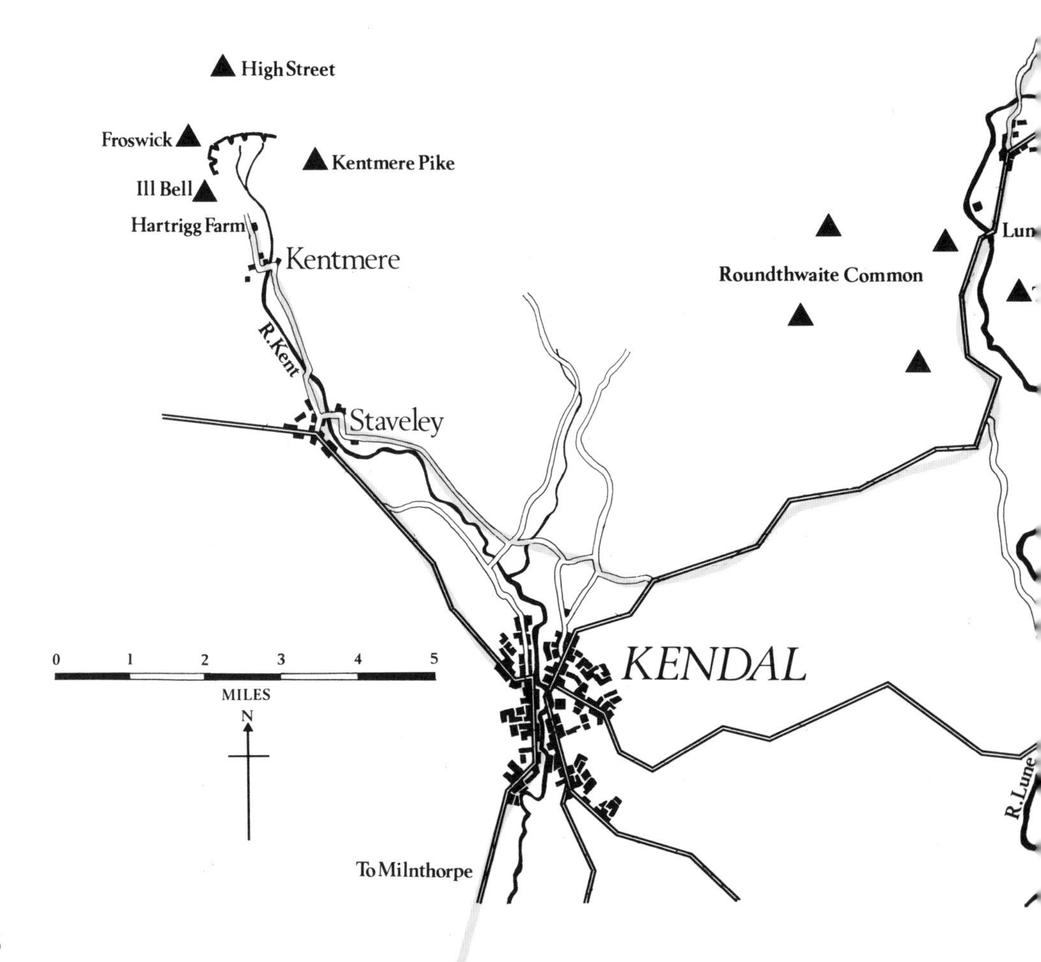

From Cauldron Snout
APPLEBY
R.Eden
Maulds Meaburn Moor

Orton Scar
ton
R.Lune
Langdale Fell

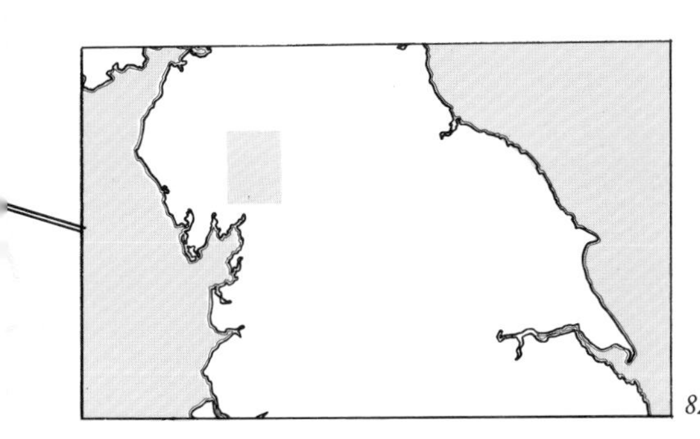

THE LUNE GAP

The valley of the Lune offered one of the few easy passages through the Westmorland Hills for Anglo-Scottish traffic. About a mile south of Tebay, the road crosses the marble-smooth gorge of the young river Lune, in Turner's day spanned at this point by two bridges. The northerly one replaced a medieval structure which had presumably now become unsafe. Turner devoted a page in the smaller composition book to this site (Ills. 81 and 82), choosing, as usual, to record his first impression as he rounded the bend in the road from Tebay.

This is a peculiarly satisfying sketch. The elegant twin bridges provide a landmark of human ingenuity amidst the bare fells raked by early evening sunlight. Human presence in a landscape, and man's achievement in direct and vital contact with the environment, are favourite themes with Turner. The Lune Farm and its bridges

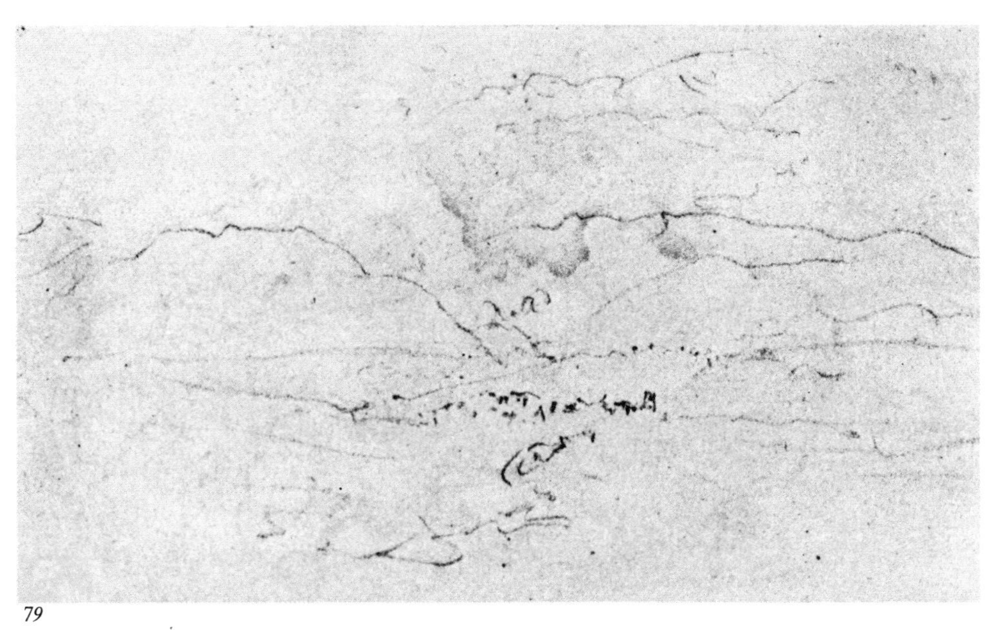

79

80

81

82

77. High Cup Nick, near Appleby.

78. Two views of High Cup Nick. Despite the fact that Turner had just struggled across the bogs from Cauldron Snout he still had enough energy to sketch the view looking towards the Lake District mountains and 'Hellvelyn'.

79. The view from Orton Scar towards the Lune Valley and the 'Road' to Kendal, Orton Church to the right. Note rain-staining.

80. View from Orton Scar of about 70 degrees. Note the way that Turner seems to compress this view in his sketch (Ill. 79), and exaggerates the apparent height of the hills.

81. Lune Bridge, near Tebay.

82. Lune Bridge and Farm near Tebay. Turner almost always sketched his first impressions, whether of the surprise view coming over Orton Scar from Appleby, or as here, rounding a bend in the road from Tebay. The nearer bridge survives, as does the farm (almost completely unchanged), but otherwise there have been dramatic changes.

KENT HEAD TO LEVENS HALL

provided him with a vivid instance.

The nature of Turner's brief as, indeed, his nature as an artist, meant that he must make direct contact with the wild countryside and the untamed forces of the elements. He never lost sight, however, of the artefacts spawned by that very urban and technological revolution which created a demand for such paintings. The newer bridge in the sketch remains, as does the farm, but the demand for ever faster forms of transport has led to dramatic change. The Kendal road no longer crosses on Turner's bridge, but glides instead across a huge flyover beyond. Anglo-Scottish traffic no longer even uses the Kendal Road. The purpose of the flyover is to carry traffic across the six lanes of the M6 motorway. Besides all this, electric trains thunder past on the five-hour run from Glasgow to London—a journey which would have taken Turner a good five days.

Monday 5 August

Turner probably spent the night at Staveley for his next sketches were made above Kentmere, at the source of the river Kent. The dale head appears at its best in cold morning light with the sun shining directly on the gaunt, rocky hills. Turner's composition sketch (Ill. 84) shows the view from just above Hartrigg Farm with Ill Bell (2470 feet.) on the left, Thornthwaite Crag (2560 feet.), High Street (2719 feet.) and Lingmell End (2183 feet.). After his tour there in 1797, Turner had largely avoided the more popular sites in the Lake District—then at the height of its fame as a tourist attraction. He preferred, on the whole, not to jostle with the pack for the best viewpoints. Most artists of the time would hardly have known of Kentmere's existence, and even today it remains one of the most secluded, peaceful and unchanged of all Lake District valleys.

He now turned southward towards Morecambe Bay. His route took him past Levens Hall, the greatest Elizabethan manor in Cumbria, which is still visited today for its medieval pele-tower, its superb panelled interiors and, above all, its unique seventeenth-century topiary gardens of shaped yew, box and privet hedges. He made a sketch for his own reference here, contriving to include both the bridge and the house in the same sketch from a viewpoint outside the main

83

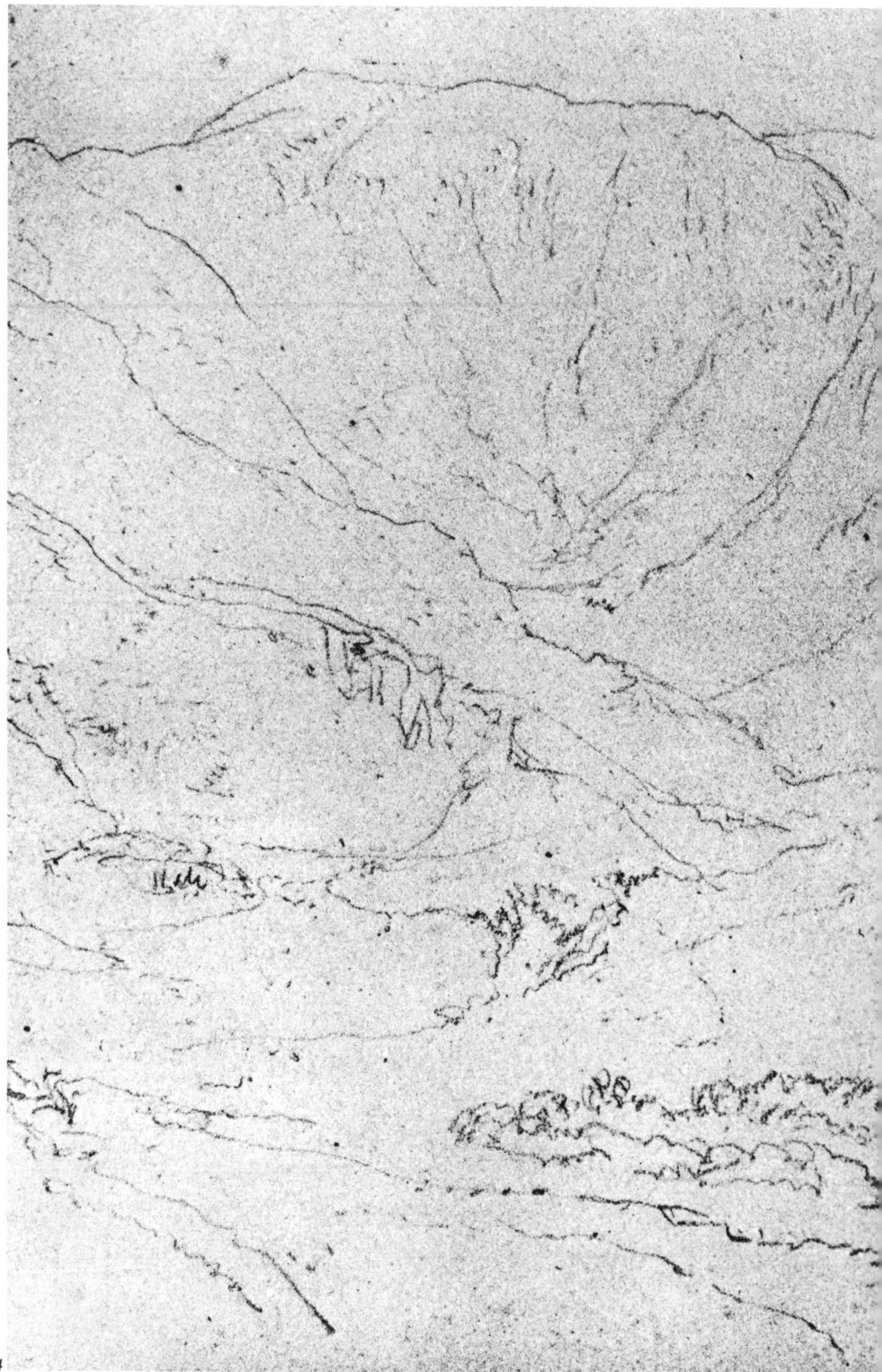

84

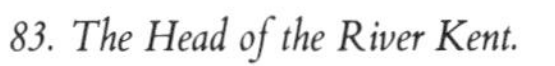

83. The Head of the River Kent.

84. The Head of the River Kent from near Hartrigg Farm above Kentmere, Ill Bell (to the left) High Street (centre) and Lingmell End (to the right). One of the most perfectly preserved of all Turner's landscapes.

85. Levens Hall and Bridge. Turner was famous in his youth for his skill as an architectural draughtsman. He never lost his interest in architectural detail and even in a quick sketch such as this was careful to note the number of window lights.

THE KENT ESTUARY

85

gates. Meticulous as ever, he noted the number of lights in each window, just in case he should ever be called upon to paint it (Ill. 85).

From Levens Hall he pressed on to Morecambe Bay. He arrrived at about two o'clock in the afternoon. The first objective was Dallam Tower, built in 1720 on the site of an old pele-tower, and the home of the Wilson family. Dallam was renowned for its grounds with stately groves of oak and beech, and Turner found a viewpoint in the deer park looking north east over the house to the Kent estuary, with Whitbarrow Scar across the sands and a backcloth of Lake District mountains, including Coniston Old Man at the extreme left and Fairfield and the Helvellyn range towards the centre. Morecambe Bay has a climate and atmosphere all of its own, and Turner was so delighted with the change of scenery that he took out his largest sketchbook for the first time since Cauldron Snout. He had been in the area several times before, but had never taken the opportunity to make a proper survey. The area had in fact been by-passed by most artists, and still has a tranquil, back-water air, which, with the tide out and the sun gleaming on three hundred square miles of wet sand, is unique.

It was late afternoon by the time Turner finished his sketch of Dallam. Low tide was at about 3.30 p.m. and the Kent can be seen snaking across the sand. The salt air and open spaces drew him down to the estuary and his next sketch was taken from Milnthorpe Sands, a panorama of 360 degrees, looking first north to Whitbarrow Scar flanked by Coniston Old Man and the Helvellyn range, and then south to the sea with Meathop, Grange Fell and Newton Fell to the right with Arnside Knott, now a National Trust property, to the left. Many tourists to the area noted the local lifestyle as one of almost primitive simplicity and observed the fishermen

86

87

staking out the sands with nets to catch fluke, plaice and salmon, and the women and children 'following the sands', cockling. Turner was no exception, and his drawing shows a crowd of figures busy at work on the sands.

He seems to have crossed the Kent estuary near Arnside, probably by ferry. The next sketch in the sequence (Ill. 86) was made from the cornfields on the banks of the Winster near Lindale at about seven o'clock looking out to sea, with the bold outline of Castle Head jutting up into the sky on the right. This is one of the few sketches from the tour which has any indication of cloud formations. When recording the landscape with his pencil, Turner made few notes of the light or weather effects, but those he did make are telling. The clouds in the distance drift away to the East and the waters of the Winster, backed up by the tide and sheltered by Castle Head, are

88

glassy and still. When we look closely at the drawing we find the essential clues that unlock this image of a quiet summer evening consist of three vertical strokes on the river's surface, a slight shading on the left slope of Castle Head and a few scribbled clouds in the distance. Within these spare sketches, apparently little more than a network of outlines, lies a highly developed shorthand so that one of them appears to us, as it did to Turner in his studio, as Castle Head at about seven in the evening on 5 August 1816.

Castle Head had revealed evidence of Roman occupation in 1795 when the foundations of the new house were being dug, but was more noteworthy for its builder than for the ancient history which he uncovered.

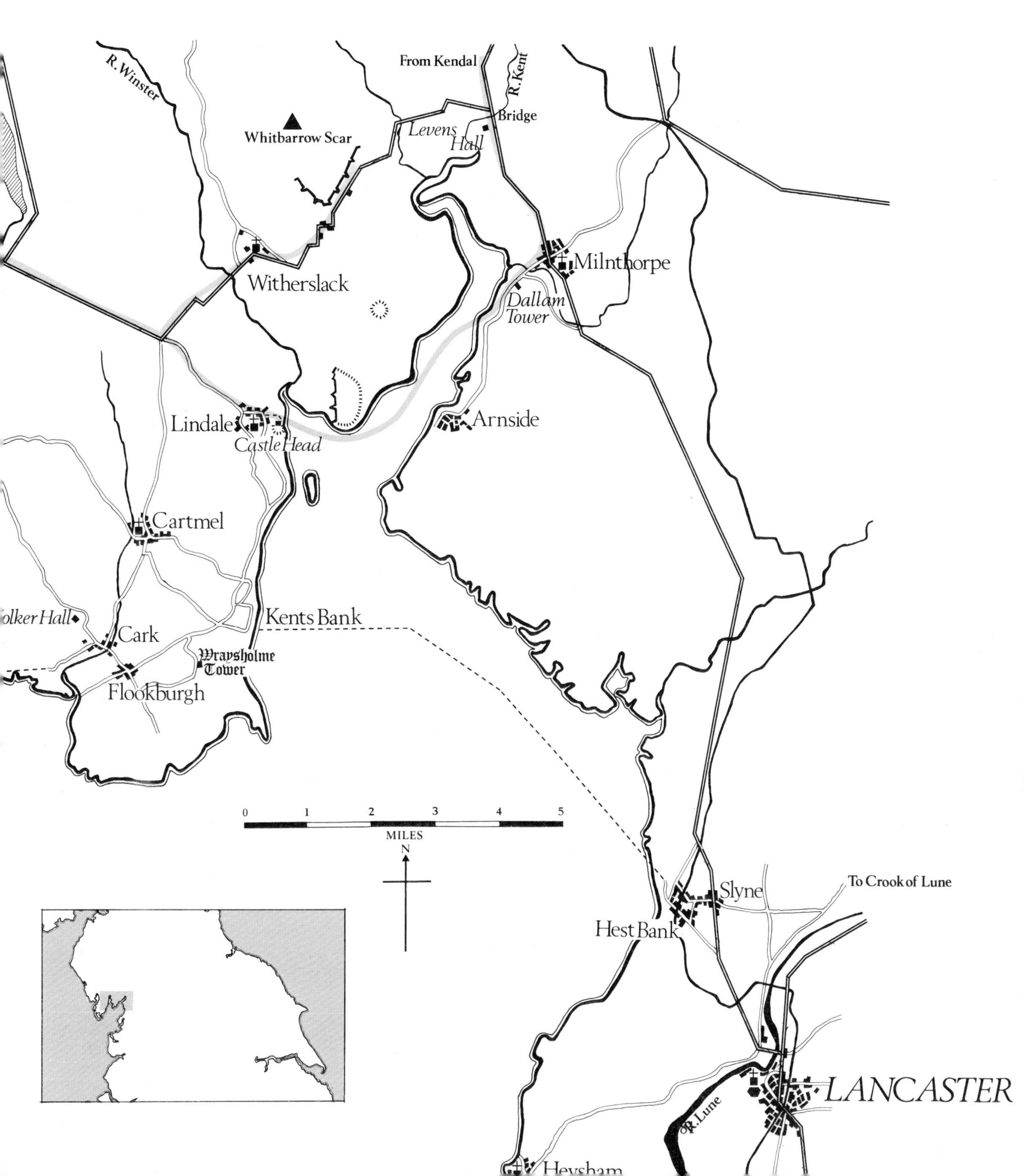

CASTLE HEAD

John Wilkinson was a local man who became the greatest iron master of the early industrial revolution with large iron works in Shropshire, Staffordshire and Wales. He made one of the first iron bridges and, in the face of almost unanimous scepticism, the first iron boat. His death in 1808 had caused a local sensation for he instructed that his body be brought back to Castle Head for burial in the grounds. Things did not work out as he had planned. On its way from Lancaster over the sands the iron coffin containing his body had to be abandoned near Holme Island when the tide came in. It was dug out the following day. When it arrived at Castle Head it was discovered that the grave carved out of solid rock was too small, and he was temporarily buried elsewhere while enlargements were made. He was finally interred as he had instructed, and his mortal remains were there when Turner visited in 1816, although he had to be moved again when the island was sold in 1828. The new owner, Mr Wright, found his presence oppressive. He had the body exhumed and reburied at Lindale. The massive iron obelisk that marked the original grave can now be found by the roadside near the village. The house has enjoyed a less disturbed

86. Castle Head, near Lindale. A drawing of great economy and precision. Note particularly how the direction of the wind is indicated by the clouds billowing up from the south-west and how the glassy stillness of the water sheltered by Castle Head is depicted with just three or four lines to suggest reflections.

87. Castle Head and Morecambe Bay from above Lindale.

88. A colour study of Castle Head and Morecambe Bay from above Lindale, c. 1818, based on the sketch made in 1816 (Ill. 89), showing the view across the sands towards Lancaster and Heysham Head, visible in the distance to the right.

CASTLE HEAD TO CONISHEAD PARK

89. Castle Head and Morecambe Bay from above Lindale with evening sunlight on Castle Head.

90. Ulverston from Conishead Park with Coniston Old Man to the left and the Kent Estuary to the right. This view appears at its best on a summer's evening when the light rakes across the Lake District fells from the left.

91. Ulverston and the Lake District fells from Conishead Park.

89

90

91

history than its builder, and survives intact today as a field study centre.

Castle Head was one of the most prominent landmarks in the area with its dark green plantation rising from the marshes, and Turner sketched it again from a hill above the village of Lindale (Ill. 89). The evening sun was shining on the island, beyond stretched Morecambe Bay over ten miles of glittering sea and sand all the way to Lancaster and Heysham Head. Turner's route to Lancaster lay across these very sands, and he must have considered their dangers as well as their beauty as the bay filled again in the evening towards high tide at 9.54 p.m. He gazed on them with anticipation and pleasure, but his route for the moment lay elsewhere. The final sketch of the day was of Witherslack Chapel from Newton Fell, as he made his way towards his accommodation for the night.

For those that came by road from Milnthorpe, Thomas West's *Guide to the Lakes,* (first published in 1778, but even in Turner's day after many reprints, still well known) offered the following information: 'From Milnthorpe to Levens (an ancient seat of the Hon. F.G.Howard where a curious specimen of the old style of gardening can be seen, as laid out by the gardener of King James the Second)—2 miles. From thence to the

recorded views in the smaller composition book, looking south west over the 'Bog' towards Castle Head, and east over more 'Bog' towards Levens, with the Howgill fells in the distance.

From Witherslack Turner rode about seventeen miles west to Ulverston, home of Margaret Fell, the Quaker, with its fine Tudor churches. He did not arrive until well into the afternoon. His principal object was to collect sketches of the Levens estuary, and his first stop was at Canal Foot, where he made a two-page panorama in his largest sketchbook looking across the plains of sand to the mountains. At the centre of the composition can be seen the ridge of Fairfield with the sun casting a clear shadow to the right, which suggests that it was by now at least five or six o'clock in the evening.

He continued down the coast to Conishead Priory, where he found a still more satisfactory panorama from the grounds of the priory park (Ills. 90 and 91). Wordsworth had recommended 'the view from the top of the hill [near Urswick], before descending to the grounds of Conishead Priory' in his *Guide to the Lakes* in 1810, and Whitaker described a similar prospect in the text of the *History of Richmondshire*: '[Ulverston] is a large, well-built town, screened from the north and west by gently rising grounds, backed at a distance by Black Comb and the Coniston Fells, and upon the verge of a small plain, apparently abandoned by the sea ...' The shadow on Fairfield suggests that the evening was a pleasant one, and Turner delighted in placing all the Lake District mountains, with Coniston Old Man at the left with Ulverston church tower visible below, sweeping round to the plain that Whitaker described and the sands of the Leven at the right. He finished off the evening with a few sketches of Conishead Priory and a view over the sands to

near end of the long causeway at Beathwaite Green — 1 mile. Then to the Black Bull in Witherslack—3 miles (which takes you by the foot of Whitbarrow Scar, a remarkable precipice of limestone rock.'

Until the new road was built between Levens and Lindale in 1818 – 23, Witherslack was an important stopping-place on the overland route to Furness. The road beneath Whitbarrow Scar was, when Turner used it, at the very end of its life. It is now a bridle path, and the once busy road to Newton over Blea Crag bridge is just a sleepy country lane. It is as hard to imagine Witherslack bustling with traffic as it is to conceive of Morecambe, on a sunny August evening, peopled by no one more garish or noisy than a few cockle-gatherers, but the *Black Bull* was then one of the busiest inns in the area. Since Turner intended to explore the 'remarkable precipice of limestone rock' at nearby Whitbarrow Scar the next day, Witherslack provided the ideal resting-place.

Tuesday 6 August

Turner spent the first part of the morning making sketches around St. Paul's Church at Witherslack, built in 1664 by the 'Reverend John Barwick STD. Born in this hamlet. Late Dean of St.Pauls' according to the tablet over the door. He seems to have been sketching largely for his own interest, filling up the blank pages in his pocket-book with a series of views of the church under its wooded banks, looking out over Morecambe Bay with Castle Head and Meathop Marshes (called 'Medup' on contemporary maps, and 'Medcup' by Turner), details of the chapel windows, and views of Whitbarrow Scar and Witherslack from various points round about. The best views were from the road under Whitbarrow Scar near the Lodge which had been built in the 1720s and laid out with gardens and ornamental trees. Turner

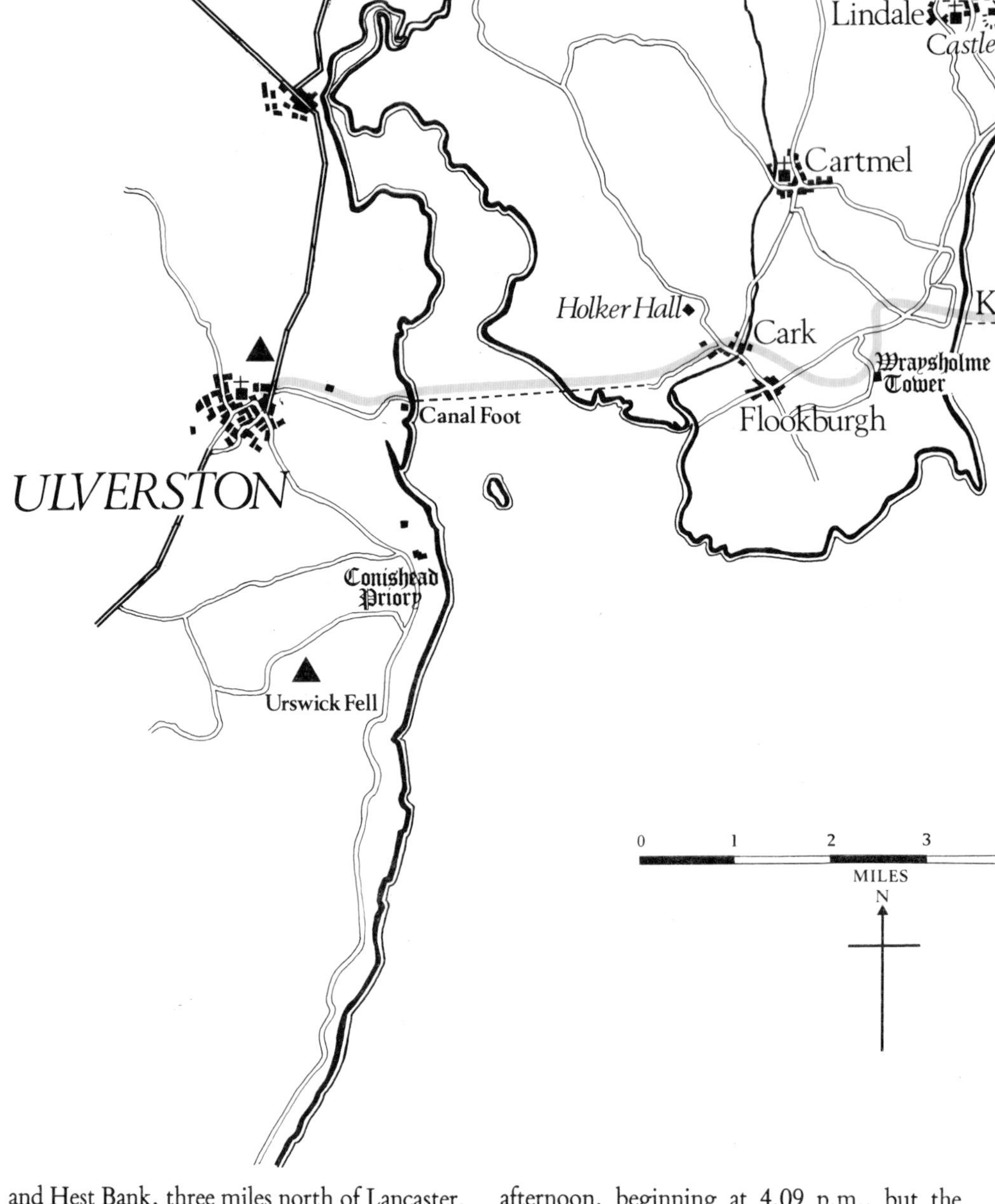

92

Cartmel before returning, presumably to Ulverston, for the night.

Wednesday 7 August

The journey to Lancaster was one of the highlights of Turner's tour. Until the opening of the railway between Ulverston and Carnforth in 1857 the main line of communication to Lancaster lay directly over the sands at low tide. The crossing held many dangers. There were three river estuaries to cross, whose courses and depth change unexpectedly, there are fogs, quicksands deep enough to swallow a coach, and a surging tide which can gather into a wall of water up to ten feet high, rushing across the sands faster than a horse at full gallop. Thomas West's *Guide*, however, was reassuring: 'The approach...to Lancaster [from Furness] hath always been considered as dangerous: but it is less so now than formerly, the sands being more solid; and in company with guides few accidents happen ... The river Kent hath its channel, and a guide on horseback is always in waiting to conduct travellers over at the stated hours ... The Leven sands are safe, yet the ford, like that of the Kent, is frequently changing by the shifting of the sands. This ford is every day tried by the guide, and in his company you are safe ... on a fine day there is not a more pleasing seaside journey in the country.'

There were two sands to cross, first the Levens estuary between Canal Foot, Ulverston, and Flookburgh, a distance of about three miles, and then between Kent's Bank, near Grange, and Hest Bank, three miles north of Lancaster, a distance of about ten miles. The guides, or 'Carters', marked the routes with sprigs of laurel called 'Brobs', and it was generally possible to cross between three or four hours after one high tide and three hours before the next—a period of about six hours, though much depended on the height of the tide and the direction and strength of the wind.

According to the tide tables published in the *Lancaster Gazette* on 3 August, high water on the 7th was at 11.03 a.m. and 11.24 p.m. The recommended crossing time was therefore in the afternoon, beginning at 4.09 p.m., but the following day a morning crossing was advised, beginning at 4.29 a.m.

In 1820 a writer in the *Lonsdale Magazine* described how his journey began at 5 a.m. when his coach driver burst into his hotel room in Lancaster exclaiming 'For God's sake make haste ... the tide is down ... if you delay we shall all be drowned.' If Turner began the crossing at first light he would have had some five hours in which to complete the twenty-one miles to Lancaster in safety.

The crossing could be extraordinarily picturesque. The *Lonsdale Magazine's* corre-

spondent went on to describe the crossing of the Kent on his journey: 'there could not be fewer than forty carts, gigs, horse-chaises, etc. with men, women, children, dogs and I can hardly tell what besides all in the river at once ... It would have been a fine model a draw the Passage of the Red Sea from.' In 1850 a traveller crossing from Kent's Bank noted, 'Sometimes the number of people and conveyances which cross from hence to Hest Bank on the opposite shore, is so great as to present the appearance of a caravan traversing the Arabian desert, but consisting of oxen, sheep, horsemen, fishermen, carriers, chaises, gigs, coaches, all in close succession, instead of the dromedaries and turbaned inhabitants of the East.'

Turner made jottings in his notebook of the Lakeland hills from the sands, and of 'Rayham [i.e. Wraysholme] The Tower' as he crossed overland between Flookburgh and Kent's Bank. The economy of these sketches indicates that progress was more important than sketching. He had made the journey on at least three previous occasions and the memory of those experiences was vivid enough to furnish material for two finished watercolours.

92. Lancaster Sands, c. *1816. One of the first of Turner's autobiographical travelling pictures, showing the Lancaster coach struggling across the sands in a rainstorm being overtaken by the incoming tide.*

93. Lancaster Sands, c. *1825, showing the coach approaching Hest Bank, near Lancaster towards the end of its journey from Ulverston, with a whole caravan of travellers straggling behind, no doubt fondly recalled by Turner from his journeys.*

93

In the first (Ill. 92), usually related to the present tour, he shows the Lancaster-Ulverston coach battling against the wind, rain and fast-incoming tide. Various coaches plied over the Sands between the *Kings Arms* at Ulverston and the *Sun Inn* at Lancaster. In 1781 there was a diligence that carried three passengers, and for a number of years around 1800 there were long coaches called 'dillies' which carried thirteen, and a heavy load of luggage passengers on top. These had an unsurprising tendency to become trapped in the sand and were replaced by smaller vehicles such as that shown by Turner. The tide is already lapping around the coach wheels and land is nowhere in sight. The driver flogs the horses in an effort to make haste, the riders bend grimly into the wind, luggage-passengers huddle on the roof, while the sky rages all around, and the line of 'brobs' leads into distances already covered by the sea.

In a later watercolour (Ill. 93), Turner recalls an assortment of tired travellers arriving at the Lancaster end of the sands just in the nick of time. The tide is about to cut off the stragglers. If the theme of the earlier watercolour was 'sublime'—man's struggle against the elements—that of the later one was more picturesque, showing the rich carnival of incidents that he had witnessed. There is a barefoot itinerant wheelwright carrying his wares on his back, there are tired horses, fretful passengers peering intently ahead towards their destination—though one at the back is apparently less concerned with his predicament than with the spectacular view of the Coniston Fells

LANCASTER

behind. There are dogs, children, mothers, tradesmen, tourists, even a babe-in-arms, all hurrying along as best they can.

Turner's first project at Lancaster was to visit the aqueduct built in 1796 to carry the Lancaster Canal over the Lune. After the sands crossing most tourists would have had quite enough for the day, but not Turner. His first view of Lancaster was from the top of the bank by Carus Farm, coming down the road from Hest Bank *via* Slyne, with the town, the church, castle, bridge and aqueduct laid out before him, and a cart making its slow way down the lane as he sketched.

The aqueduct was the largest of its kind in the country, a worthwhile subject in its own right, and he made a drawing of its architectural details, noting the number of modillions ('11', though there are in fact twelve) and particulars of the banding on the bases. He had first sketched it when it was brand- new, looking through one of the arches to the town, but now, perhaps having had his viewpoint chosen for him, the aqueduct served as a grandstand for the view (Ill. 94) it offered from the southern end, over the riverside fields and mills, to the new bridge, St. John's Church, with the town crowned by the castle and the ancient parish church of St Mary. Whitaker, curiously, devoted considerable space to Lancaster in his *History of the County of York*. Whitaker's 'Yorkshire' indeed included everything north of the Ribble, including large portions of Westmorland. His justification was that in Norman times all this was actually part of Yorkshire. This may sound like the logic of a Tyke, but Whitaker was in fact born in Norfolk. Call it instead the logic of an antiquarian.

He described Lancaster as a 'pleasant but not very populous or opulent town' whose principal attraction was that it was untouched by industrialisation. He was particularly impressed by the 'absence of commercial bustle, of smoke and dust; [and the] ... natural beauties of the place ... the near neighbourhood of the finest scenery in the kingdom, the opportunity of sea-bathing, the productive plenty of the adjoining county, the abundance of the market in fruit, fish and grain.'

The modern visitor to Lancaster will find it a quiet and prosperous town. Although it remains the capital of one of the most industrial counties in England, it is dwarfed by its *confrère* cities such as Liverpool and Manchester. Its days of glory are past. It is curious to reflect that it started in obscurity too. In the Domesday Book, it is recorded as a hamlet of the manor of Halton—a tiny village by the Crook of Lune. Within 400 years however, it had given its name to a huge county, one of the greatest duchies in the land, and a royal dynasty. The history of the castle is one of constant bloodshed: restored by

94

95

94. Lancaster from the Aqueduct Bridge, c. *1825.*

95. Morecambe Bay and the Lake District Fells from Heysham. One of Turner's most extensive panoramas taking in an angle of nearly 180 degrees and tracing his journey around and across the bay, from 'Black Combe' to the left, past Coniston 'Old Man', 'Holker Hall', 'Floo[kburgh]', 'Castle H[ead]' and 'Arnside'.

96. Lancaster from above the Aqueduct.

96

John of Gaunt, fortified to resist the Armada, fought over in the Civil War, thousands of people have been confined, tortured and put to death here; the shackles and the gallows are still in place. In the chapel, a section of the gallery is railed off for those prisoners already condemned to die. Torture instruments are on display. In the Crown Court, formerly the great hall, there is a branding iron and a clamp which held the prisoner's hand as, in full view of the court, 'M' for 'Malefactor' was burned into it. This practice stopped in 1811, just five years before Turner's arrival. More people have been condemned to death on this spot than anywhere else in Britain, among them the ten Lancashire witches and at least twenty people condemned for their faith. In the four years after Waterloo, the very period during which Turner came here, 240 people were condemned and executed in this court.

It is a city steeped in law. The castle library has a complete collection of English laws since 1225, and the Shire Hall is decorated with hundreds of shields, bearing the coats-of-arms of Constables of the tower, Royal coats of arms from the thirteenth century to the twentieth, and those of every sheriff who has ever come to Lancaster for the June assizes. The church, incidentally, has some of the finest and most intricate carved fourteenth-century stalls in the world.

When Turner came to paint his finished watercolour (Ill. 94), he chose to contrast the modern industrial life of the canal barges, carrying coal and lime to south Lancashire, with the still agricultural economy of the country town. One benefit of the modern world was, apparently, leisure, for while the work still goes on in the fields, everyone on the canal is resting. On the left a boy fishes from a barge, at the right another figure snoozes in the shade of the parapet, and even the barge horse is allowed to graze contentedly while the bargeman and his wife sit on the towpath enjoying the warmth of the sun.

HEYSHAM

Turner believed that industry had its joys and its beauties. Doubtless reflecting on this notion, he finished off the day by returning to his first viewpoint to make a detailed drawing of the prospect of Lancaster, this time making a feature of the aqueduct itself.

Thursday 8 August

The morning was passed in exploring Heysham. He began with a sketch from the foreshore. A group of fishermen was at work. He recorded them with a net lying on the beach beside them. The rocky cove is called St. Patrick's Skeer after the legendary landing of the Irish saint, and Heysham Head is crowned by a ruined Saxon chapel, famed still for a family of graves cut into the living rock. The next sketches were made from the 'red scar' seen to the left of the first, looking out over the village with Heysham Tower at the left and Morecambe Bay spread out over an angle of about 180 degrees, the Lakeland fells far beyond.

For Turner, the view was an opportunity to review his progress around and across the bay over the previous few days, and he recorded the names of places he had seen, from 'Black Combe' at the left, over '[Coniston] Old Man', 'Holker' Hall, 'Floo[kburgh]', 'Castle H[ead]' and 'Arnside' (Ill. 95). A heavily laden haywain was making its way down the village, and both the laboriously gleaned crop from the stony fields and the shallow water sparkling in the bay were lovingly recalled in his finished picture (Pl. 15).

From Heysham Turner returned to Lancaster and spent several hours making a detailed survey of the town, starting with views around the dock, showing the busy St Georges Quay with its moored boats, warehouses and Customs House, and its constant, bustling industry: 'Shipbuilding', 'Float of timbers' and 'Linen'. The

THE LUNE VALLEY

97

98

medieval bridge still stood then, broken and ruined, though it had been intact when first he had visited Lancaster. He sketched it now in its dilapidation, before moving upstream to make a large composition of its successor, the elegant five-arched structure built in 1788 by Harrison of Chester. He completed his exploration with a two-part panorama (Ill. 98) from the south, looking out over the castle to the Cumberland fells beyond, and over the town to the aqueduct and up the Lune valley, where his route now lay.

In his *Guide to the Lakes*, Wordsworth had recommended 'The direct road [from Lancaster] to Kendal is twenty-two miles, but by making a circuit of eight miles, the Vale of Lune to Kirkby Lonsdale will be included.' The whole tract is pleasing; there is one view mentioned by Gray and Mason especially so. In West's *Guide* it is thus pointed out:—''About a quarter of a mile beyond the third mile-stone, where the road makes a turn to the right, there is a gate on the left which leads into a field where the station meant will be found .' Turner avoided the turnpike road from Lancaster and approached instead through the village of Halton, probably in order to see the famous stones, which include a Roman altar dedicated to Mithras, the sun god, and an extraordinary cross of the time of the Danish conquest. At the Crook of Lune, the river makes an extraordinary loop around a bluff that blocks its otherwise lazy passage. It is still a popular spot for paddlers, picnickers and fishermen, though the well-wooded banks have now grown into a jungle that obscures whatever attraction it had for Turner. The Crook was originally famed for its 'prospect' and Whitaker devoted one of his most eloquent descriptive passages to it. 'The noble windings of the river, the fruitful alluvial lands upon its banks, the wooded and cultivated ridge which bounds it to the north-west, the striking feature of Hornby Castle in front, and, above all, the noble form of Ingleborough—form an assemblage of features—[with no]—rival—in the kingdom.'

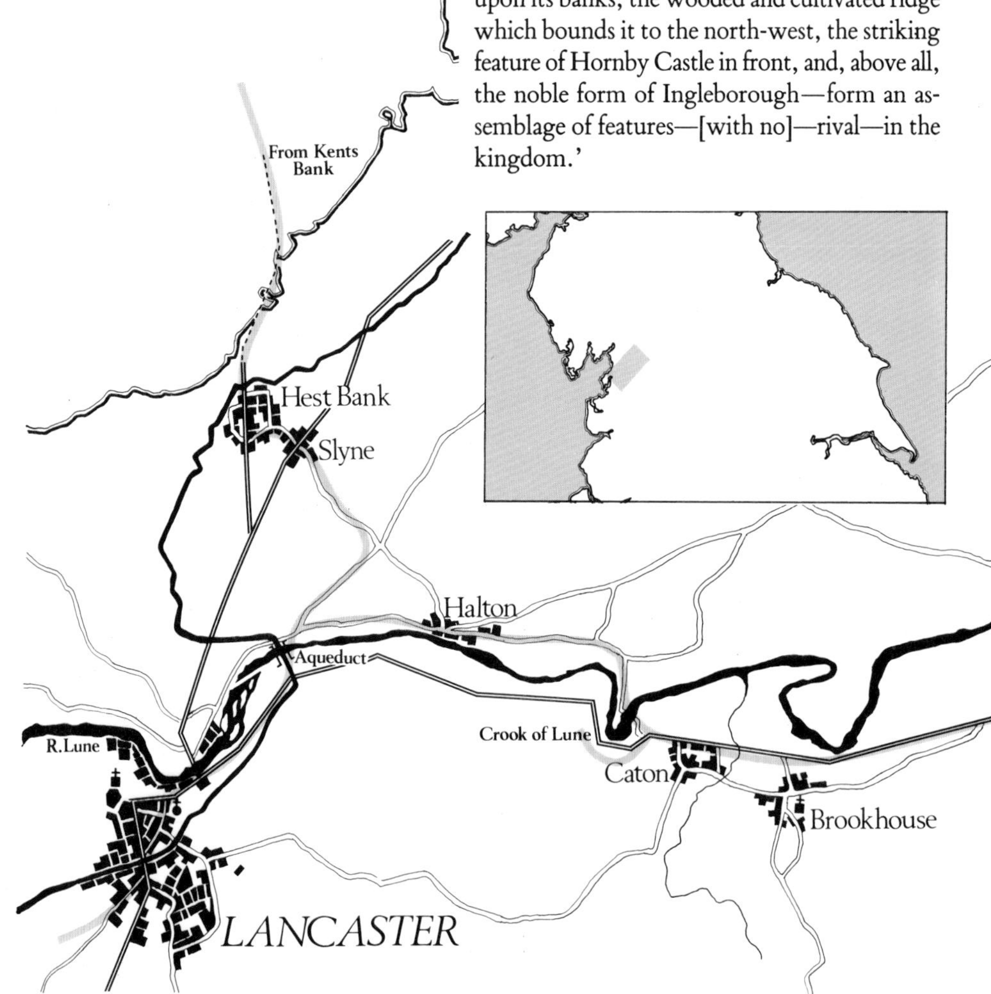

THE CROOK OF LUNE

Turner arrived along the lane from Halton, which runs down the bluff to the bridge. He seems to have needed to come to terms with the subject rather circumspectly. He made a series of trial notes in his pocket-book before deciding on the final composition. His first impression was taken from the road, and he followed this with sketches of the bridge looking up-river, a third from the crown of the promontory, and others of the bridge, the 'furze'-topped Crook, and the road down which he had come, and a view from the Crook looking down-stream towards Lancaster with a 'Girl driving cows to milk.'

The best viewpoint, he decided, was not far from that advised by West and Wordsworth, from the quarry above the main Lancaster road. The quarry was, according to Mrs. Hunt, 'of special local interest—a very peculiar stone is said to be found there,' and Turner, as an illustrator, never missed a characteristic point of that kind. He sketched a lifting tripod and a horse yoked to a sled, and developed the theme in his finished watercolour (Pl. 16) with a quarryman working with a pickaxe in the foreground. He made other notes on the sketch (Ill. 99), of the 'Road with Walls', 'Corn' and 'G[rass]' in the fields, and every detail of the landscape laid out before him, including Caton Bridge and Brookhouse

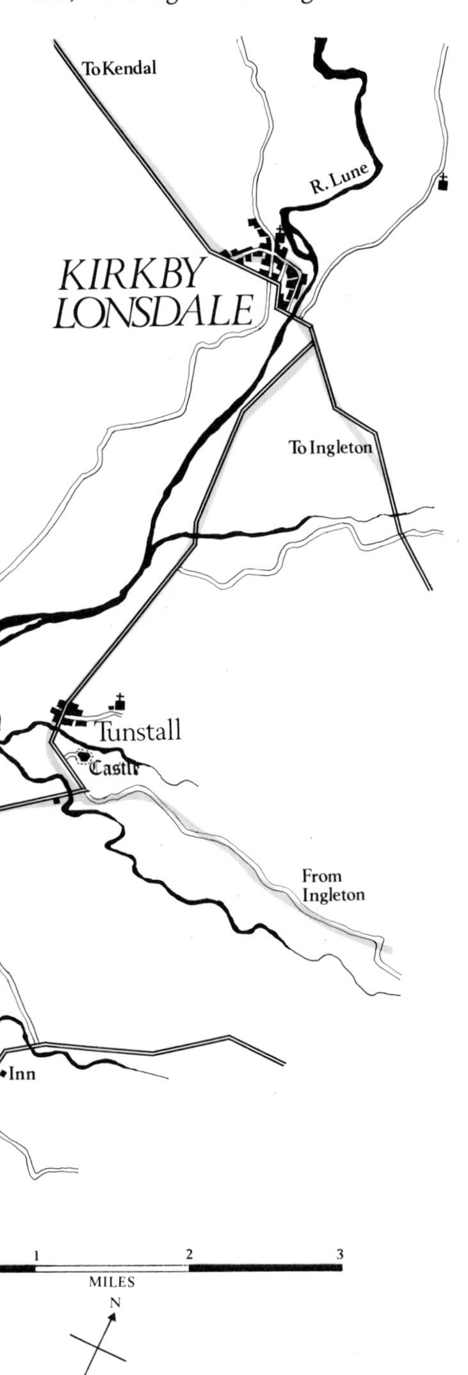

97. Lancaster from the South.

98. Lancaster from the South, a two-part panorama with the view over the castle to the Lake District fells above, continued to the right below, with the old Town Hall, the spire of St.John's Church and the Aqueduct.

99. The Crook of Lune.

100. Colour study of the Crook of Lune made in 1818 as the basis of the finished watercolour (Pl. 16).

99

100

HORNBY CASTLE AND TATHAM

Church to the right, and the medieval bridge (replaced in 1883), with its gatehouse sketched in the bottom left-hand corner. This was Turner at his best and most relaxed, and the quality of his pencil work conveys his sense of delight. The finished watercolour sets the time at about half-past seven in the evening, and he shows smoke rising steadily through still air from a distant chimney. Sound carries far when the air is still, and with cows being taken for milking and sheep being herded along the road, the dale echoed to lowing and bleating as Turner made his way to Hornby to find his bed for the night.

101

102

103

Friday 9 August

Turner's next assignment was to take sketches of the view from Hornby Castle terrace and a view of the castle from near Tatham. He probably stayed at the *George* nearby and was up and sketching early. Hornby Castle was begun in the twelfth century during the reign of King Stephen, but had been rebuilt on many occasions, latterly during the late eighteenth century to fit it up in the modern style. Whitaker was enraptured by its setting: 'Perhaps no situation in the northern dales can boast of equal fertility. Situated on a steep insulated hill, on a curvature of the Wenning, near its junction with the Lune, it commands an enchanting view of the fine river under curving woods and diversified grounds, and terminated by the vast bulk of Ingleborough which is here seen to the greatest advantage, distinct and majestic. In front is a long reach of the winding Lune, seen from a commanding elevation on the terace in front of the castle, which as much surpasses that of Windsor in variety of landscape, as it falls short of it in its own extent, and the majesty of the pile which it encircles.'

The view required no preliminary research. Turner worked directly in his largest sketchbook, plotting the line of the river Wenning up to Tatham, with the Hindburn running across the meadows from the right to join it, and the wooded slopes hanging over the water at the left. The summit of Ingleborough was evidently obscured by clouds, for Turner had to miss it out of his sketch, and suggests stillness by noting the sound of the 'Rush of W[ater]' drifting up to him on the cool morning air. The idea of sound was further explored in the finished watercolour (of which the engraving is reproduced as Ill. 103). by the introduction of a peacock hooting in the foreground and the quizzical faces of distant cattle, turned up as if to enquire what the noise is. It is particularly noteworthy that the picture has no human figures in it, though there are signs of human activity in the water-carrier and watering-can left out overnight. The only person abroad is the artist, catching the world in its quiet hours while everyone else is still in bed.

After breakfast Turner went to Tatham to take the view of the castle looking back towards the terrace. He made a preliminary sketch of the view from near the bridge in his pocket-book, but found a more varied and incident-packed view from just above the *Bridge* Inn where he could include the road, bridge and inn, as well as Tatham church to the right. Across the

HORNBY CASTLE AND TATHAM

104

'meadow' in the foreground he could see the 'River sparkling among the trees', noting that the trees were in fact 'alders'. The *Bridge* Inn was built in 1744 and the initials of its first occupier 'C W A' are carved over the door. The cottage next door dates from 1642, and, on the evidence of the watercolour, was in need of repair when Turner saw it.

He spent quite some time in making this sketch (Ill. 104), for the finished watercolour (Pl. 18) is one of the most elaborate compositions of the tour. While he worked a whole carnival of incidents seems to have passed by: there is a difficult-to-make-out note on the sketch about an 'Ox the Harness on [-?]', which later served to remind Turner of a road packed with incident. In the watercolour a gig passes the inn, a ladder stands propped against the wall of the cottage where repair work is being carried out, a man rides a rather broken-down looking creature in the direction of Hornby, stopping to chat to a mother with a brood of five children. One of them has spilt milk on the road, and a cat steps forward boldly to take advantage of the accident; a milkmaid obtains further supplies while one cow gazes patiently at the scenery and another scratches her head on the wall.

From Tatham, Turner returned to Hornby, first to take a closer view of the castle (Ill. 101) from the same angle as his view from the *Bridge* Inn, so that his details would be accurate in the finished watercolour, and secondly to take a few sketches of the castle, bridge and church (with its unusual octagonal tower) on his own account. This attention gives the impression that he would like to have made more of the castle, and that he was contemplating some way of working the building into his view from the terrace, for his final sketch shows him noting the exact profile of Ingleborough now that it had cleared, and panning round from the terrace to include a study of the house.

Turner set the time of his Tatham Bridge watercolour at mid-morning, so it was afternoon when at last he left Hornby. His route took him past the now largely-hidden Thurland Castle at Tunstall. Thurland, like Hornby, has a long history. It had recently been modernised as a comfortable dwelling-house. In many ways it enjoys a better setting than its neighbour. It stands on a natural eminence commanding the rich fertile plain near the junction of the Greta (not the same as the Greta which flows into the Tees) and the Lune. Turner was particularly struck with the first impression coming down the road from Welling, with the castle on its rock rising out of the plain, and the Lune Valley hills all around, but decided on a view of the castle from the west (Ill. 105), showing the old barbican, for one of the principal features of the castle was its moat. He also managed to include a view of Ingleborough to the left but the proposed illustration was a casualty of Longmans' cancellation of their agreement. They used an inferior engraving which, if it had no other virtues, cost just £5.10s.—one-twentieth the price of a work by Turner.

It was late afternoon when Turner arrived at Kirkby Lonsdale, and after stabling his horse he

105

101. Hornby Castle. A close-up sketch of the castle which Turner made to record details for the finished watercolour (Pl. 18).

102. Hornby Castle.

103. Ingleborough from Hornby Castle Terrace. *The engraving by Charles Heath published in 1822.*

104. Hornby Castle from above Tatham Bridge Inn, with Tatham Church to the right and 'River sparkling among the trees' written as a rough note on the sketch.

105. Thurland Castle, Tunstall, with a profile of Ingleborough above.

KIRKBY LONSDALE

had time to take a stroll down to the river. Whitaker particularly recommended that the visitor should see the Devil's Bridge; 'a noble specimen of architecture, of which I regret that the antiquity is unknown. Its appearance is very fine, as the best possible situaton was chosen, where a chain of projecting rocks thrown across the Lune afforded a groundwork durable as the earth itself for the piers of the arches.' There is a record of the bridge dating from as early as 1272 and it was said that the devil had appeared to an old woman on this spot. She was anxious to cross the Lune and the ford was deep underwater. The devil therefore offered to build a bridge for her on the condition that the first creature to cross it would be his. She agreed and, as soon as the bridge was complete, threw a bun over it. A small dog chased it and therefore was the first across.

106

Turner had also dabbled in architecture, and only two years earlier, had designed his own house at Twickenham. It was with an expert's regard, therefore, that he scrambled down the bank to examine the satanic masonry at close quarters. Perched on rocks in the river, he sketched the bridge and its foundations, with the arches framing cameos of the riverbanks beyond.

These close-ups, however, did not permit him to relate the bridge to its surroundings. He had to climb up into the fields by the side of the Lancaster road to take a view of the town, the bridge before it, the mountains of upper Lunesdale beyond. This study immediately satisfied him as the basis for a finished picture, for he made a composition study at the corner of the page.

Pleased, no doubt, that he had got the measure of the subject, he now made his way back to the town, stopping at the bottom of Mill Brow to sketch the steep street leading up to the church and churchyard at the top, the old mills and factories of snuff, calico, horseblankets, rope, which tumbled down the streamside. The mail coach from Settle rattled into town up this street,

107

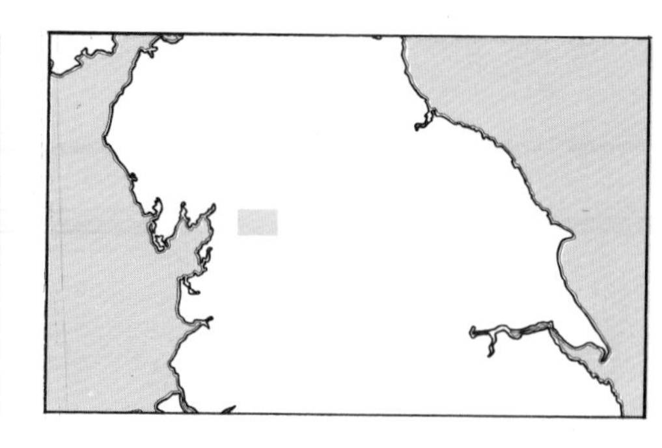

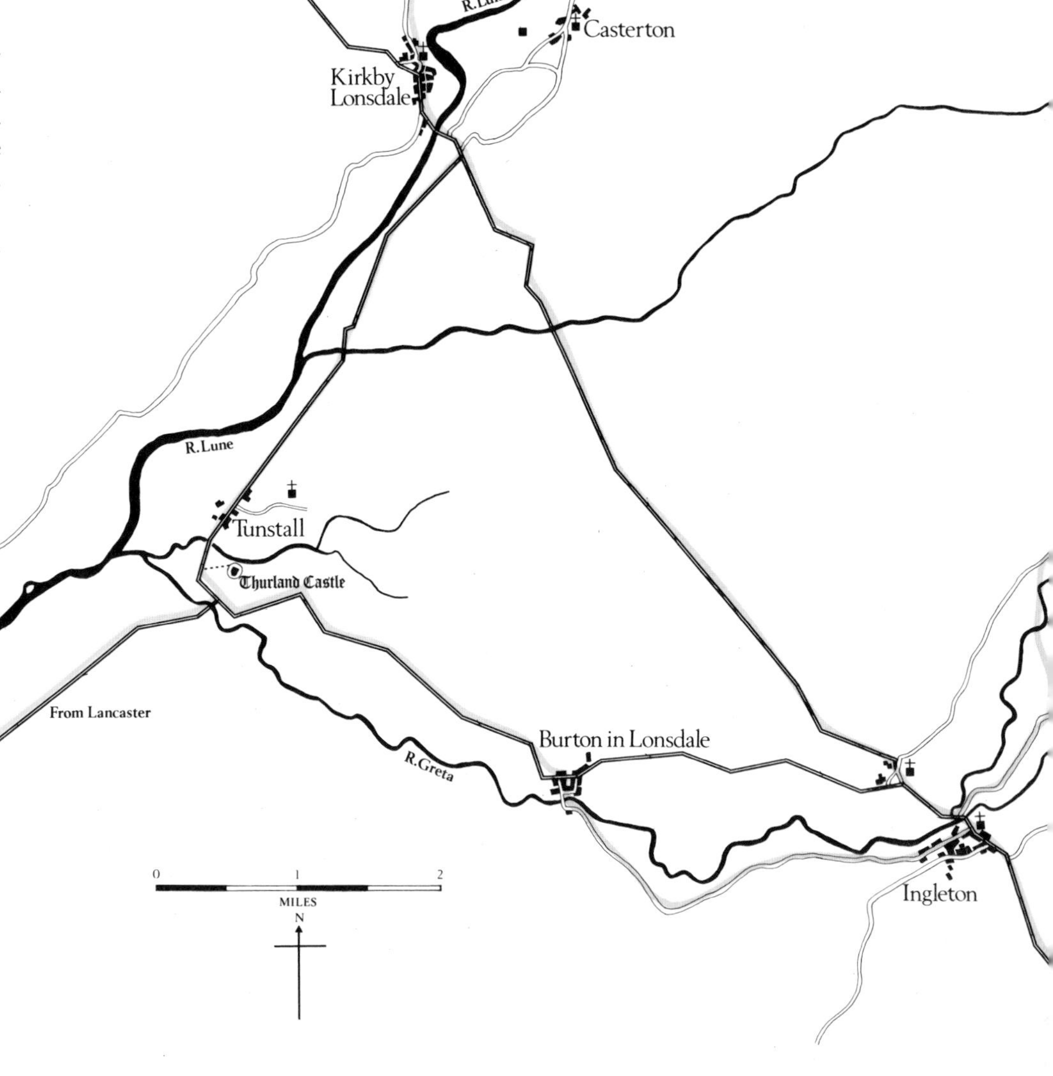

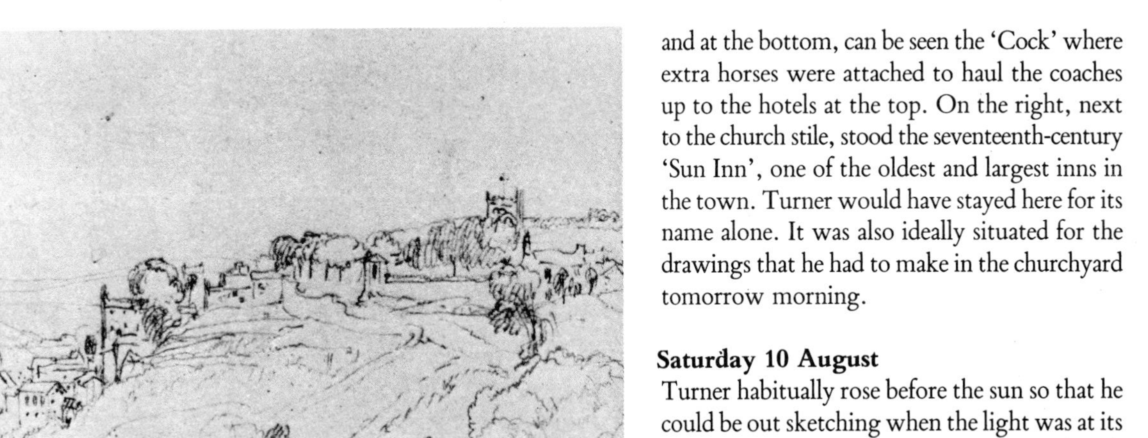

108

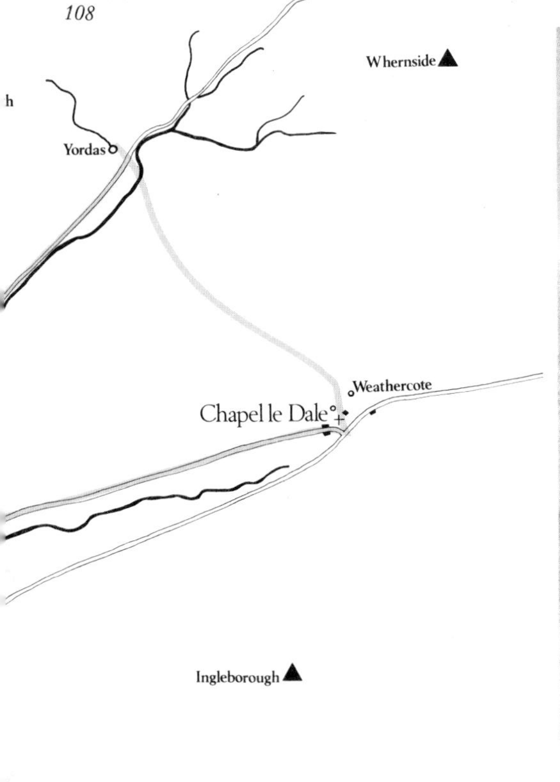

109

and at the bottom, can be seen the 'Cock' where extra horses were attached to haul the coaches up to the hotels at the top. On the right, next to the church stile, stood the seventeenth-century 'Sun Inn', one of the oldest and largest inns in the town. Turner would have stayed here for its name alone. It was also ideally situated for the drawings that he had to make in the churchyard tomorrow morning.

Saturday 10 August

Turner habitually rose before the sun so that he could be out sketching when the light was at its best. This morning was no exception, and with the air clear and a breeze blowing from the south east, he set out to make his commissioned drawing of the view from the churchyard. 'If,' enthused Whitaker, 'setting aside every idea of accommodation, beauty alone had been attended to in the choice for a capital, of perhaps the finest valley in the Kingdom, Kirkby Lonsdale must have been the place. On a plain above the Lune, sufficiently elevated to command the soft foreground, where that river, already majestic and powerful, makes a graceful curve about a peninsula of meadow and pasture, exuberantly fertile, and spotted with standard forest trees, while this soft scene is contrasted by the noblest of backgrounds, the long ridge of Grey Garth, and the towering height of Ingleborough to the south east, and the piked points of Howgill to the north, announcing the commencement of that bolder style of rock and fell which characterises the wildest parts of Westmorland and Cumberland, I know not that the site of Kirkby Lonsdale, however admired, has ever been applauded beyond its deserts.'

Whitaker may have based his choice of view on Wordsworth's recommendation for the *Guide to the Lakes*, 1810, instructs the visitor to Kirkby Lonsdale to 'by no means omit looking at the Vale of Lune from the Churchyard'. Unfortunately this view includes hardly any of the features that Whitaker extolled, and Turner preferred to draw first a detailed panorama of the town from the north (Ill. 108). The newly risen sun was in the north-east quarter and the low light, raking across from the left, brilliantly picked out the buildings. We see the church and

106. One of two experiments (see Ill. 109) with different effects of light and weather for the watercolour of the view from Kirkby Lonsdale Churchyard (Pl.19).

107. The view from Kirkby Lonsdale Churchyard.

108. Kirkby Lonsdale from the North. The viewpoint of the finished watercolour (Pl. 19) can be seen among the trees to the left of the gazebo.

109. The second colour study of the view from Kirkby Lonsdale Churchyard.

110

the churchyard on the right, with the gazebo at the end of the rectory garden. Mill Brow on the left leads down to the point where Turner had sketched the previous evening. Beyond can be seen the Devil's Bridge with Ingleborough's head jutting up over the distant hills. In this single drawing Turner captured the peculiar situation of the town and contrived to include both the bridge and the most important landmark around. He must have been confident that he could persuade Whitaker to accept this view instead.

He then made his way back to the prescribed viewpoint at the far side of the gazebo. The view may have seemed exceptional to Wordsworth but it offered Turner hardly any detail with which to work, so little, in fact, that his drawing of the scene remained unidentified until 1980. Even though Turner exaggerated the height of the hills and emphasised the meandering rhythms of the river, and even though the gazebo is included at the left and Casterton Hall at the right, there is nothing in the view to tell us at what or from where he was looking. There is no sign of Kirkby Lonsdale, nothing distinctive of the Lune valley, no sign of Ingleborough.

In an attempt to add interest to the subject, Turner continued it to the right in a separate drawing covering the landscape from Casterton Hall to Ingleborough. He evidently wanted to remind himself to take the matter up when he returned home, for he labelled the drawing 'the continuation of K.L.C[hurch]yd View', as if to say that the continuation was probably more interesting than the original view. At least it included 'Ingleboro', and Turner labelled it with all the emphasis due to the mountain then thought to be the highest in England and Wales.

Now that he had finished his work for the commissioned watercolour (Pl. 19) and had made drawings of his own which might answer the

purpose better, Turner could settle down to study the Devil's Bridge without feeling that he must relate it to its surroundings. It was now nearly midday, and the sun shone on his back from the right as he sat by the river.

The air was still, the calm water reflecting the bridge and the view through its arches. Turner chose a rocky promontory just downstream from the bridge as the best viewpoint, and was impressed enough with it to take out his largest sketchbook and to spend the best part of an hour noting down every detail in his most careful pencil style.

The bridge is more likely to have been built by the monks of Fountains' Abbey than by the Devil, to carry wool from their granges in the Lake District back into Yorkshire. Its scale is in keeping with that of their abbey and one of its most impressive features is the loftiness of its arches. Turner was so concerned to capture this that he considerably exaggerated the height of the piers up to the springing of the arches. 'Always paint your impressions,' he advised his fellow-artists, and in this case, again, the impression more closely resembles our perception of the place than any photograph.

He had first seen the bridge as he descended the bank to the left and he now explored this first impression in another detailed sketch which concentrated on the bridge as first seen through the tangled growth of riverside trees. One of the trees he included, a bent sapling, has all the makings of a fully grown tree to be seen here today. He was most fascinated, however, by the reflections, and he returned to them in a third sketch (Ill. 110) made from slightly further away and to the right of the first. It is said that Turner derived his love and knowledge of reflections from the many hours he spent staring at the water while fishing, and it was with evident pleasure that he noted down the colours shining darkly in the depths of the Lune. In the first sketch 'Sky Light' and the 'V Dark' again to the right, the 'S[ky]' between rocks in the foreground, themselves reflected 'yello[w]' in a pool to the left. Meanwhile a constant stream of traffic passed over the bridge. Pedestrians made their way home from Kirkby Lonsdale, two horsemen rode towards Kendal, a loaded cart lumbered its slow way into Yorkshire. At last he closed the sketchbook, mounted and rode off towards Ingleton.

Turner's first sight of Ingleton was from the bank dropping down from Thornton-in-

111

110. The Devil's Bridge, Kirkby Lonsdale. In a comparison with the photograph (Ill. 111), Turner seems to have exaggerated the height of the piers, but the impression the bridge gives in fact is one of imposing loftiness, much closer to the sketch than the photograph.

111. The Devil's Bridge, Kirkby Lonsdale. The bent trunk of the tree in front of the left-hand arch appears as a sapling in the sketch.

INGLETON AND INGLEBOROUGH

112

Lonsdale, with Ingleborough now towering immediately behind the town. He stopped to make a quick note of the scene and became so engrossed that he put much more detail into the drawing than was normal for the notebook, recording not only the buildings of the town but even every window. He made separate studies of the church tower and Ingleton Hall at the top of the page.

Ingleton had been famous among tourists for its waterfalls and caves since the latter half of the eighteenth century, and a number of guidebooks had given accounts of them over the years. They were not so familiar in paintings, however, and London artists were only just beginning to think about capitalising on the interest. William Westall published an illustrated guide to the caves in 1818, and presented a copy to Turner. Turner had beaten Westall to most of the sites by several years, however, and had made watercolours of *Ingleborough from Chapel-Le-Dale* (Ill. 112), *Weathercote Cave* (Ill. 113), *Gordale* and *Malham Cove* (Ill. 9) following his tour of 1809, though these were made for Fawkes, not for publication. Whitaker required a view of each for his *County of York*, together with one of Thornton Force, and Turner spent the afternoon making a thorough exploration of all the required sites in the vicinity, together with a few thrown in for his own interest.

He made his way up the road to Chapel-Le-Dale under Twisleton Scar, making sketches of the views over to Ingleborough. Torrington had graphically recorded the same experience in 1792: 'All the Yorkshire around, tho' black, and frightful, seem of small account in the comparison of Ingleborough ... There fell many storms of rain; and these come upon you, in a mist, from the mountains, without giving the least warning ... I then [came] ... to a vale, called Chapel-in-dale; where ... the first house ... was the habitation of a jolly shoe-maker, a fine bold-looking fellow: and his wife ... he is the guide to the neighbouring caves, the noblest of which, Wethercote, is adjoining to his house ... Perhaps there is no corner of this island that can afford wilder scenery; but Jobson thinks it is a paradise: chas'm, just below his house, call'd Gingle-pot; down which we peep'd, and three stones. But how shall I describe the wonders of Wethercote-Cave (Cove pronounc'd)? From the top of this perpendicular cave are to be seen the falls of water that lose themselves at the bottom; and to which we approach'd by a most laborious descent; here the two cascades are to be seen thro' upon a small passage leading into a horizontal cave: much wetting is to be encounter'd, and some danger apprehended.—These cascades fall with an horrid din, filling the mind with a gloom of horror.'

The weather conditions were precisely those encountered by Turner on his visits to Ingleton. His 1808 sketch of Ingleborough and the church of St. Leonard at Chapel-Le-Dale shows figures sitting under umbrellas, and the weather is the

112. Ingleborough from Chapel-Le-Dale, *1809. Previously known as* Patterdale Old Church, *this watercolour was made for Walter Fawkes, following Turner's first visit to Farnley and a tour of the Craven dales in 1808. His visits to the area seem to have been invariably accompanied by bad weather. The sketch on which this watercolour was based shows figures sheltering beneath umbrellas and on the visit in 1816 nearby Weathercote Cave was flooded.*

113. Weathercote Cave, *1809. A companion-piece to Ill. 112, also made for Walter Fawkes. On the earlier visit in 1808 Turner was able to make the descent of the 70 foot deep chasm, and paint the view looking out of the cave with an artist sketching the waterfall.*

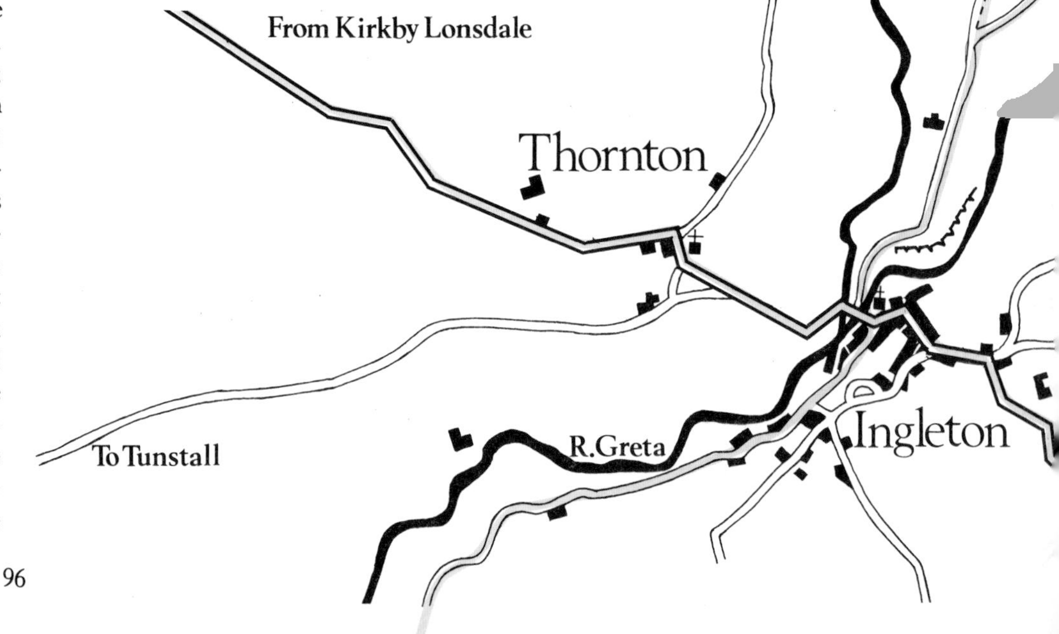

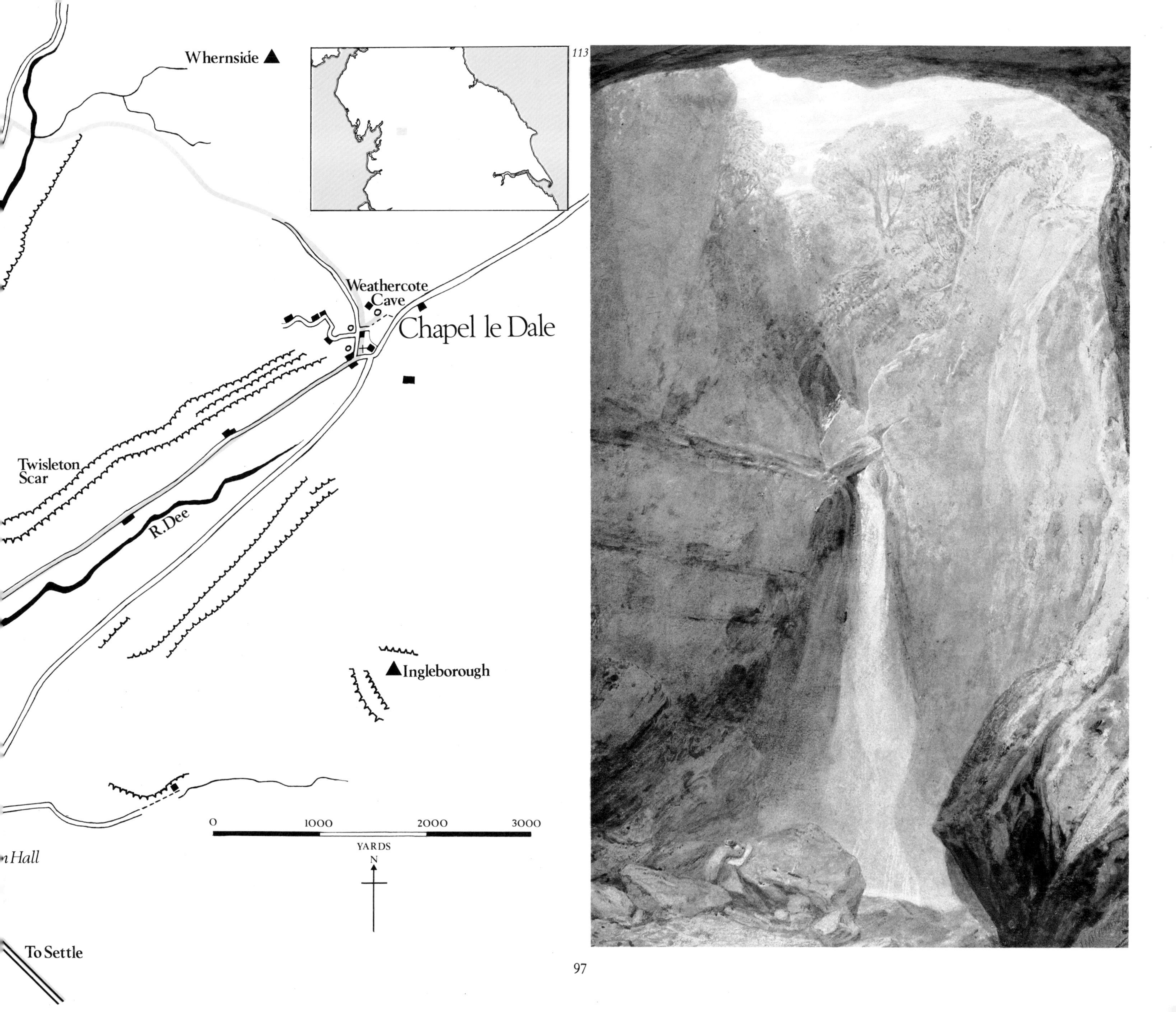
Whernside
113
Weathercote
Cave
Chapel le Dale
Twisleton
Scar
R. Dee
Ingleborough
0
1000
2000
3000
YARDS
N
n Hall
To Settle

114 115

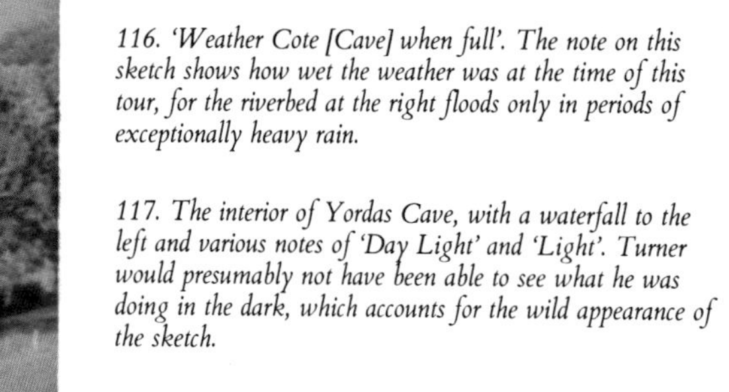

114. Ingleton and Ingleborough beyond. Ingleborough was popularly thought, at 5,280 feet, to be the highest mountain in Britain after an over-enthusiastic eighteenth-century survey. It is in fact a more modest 2,373 feet, but Turner drew what he knew, not what he saw, and having sketched the profile of the mountain once, enlarged it to conform with his expectations.

115. Ingleton and Ingleborough from the West.

116. 'Weather Cote [Cave] when full'. The note on this sketch shows how wet the weather was at the time of this tour, for the riverbed at the right floods only in periods of exceptionally heavy rain.

117. The interior of Yordas Cave, with a waterfall to the left and various notes of 'Day Light' and 'Light'. Turner would presumably not have been able to see what he was doing in the dark, which accounts for the wild appearance of the sketch.

118. Pen-y-ghent from Upper Winskill.

116 117

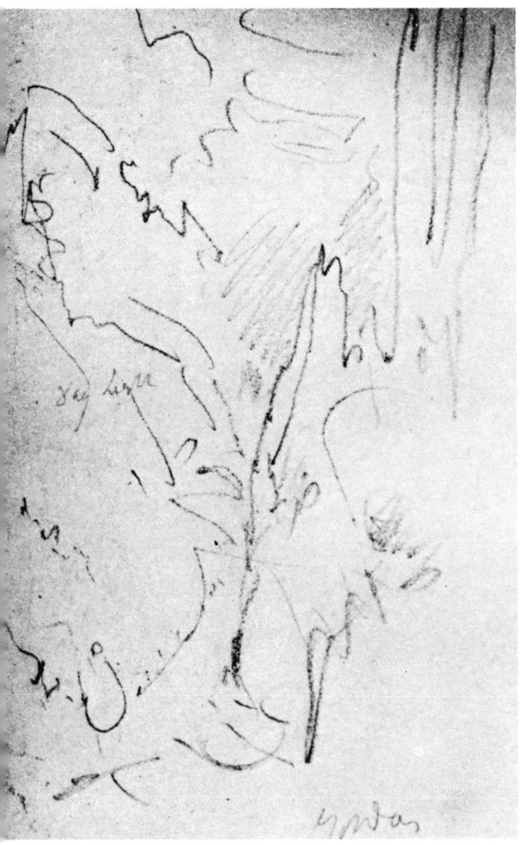

principal feature of the finished watercolour. Clouds swirl around the head of the mountain. A squally shower approaches. An alarmed figure makes for cover as lightning flashes through the dark clouds overhead.

Turner had first visited Weathercote in 1808, and made the same descent as Torrington, through the cave at the bottom of the seventy-foot deep hole, to stand at the bottom and admire the cascade falling out of sunlight into the shaded depths below. In 1816, however, he was in for a surprise. So wet had it been in recent weeks that the water table had risen and the normally dry riverbed at the right was now in spate. The cave itself was half-filled with water. Descent was out of the question. He had to make do with a view from the top (ill. 116), where he recorded both waterfalls in spate, and made virtue of the unusual conditions. He noted the fact in his sketch: 'Weather Cote when full' and the publishers were proud to advertise the rarity of their view, calling it 'Weathercote Cave, when half filled with water' and adding 'and the Entrance Impassable' when it came to selling the watercolour in 1822.

Turner fixed the time of day in the watercolour as mid-afternoon, with the sun shining from the left, and may have been lucky enough for a shaft of sunlight to cast a rainbow in the spray, for he introduced one into his finished watercolour. He may also have had in mind the account given in 1781 by John Hutton in his *Guide to the Caves in the Environs of Ingleborough and Settle in the West Riding of Yorkshire*: 'The sun happening to shine very bright, we had a small vivid rainbow within a few yards of us for colour, size, situation, perhaps nowhere else to be equalled.'

Turner shared Torrington's route as well as his weather. 'Crossing a nasty, stoney brook, we arrived at Yordas Cave; where, leaving our horses at the entrance, and lighting our candles, we enter'd the cavern: It is well worthy of inspection, not too tedious, and beautifully closed by a cascade. —Jobson stuck up candles by the way, which gave a most fanciful effect.' Popular legend has it, unsurprisingly that a giant lived here. The rocks within the cave are named accordingly: the giant's throne, his flitch of bacon, his water bowl and his great oven.

Even in the dark cave, unable to see the drawing that he was making, Turner worked furiously in his notebook, making scribbles which in the light of day would need some annotation to make sense (Ill. 117). 'Loose stones', 'Roof', 'Light Gr', 'Day Light', can be picked out from the otherwise unintelligible scribbles, though there are one or two recognisable features in the best of the drawings, especially the waterfall to the left. For Turner sketching was his means of registering what he saw. Without the action of hand and pencil, the experience remained mere sensation, lacking significance or form. Turner had to draw a thing to understand it properly.

He drew what he understood, what is more, not merely what he saw. When he returned to Ingleton, having first sketched Thornton Force with a torrent of water in it, he returned to draw the view of Ingleborough from the Thornton road. Gray had described the mountain as a 'huge creature of God', and a wayward eighteenth-century surveyor, called Jeffreys, had measured its height at 5280 feet. It was believed, therefore, to be the highest mountain in Britain. It is, in fact, a more modest 2373 feet. Turner enlarged the profile of the mountain to conform with what he expected (Ills. 114 and 115).

Ingleborough, Pen-y-ghent and Whernside are now, of course, principally famous as the Three Peaks of Yorkshire. In 1887, two teachers from Giggleswick School walked over Ingleborough to have tea at the Hill Inn, Chapel-Le-Dale. So invigorating is a Yorkshire tea that they then felt compelled to walk over Whernside and Pen-y-ghent as well. Anyone who can cover the 20¾ miles within twelve hours is entitled to membership of the Three Peaks of Yorkshire Club, but there is a race each spring for three peaks walkers and each autumn for cyclists (who have to carry their bicycles for long stretches at a time). Both groups now complete the race in less than three hours. Ingleton still attracts tourists and painters, more for its site than for its buildings. Some of the houses scramble up the hill. Some perch high above the gorge, the Greta roaring below, now spanned by an 800-foot railway viaduct. From here, travellers climb Ingleborough for its magnificent views out to the Irish Sea or make the five-mile walk down the valleys of the Greta and the Kingsdale Beck in order to see the descending staircase of falls—Pecca Falls, Thornton Force, Beezley Falls, Black Hole Falls, with a pool eighty feet deep, Baenghyll Gorge,

118

TO FARNLEY HALL VIA KENDAL

119

Yew Tree Gorge and the foaming White Snow Falls.

After Ingleton Turner rode west to Tunstall, then north to Kirkby Lonsdale again, and, finally and surprisingly, twelve miles north-west to Kendal. We might have expected him to head directly for Farnley at this stage of the tour. There is in fact, no logical explanation for the twisting route, which meant an arduous ride the next day. However, the order in which the drawings of Kendal appear in the different sketchbooks leaves little doubt that this curious detour occurred, though the reasons for it remain unknown.

Sunday 11 August

By the time he reached Kendal, Turner had just one blank page left in each of his large sketchbooks. His pocket-book shows how he explored the town with views from near the river to the south, the mill buildings, the church and the castle, before settling for a viewpoint on the Kirkby Lonsdale road near The Lound (Ill. 119). Here he could survey the whole town and the Kent valley leading up to the fells beyond. It was still early in the morning to judge from the shadows cast by the castle and the trees in the middle of the composition, and having made a final drawing of the parish church and its nearby bridge, together with details of the castle and the church itself, he had finished all that the publishers had demanded of him.

Looking forward to the shooting party at Farnley the next day he set off from Kendal as soon as he could and made all possible speed over the sixty miles back to Otley. He nevertheless made a number of notes in his pocket-book on the journey, a couple at Kirkby Lonsdale, others of Ingleborough as he passed by on the road to Clapham, and views of the Castleberg at Settle and Pen-y-ghent from nearby.

It was late afternoon when at last he arrived at Skipton, and although he was only seventeen miles from home, had covered 550 miles since he left Farnley on 17 July, and had made 450 sketches on the way, he was conscientious and professional enough to take his customary care over the research of his final subject.

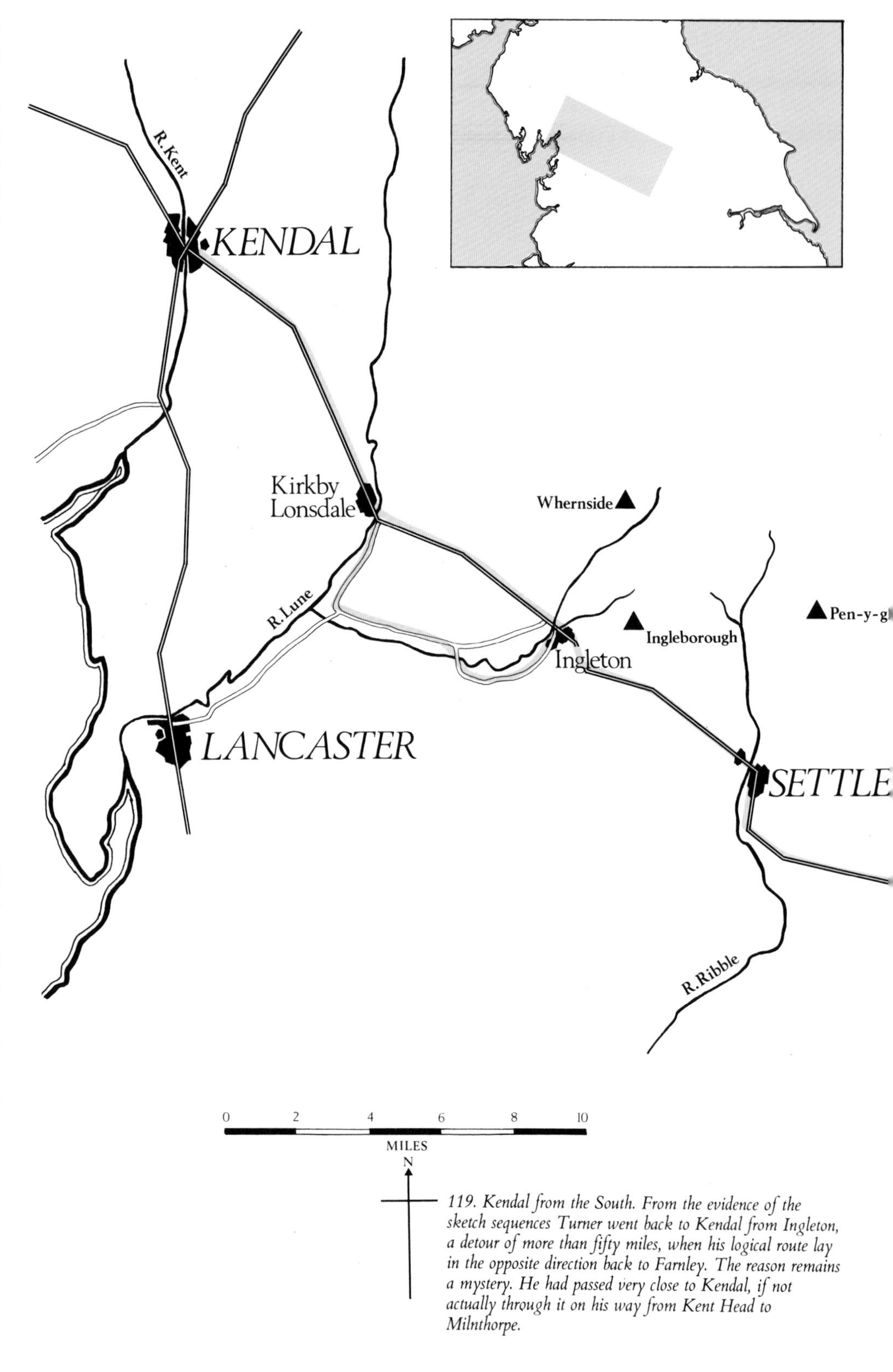

119. Kendal from the South. From the evidence of the sketch sequences Turner went back to Kendal from Ingleton, a detour of more than fifty miles, when his logical route lay in the opposite direction back to Farnley. The reason remains a mystery. He had passed very close to Kendal, if not actually through it on his way from Kent Head to Milnthorpe.

120. Skipton Castle from the North. Turner's final sketch on the tour, and the conclusion of his search for a view of the castle which would include Eller Beck and the church, begun more than three weeks, 550 miles and 450 sketches earlier.

120

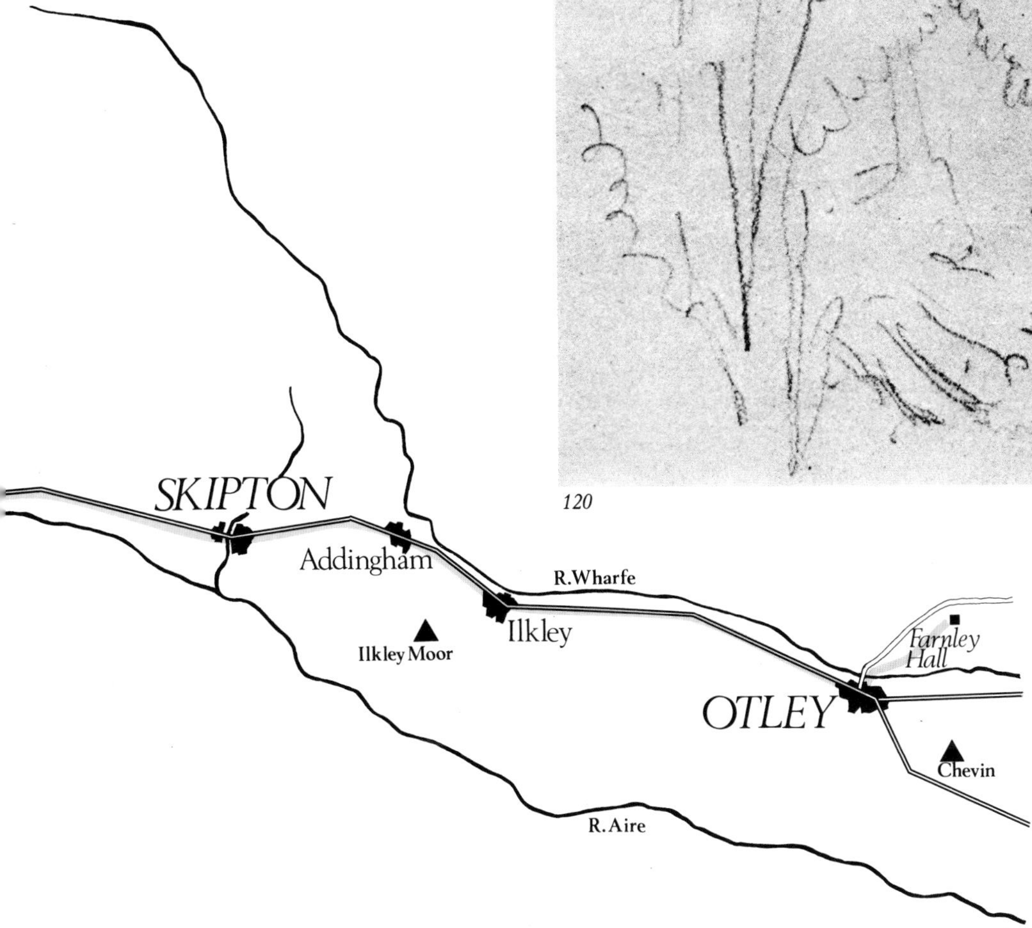

His first exploration of Skipton on 17 July had been inconclusive. This time he decided to seek a view from the northern approaches to the castle. He started at the north gates and made a number of notes as he moved back along the buttress wall, again showing the railway trucks that had been visible in the earlier sketches. As he progressed up the east side of Eller Beck, a much more satisfactory prospect came into view. The castle was now clearly visible, as was the church, and in one sketch he also managed to include Eller Beck Mill and the fells over Airedale to the south. The view on which he finally decided shows the northern defences of the castle, looming dauntingly over the beck and valley with its ponds which Whitaker described all set against a background of fells (Ill. 120).

This was his final sketch, and it was evening as he now shut his sketchbook, his task at last complete. He must have felt well pleased at the amount of work that he had managed to cram into the journey, and, perhaps, relieved that the job was completed. It had been the most intense, sustained, and arduous tour that he had ever made, and the high point of his sketching tours in Britain. He had good cause to celebrate, and now he happily contemplated the prospect of comfort and companionship as he rode the last few miles to Farnley with dusk closing in on Wharfedale.

In her diary for 12 August, Mrs. Fawkes records that all the gentlemen went to the moors. Turner went armed with his pencil and with a particu-

FARNLEY HALL

larly large and luxurious sketchbook, the *Large Farnley*, which he seems to have brought specifically for this purpose. Here are fine pencil drawings of the marquees on the moors, the guns, the dead birds, the beer-barrels scattered about. Here are the alert sportsmen scanning the heather on Beamsley Beason, or resting by their horses in Kex Gill. It is an exuberant record, and the finished watercolours, being related to a specific, keenly observed event, have a vividness rare in sporting pictures (Ill. 121). *Shooting Party on the Moors, 12 August* depicts the end of the day. The bag is being prepared for the spit; dogs and beaters rest, sprawled after their exertions; gentlemen swap stories; the marquees, the guns and the beer-barrels are all here, all painted with relish as Turner recalled a happy day.

He was never loath to consume his fair share of the available ale, which appears to have been copious. Perhaps, as it had its effect, he regaled the company with the song he had copied down in his largest sketchbook:

Here's a health to Honest John Bull
When he is gone, where will you find such another/
So with Hearts as with Bumpers quite full,
Here's a health to Old England his mother ...

and so on through six verses which he had copied down inside the cover of his sketchbook, no doubt at an inn somewhere on his tour.

Next day, the 13th, there was a tragedy. Richard Hawkesworth Fawkes, Walter's younger brother, was wounded in a shooting accident. On the 14th, Mrs. Fawkes wrote that he seemed 'pretty well', and again, on the 15th, 'Richard pretty well until evening'. But his condition deteriorated suddenly. That night the doctor was called out suddenly and 'said he was dying'. 'Poor Richard' died at five o'clock in the morning on the 16th. The party broke up immediately. The diary records the guests' departures, one by one, between Saturday 17th and Monday 19th. Turner stayed on to comfort his old friend. Then he too left the house, riding towards Central Yorkshire, with a new pocket-book and composition book, as well as the *Large Farnley*. He had spent so much of this summer alone that he was now beginning to make a virtue of solitude. Later, on the road, he began to compose a verse on 'Independence' inside the cover of one of his sketchbooks:

Sweet Independence, rough is thy nature, hardy, sincere,
Though gives the humble roof content, devoid of fear
Even of tomorrow's fate, and add a blissful joy
To its perhaps lone inmate, love without alloy.

He had indeed been under a number of humble roofs this summer, and one of the principal characteristics of the work that he produced as a result of the tour is the joy and love he felt for his subject-matter. A journey through the sketchbooks suggests the drawings were sometimes more an end than a means, each one the record of a moment of the summer, of which a few would be recreated in his studio during the winter. The beauty and greatness of his art lies in its power to convey the feelings that these experiences held for him, and the rich response it is possible to have to the world around us.

121

121. Grouse-Shooting: Beamsley Beacon, *1816. Turner hurried back to Farnley Hall to join in the shooting-party on the moors on 12 August. The festivities ended in tragedy, however, for Richard Fawkes was wounded in an accident on the 13th and died three days later. Although this picture held unhappy memories, it captures very vividly the atmosphere of the bleak windswept moors above Bolton Abbey.*

—THE— ALBUM

POSTSCRIPT

By the time he returned to Farnley on 11 August, Turner had completed the sketches necessary for the first part of the *County of York*, namely the *History of Richmondshire*. When he left Farnley on 20 August, he made a week-long tour of central Yorkshire, and then some time between 27 August and 12 September made a further tour, or possibly separate expeditions, to a number of sites, including Bolton Abbey, Scarborough, Gledhow Hall and Leeds.

The finished watercolours for the *History of Richmondshire*, which as we have seen was the only part of the grand undertaking to be published, were delivered to the publishers for engraving in two groups, twelve on 12 April 1817, and eight on 31 December 1818. All the finished watercolours are reproduced in the following pages, with the exception of three, of which two remain untraced and a third was destroyed by fire in the last century. These are represented by their engravings in the main text. In the commentaries which precede the plates, the titles are those used by the engraver, and where these are either mis-spelt or old-fashioned, the spelling used by the modern Ordnance Survey is followed in the text. It is possible to assign most of the pictures to the group in which they were delivered and the date given after each title (i.e. 1816–17 or 1817–18) refers to their probable date of execution where no more specific information is available. The measurements are in millimetres, height before width. The catalogue numbers beginning 'TB' refer to the Turner Bequest inventory, 'R' to W.G. Rawlinson's, *The Engraved Work of J.M.W. Turner* (2 vols, London 1908 and 1913) and those beginning 'W' to Andrew Wilton's *The Life and Work of J.M.W. Turner* (London 1979). The watercolours appear in the order in which Turner visited the sites in 1816.

122

122. Leeds, *1816. Turner sketched the view of the city from Beeston Hill, probably at the beginning of September 1816. At the centre can be seen the spire of Trinity Church on Boar Lane, with the towers of St. John's Briggate to the left. To the right stands the tower of the parish church, St. Peter's. Leeds was one of the fastest-growing cloth towns in the North at this time and Turner made a feature of the mills on which its prosperity was founded.*

123. Gledhow Hall, *1816. Sketched in the same sketchbook as the drawings of Leeds and engraved at the expense of John Dixon, the owner of the Hall. Gledhow has now been overtaken by the northern suburbs of Leeds, although the valley is preserved as a park.*

123

COMMENTARIES

1. Simmer Lake, near Askrigg

1817-18, 287 x 412 mm
Inscribed: (lower right) *'J.M.W.Turner RA'*
British Museum, Salting Bequest 1910 – 2 – 12 – 280
Engraved by A. La Keur 6 June – 25 September 1821, 80 gns. McQueen paid December 1821 for print. 160 India, and 400 plain. Publication date 25 October 1822.
REF: W.571, R.180

Semer Water lies in a hidden valley above Wensleydale, three miles south-west of Askrigg. Turner's view is perfectly visible today, looking from the northern edge of the lake over the Carlow Stone to Raydale (centre), Bardale (right) with the fells of Fleet Moss and Cragside Moor (about 1900 – 1950 ft.) forming the skyline. Turner's road over the Stake Pass from Wharfedale is visible to the extreme left. The time of day in mid-afternoon, and the foreshore is busy with ruminating cows and their minders, and reed-cutters unloading boats to the right. Turner adapted the details of his sketch (TB CXLVII 3a-4, see p.48) to give a higher apparent viewpoint, together with greater emphasis to the surface of the lake and proportion to the distant fells.

Semer Water is the largest of Yorkshire's few natural lakes, and has a legend regarding its miraculous origin, described in the main text.

2. Moss Dale Fall

1816-17, 291 x 418 mm
Fitzwilliam Museum, Cambridge (571)
Engraved by S. Middiman, paid 120 gns. between 2 October 1821 and 10 August 1822. Lettering paid for 19 December 1822. H. Triggs paid for printing, 160 India, 400 'French', February 1823. Publication date 22 August 1822.
REF: W.572, R.181. M.Cormack, *Turner: Drawings and Watercolours in the Fitzwilliam Museum, Cambridge*, 1975, No. 16

Mossdale Falls are situated on the lower slopes of Widdale Fell, half a mile to the left of the Sedbergh road, three miles beyond Hawes. A small stream tumbles down a rock staircase to meet Mossdale Beck, which runs down to another fall by Mossdale Head farm, before joining the Ure a few hundred yards further down. Mossdale has a dreamy remoteness on a fine late evening in July, which could only take on the apocalyptic atmosphere of Turner's vision in conditions of extreme violence. Much of the left-hand side of the picture is now obscured in a larch plantation, but the falls at the right in Mossdale Beck, and the rock bluff in the centre are still to be found. Turner evidently remembered it as being rather larger than in fact, and as it was without trees when Turner sketched it (TB CXLVIII 16 – 17, see p.52) it must have seemed rather larger than it does now.

When Mrs. Hunt visited the site when writing her descriptions for *Richmondshire Illustrated by Twenty Line Engravings...* (1891) she was forced to confess: 'Mossdale Fall in broad simple daylight is a very different thing from the transfiguration of it by a sunset effect which Turner has given us. The engraving is full of examples of his truthfulness in little things, and, if a certain enlargement of scale, due to the remembrance of an effect, be allowed for, in great ones also. Let it be confessed at once that Mossdale is a very small furrow in a moorland dale, with nothing Alpine about it, and that the descent from the heights above and to the right of the Fall, where the mists are gathering and a great peak appears to lift itself, down to the spectator's view at the bottom of the Fall, can be accomplished in a few minutes.'

3. Hardraw Fall

1816-17, 292 x 415 mm
Fitzwilliam Museum, Cambridge (PD 227—1961).
Etched by S. Middiman (13 prints paid for 22 July 1818). Engraved by John Pye, paid 80 gns., 27 August 1818. Engraved lettering paid for 8 December 1818. Printed by Hayward, paid 21 July 1819. Publication date, 1 October 1818.
REFS: W.574, R. 182, Cormack *op cit* No. 17

Hardrow Force is one of the chief wonders of Wensleydale, and reputed to be the highest unbroken fall in England. It stands at the end of a narrow horseshoe shaped gorge, surrounded by cliffs nearly 200 ft high, from the centre of which the stream leaps down to a depth of 96 ft. Access is through the *Green Dragon* hotel in the village, where Turner probably stayed. A small charge is payable and a good path has been made. Turner shows the gorge in the early morning with the cliffs casting deep shadows over the path, while the meadows opposite are bathed in warm sunlight and was at pains in his sketches (TB CXLVIII 15, 28a – 15) and his colour-beginning (see p.53), to work out a way to draw the eye in along the path to give an impression of scale. Not surprisingly, in view of its pre-eminence, *Hardraw Fall* was the first watercolour to be sent to the engraver, and it was published by 1 October 1818, eighteen months after delivery amongst the first group of watercolours on 12 April 1817. It is one over which John Pye, the engraver, is said to have taken particular care, and he especially prided himself on the results. Whitaker took equal pride in his account of Hardrow in the text and recorded that, 'In the great frost of 1739 – 40, the fall of Hardraw became a hollow column of ice; a fixed and stately object; during which the unfrozen current was distinctly seen to precipitate itself through a tube in the centre, while the country people, surprised and delighted by so novel an appearance danced around it.'

4. Aysgarth Force

1816-17, 280 x 404 mm
Inscribed: (lower right)*'J M W Turner RA'*
Indianapolis Museum of Art, Bequest of Kurt F. Pantzer Sr.
Engraved by J. Scott, paid 80 gns., 12 May 1820. Printing and lettering paid for 5 June 1820. Publication date, 1 June 1820.
REFS: W.570, R.179

Aysgarth has been one of the principal highlights of any Yorkshire itinerary since the days of Bishop Pococke, who in 1751 discovered in Wensleydale one of the finest landscapes he had encountered, and among '...the grandest natural curiosities of the Youre [i.e. Ure], the falls of water at Aysgarth.' There is now a modern car park and Yorkshire Dales National Park tourist centre with excellent amenities situated not far from the bridge. Whitaker enjoyed his visit, noting: '...Aysgarthe. The vulgar pronunciation Escar, or Ayscar, leads to the true meaning of the word [i.e. rocky river]. To account for this let it be understood, that in the line of the Ure, and immediately beneath the parish church, the course of the river lies over a rocky and irregular channel of limestone, broken into two deep and beautiful descents, one above and the other beneath the bridge...'

Mrs. Hunt was particularly impressed by the 'great artist's power of making a picture of a place wonderfully like the place, when he chose. The geological facts, however as Turner has seized them, are verifiable now. Perhaps it may be well to admit—for fear of being supposed to confuse the truth of an artisitic portrait with that of a scientific or photographic one—that Turner may have unwittngly compressed very slightly the width of the river's channel, and proportionately increased the height of the Fall, but the effect of the whole scene must have been of a wilder and grander kind when there was no line of tall trees at the back of the Fall.

Turner's picture is probably still the most characteristic and well-known image of Aysgarth. Its power was such that when plans were drawn up in the 1880's to build a brick railway bridge across the river near the Falls, the watercolour was put on special display at Agnew's in Bond Street, London, to support the opposition led by early conservationists, amongst them John Ruskin and William Morris.

5. Merrick Abbey, Swaledale

1816-17, 282 x 413 mm
Private Collection, England
Etched by December 1821 when Cox & Co. were paid for printing 12 impressions. Engraved by J.C Varrall, paid, £10 on account 22 December 1821, and paid the balance of £42.10.0., making 50 gns. on 12 December 1822. 'Coat B' paid 20 December 1822 for printing 160 India and 400 'French' impressions. Publication date, December 1822.
REFS: W. 569, R. 178.

The remains of Marrick Priory, founded for Benedictine nuns in about 1150, are situated about three miles from Grinton on the banks of the River Swale. Unfortunately Turner's viewpoint is now forested, but it is clear from the original sketch (TB CXLVII 18a – 19, see p.60), that Turner made a number of changes to the landscape of the finished picture for effect. Turner followed the basic structure but exaggerated the profile of the hill to the right, and reduced the size of the farmhouse, to give emphasis to the church tower, which he made thinner and apparently taller. He further emphasized the scale by the introduction of tiny cattle at the bottom left, to suggest the reality as it was imagined, rather than the raw material that was observed.

Turner's recollection, however, had a disquieting aspect to it. Mrs. Hunt considered that 'the touch of cruelty which has made Turner introduce a sportsman who, gun in hand, is stealthily bearing down on the unhappy rabbit which is enjoying its innocent little meal, is unpleasant.' This seems to imply some form of black humour in the artist, but at the time the picture was painted the tragedy of Richard Fawke's death at Farnley in 1816 would still have been fresh in his mind, after which it seems impossible that he could have treated this sort of subject with any relish. It is rather an incident intended to disturb. Before the lurking gunman is noticed, all is calm and contentment. Cattle drink by the river, sheep graze on the banks, the Swale gurgles by, and a rabbit enjoys, as we do, the afternoon sunshine in peace. Very soon all that is to be shattered, a shot echoing around the hills, and the rabbit lying dead and blasted at our feet. The idea of death arriving unexpectedly to Richard Fawkes could not have been far from Turner's mind. We must confront, contemplate and come to terms with, the possibility of death even in a landscape such as this.

6. St.Agatha's Abbey, Easby

1817-18, 288 x 415 mm
British Museum, Sale Bequest (1915 – 13 – 13 – 48)
Engraved by J. Le Leux, paid 80 gns., 18 February 1822. McQueen & Co. paid for printing 160 India, 400 plain, June 1822. Publication date 14 February 1822.
REFS: W.561, R.171.

Turner first visited St.Agatha's in 1797 and he used a sketch made then (TB XXXIV) as the basis of the present watercolour, though he made a fresh note of the view in 1816 (TB CXLV 112). He was particularly concerned with the colour scheme and lighting of the watercolour and he made several trials (TB CCLXIII 360, see p.61, TB CCLXIII 89, and a third in a private collection, W. 892), before beginning the final watercolour. When *St.Agatha's* was exhibited in W.B. Cooke's gallery in 1823, Robert Hunt remarked in *The Examiner* for 5 January, on Turner's 'rich arrangement of colour,' which, he said, was obtained by the use of 'very little else besides yellow, grey and blue. Connected, blended, and sometimes delicately contrasted as these colours are—his effects are exquisitely tender, but not without sufficient force, from a certain magic arrangement, a graphic secret of his own.'

7. Richmond Castle and Town

1816-17, approx. 290 x 420 mm
Untraced
Engraved by J. Archer, paid 50 gns., 30 May 1820. Printing paid for 5 June 1820. Publication date, 6 June 1820.
REFS: W.560, R.170

The watercolour on which the engraving (see p.62) was based is one of many Turners that remain unaccounted for. The only unequivocal record of it appears to be its appearance in Leeds at the exhibition of the Northern Society in 1822, No. 121, 'Richmond Castle and Town —South', when the price was 25 gns. It was one of a group of six watercolours from the series, including Nos 122 'Aysgarth Force', 123 'Junction of the Greta and Tees at Rokeby', 125 'Brignall Church', 126 'St.Agatha's Abbey' and 127 'Weathercote Cove, when half filled with water, and the Entrance impassable', which Longmans or their partners were selling off at cost. From the evidence of Archer's engraving it must have been one of Turner's most elaborate productions — appropriately so, for he had sketched the view on two separate occasions in 1816, first in July on the tour described in this book (TB CXLVIII 12a – 41a), and secondly in August on his tour of central Yorkshire (TB CXLVI 27).

8. Aske Hall

1816-17, 280 x 413 mm
Inscribed: (lower right) *'J M W Turner RA'*
The Marchioness of Zetland
Engraved by John Scott, paid £30 on account, 27 January 1821, and balance making 80 gns. on 25 August 1821. Cox & Co. paid for printing 162 India and 400 French, December 1821. Publication date, 28 August 1821.
REFS: W.562, R.172

Aske Hall was built around a fifteenth-century pele-tower, but after extensive improvements in the eighteenth-century was described by Whitaker as a house of 'surpassing beauty'. It is a private house but much of the road from Richmond to Gilling and the view over to the house remains recognizable.

9. Richmond, Yorkshire

1816-17, 290 x 417 mm
Victoria and Albert Museum, London (P.17—1938)
Thirteen proofs of etching paid for 29 July 1818. Engraved by W.R. Smith, paid £42 on account 12 January 1819, and balance totalling 80 gns. in March 1819. Hayward paid for printing in July 1819. Publication date, 3 March 1819.
REFS: W.559, R.169

Based on Turner's final sketch at Richmond in 1816 (TB CXLVIII 10a – 11, see p.66), in which he reviewed his exploration of the town, the finished composition was one of the first to be sent for engraving in 1818. He had made a particularly detailed exploration of Richmond, and derived evident pleasure from re-creating and re-exploring every street, building, alleyway and footpath, all in the utmost detail. Ruskin owned three of the four Richmond watercolours based on Turner's 1816 sketches: 'The most beautiful of the three...[*Richmond from the Moors*, see p.64]...I gave to Cambridge. The second subject, though a lovely drawing I got provoked with for having a manufactory in it...This last one, I don't think anybody is likely to get while I live. There is no more lovely rendering of old English life; the scarcely altered sweetness of hill and stream, the baronial ruins on their crag, the old-fashioned town with the little gardens behind each house, the winding walks for pleasure along the river shore—all now in their reality, devastated by the hell blasts of avarice and luxury.' Richmond, thankfully, has now reverted to something like the condition in which Turner recorded it.

10. Junction of the Greta and Tees at Rokeby

1816-17, 290 x 414 mm
Ashmolean Museum, Oxford
McQueen paid for printing 12 impressions of the etching by S. Middiman, 29 October 1818. Engraved by John Pye, paid 80 gns., 6 July 1819. Haywards paid for printing 162 India and 400 plain, December 1819. Publication date, 2 August 1819.
REFS: W.566, R.175, L. Herrmann, *Ruskin and Turner*, London 1968, No.79.

When Turner visited the meeting of the waters at Rokeby in 1816 he does not appear to have seen them at their best. He was alone, it was pouring with rain, and the study he made suggests that he was in a hurry to get the experience over with as quickly as possible (TB CXLVIII 29a). When it came to making the finished watercolour he probably discovered that his sketch was lacking in information. The main lines were there, but of specific detail hardly anything, and of Rokeby Hall, no trace. The house was not forgotten, however, nor the dairy bridge and cottage, nor the quiet wooded course of the Tees being interrupted by the youthful rock-tumbling impetuosity of the Greta. Ruskin gave the picture to the Ruskin School, Oxford in 1875 as a 'faultless example of Turner's work when it is most exemplary.'

Rokeby Hall, the private home of the Morritt family, was owned by J.B.S. Morritt in Turner's day, and was frequented by a number of artists and writers, including John Sell Cotman in 1805, Sir Walter Scott in 1809, 1811, and 1812, Robert Southey in 1812 and 1819, and Charles Dickens in 1832. The meeting of the waters is a delightful spot to this day, and may be approached on foot along the road to Mortham Tower.

11. Wycliffe, near Rokeby

1816-17, 292 x 430 mm
Walker Art Gallery, Liverpool
Engraved by John Pye, paid 100 gns., 21 February 1823. Printed by H. Triggs, 200 India, 400 plain, paid May 1823. Publication date, 1 March 1823.
REFS: W.568, R.177

Wycliffe Hall is about two miles downstream from the meeting of the waters at Rokeby, and Turner made a number of sketches there on his visit in 1816. The sketch on which the watercolour was based (TB CXLVII 26/27, see p.70) extended further to the right to include a lane with a cart passing from which he seems to have derived his idea for the finished composition.

12. Brignall Church

1816-17
Destroyed by fire (see Thornbury 1877, p.597)
Engraved by S.Rawle, paid 30 gns. on account, 6 June 1821, and the balance making 60 gns on 21 August 1821. McQueen paid for printing 160 India and 400 plain, December 1821. Publication date 25 October 1822.
REFS: W.567, R.176

Turner obviously enjoyed Brignall's woods in 1816, and he made a particularly detailed survey of the area in his sketchbooks (see p.70 – 71). Ruskin wrote in*Pre-Raphaelitism*, 1904 ed., vol xii, p. 371.

'I shall never cease to regret the destruction, by fire, now several years ago, of a drawing which always seemed to me to be the perfect image of the painter's mind at this period—the drawing of Brignall Church near Rokeby, of which a feeble idea may still be gathered from the engraving [in the Yorkshire series, see p.71]. The spectator stands on the "Brignall Banks", looking down into the glen at twilight; the sky is still full of soft rays, though the sun is gone, and the Greta glances brightly in the valley, singing its evensong; two white clouds, following each other, move without wind through the hollows of the ravine, and others lie couched on the far-away moorland; every leaf of the woods is still in the delicate air; a boy's kite, incapable of rising, has become entangled in their branches, he is climbing to recover it; and just behind it in the picture, almost indicated by it, the lowly church is seen in its secluded field between the rocks and the stream; and around it the low churchyard wall, and a few white stones which mark the resting-places of those who can climb the rocks no more, nor hear the river sing as it passes.'

13. Egglestone Abbey, near Barnard Castle

1816-17, 286 x 419 mm
Private Collection
Engraved by T. Higham, paid 55 gns., 13 December 1822. Hayward paid for printing 160 India and 400 small. 20 December 1822. Publication date December 1822.
REFS: W.565, R.174

Egglestone Abbey lies between Rokeby and Barnard Castle, and was founded in about 1195 for Premonstratensian canons. By Turner's day parts were in use as a farmhouse, and the abbey mill was used by Henry Cooke for making paper, as described in the text (pp.70 – 71). When Turner saw it in 1816 there were builders at work at the mill, repairing damage caused by a fire (TB CXLVII 31a). The finished composition is an example of Turner's anecdotal imagination at full power recalling his particular experience of a site, and a close examination will reveal a fisherman and a woman washing and laying out paper to dry, cows drinking in the river, a girl carrying a pail on her head across the (still-standing) packhorse bridge to the right, scaffolding, builders at work, one leading a horse, a figure crossing the field in the distance, more paper hanging on the abbey walls, a girl feeding poultry outside the farmhouse, and, in the foreground, a coat hanging over a bush and a bundle of sticks waiting to be collected. Most of the buildings can still be identified today, and a similar view enjoyed from the Barnard Castle road.

14. High Force or Fall of Tees

1816-17, 285 x 407 mm
Private Collection
Twelve impressions of etching paid for on 29 October 1818. Engraved by J. Landseer FSA, paid 80gns., 4 September 1821. Trigg paid for printing, 23 February 1822. Publication date 12 September 1822.
REFS: W.563, R.173

High Force, about six miles above Middleton in Teesdale, has long been regarded as one of the finest waterfalls in the land, and Turner made a number of sketches on his visit there in 1816 (see pp.72 – 75). The basis of the present watercolour was his first large sketch at the site, which proves that the weather occasionally gave some sunshine, for he recorded a rainbow in the spray. In Turner's day the water usually flowed in two channels, one on either side of a large central bastion of rock, but in recent years it has done so only in times of floods. It is possible to stand on the summit of the central rock, and Turner managed to do so, but it is possible to be stranded by the rapidly rising river. More than one unwary tourist has been swept to his death as a result.

Turner was always keen, where appropriate, to include some characteristic activity of the place. As a keen fisherman he would have been particularly interested in the fact that High Force is an impassable barrier to salmon, and the pool at its base was often full of fish. He includes what must have been a common sight in reasonable conditions, a fisherman casting a fly and an assistant waiting with a landing-net.

15. Heysham and Cumberland Mountains

1818, 290 x 424 mm
Inscribed: (lower right) *'J M W Turner 1818'*
British Museum (Salting Bequest 1910 – 2 – 12 – 274)
Engraved by W.R. Smith, paid 80 gns., 10 August 1822. Hayward paid for printing 160 India and 400 small, 20 December 1822. Publication date 22 August 1822.
REFS: W.579, R.187

Turner had a particular feeling for the wide-open expanses of sky and space as he looked out over the shore at Heysham, and his sketch (TB CLXVII 41, see pp.86 – 87) spreads out over an angle of nearly 180 degrees. The detail of the watercolour is not only characteristic of the place, but also of the very day on which Turner saw it, with a hay cart going down the hill, and the dry, stony fields giving up their harvest only grudgingly. The fields are still visible, still full more of the golden rod and thistles than of grass or corn.

16. Crook of Lune, Looking towards Hornby Castle

1817-18, 280 x 417 mm
Courtauld Institute Galleries
Engraved by J. Archer, paid 40 gns. on account, 7 May 1821. Charles Heath paid 25 gns. for 'finishing Archers plate Crook of Lune', 28 September 1821. Printing of 160 India and 400 plain paid for 21 February 1823. Publication date, 10 August 1821.
REFS: W.575, R. 183

The Crook of Lune about four miles from Lancaster near Caton has been popular since the description of it by Thomas Gray was included in most late eighteenth-century guidebooks to the area. 'Here Ingleborough, behind a variety of lesser mountains, makes a background of the prospect: on either hand of the middle distance, rises a sloping hill; the left clothed with thick woods, the right with variegated rock and herbage: between them, in the richest of valleys, the Lune serpentizes for many a mile, and comes forth, ample and clear, through a well-wooded and richly pastured foreground. Every feature, which constitutes a perfect landscape of the extensive sort, is here not only boldly marked, but also in the best position.'

Turner spent considerable time tracing the 'serpentizing' of the Lune (see pp. 89 – 90), and as Mrs. Hunt pointed out:

'A more difficult subject than the "Crook of Lune" could hardly be set to any landscape designer. The windings of a river seen from a considerable height are hard to draw, and even when drawn rightly themselves require a good deal of management in the composition of the landscape around them, in order to make them illusively pleasant to the eye.'

Turner worked out the composition he wanted in a trial colour-beginning (TB CXCVII I, see p.89) and having satisfied himself with the basic structure, then applied himself to one of the finest watercolours in the whole series.

17. Ingleborough from Hornby Castle Terrace

1818, 286 x 419 mm
Signed and dated 1818 (Armstrong, 1902)
Untraced
Engraved by Charles Heath paid 80 gns. 28 September 1821. McQueen & Co. paid for printing 160 India, 400 plain, June 1822. Publication date, 2 January 1822.
REFS: W.576, R.184

The watercolour on which the engraving (see p.90) was based is presently untraced, and was last recorded in the collection of W. Law Esq. at the beginning of the century, having achieved a record price of 2,000 guineas at the sale of C.S. Bale's collection at Christies in 1881.

Mrs. Hunt remarked that 'Hornby Castle stands on what was regarded even by the Romans as a beautiful site...'A very fine view of Ingleborough—"that huge creature of God", as the poet Gray calls it in one of his delightful letters—is obtained from the terrace at Hornby Castle, and of all—

The Mountains high
Of Craven, whose blue heads for caps put on the sky

it is the most striking, though it has no right to the distinction claimed for it in the local rhyme:

Ingleborough, Pendlehill, and Penyghent,
Are the highest hills between Scotland and Trent

for Mickle Fell is higher than any of them, and so is Whernside, but Ingleborough is so remarkable in shape that it is pre-eminent as a landmark never to be ignored or mistaken. It serves in this capacity even to ships on the Lancashire coast.'

Turner seems to have seen the view with morning mist swirling around the summit of Ingleborough, and in order to make the earliness of the hour more emphatic, has banished all people from sight. It is that quiet hour between dawn and rising. At the right a peacock sounds the reveille, Turner's call to us to take notice of the world that we ordinarily miss.

18. Hornby Castle from Tatham Church

1817-18, 292 x 419 mm
Victoria and Albert Museum (88)
Engraved by W. Radclyffe, paid 35 gns. on account, 31 January 1822, and balance making 70 gns. plus 9 s. for etching, 25 May 1822. Warren paid for printing 160 India, 400 French, 24 April 1823. Publication date, June 1822.
REFS: W.577, R.185

There are marvellous touches of colour in this watercolour. Pinks, greys, yellows and blues in the distance, deeper blues and local colour in the foreground, and a sharpness of touch and detail, that would reward close examination with a magnifying-glass. W.G.Rawlinson misquoted Mrs. Hunt, giving the impression that the drawing was faded. Mrs. Hunt actually said 'unfaded, as we believe'. The scene is described in detail in the text (pp.90 – 91).

19. Kirkby Lonsdale Churchyard

1817-18, 286 x 415 mm
Private Collection
Engraved by Charles Heath, paid 80 gns. 29 January 1821. McQueen & Co. paid for printing 130 large and 400 small, 17 July 1821. Publication date 25 January 1822.
REFS: W.578, R.186

Wordsworth had recommended 'by no means omit looking at the Vale of Lune from the Churchyard', but the sketches that Turner made in the churchyard in 1816 betray a sense of unease with the view from an artistic point of view, as containing no information as to what was being seen, nor any really characteristic features of the site, nor any clues as to the viewpoint. His problem was to transform the material he had acquired into an image that would reward thoughtful and prolonged contemplation.

He solved the first problem via two colour studies which are extremely beautiful in themselves. In the first (TB CXCVIV, see p.93), he opted for a blustery day with clouds scudding across the sky, its freshness made emphatic by the evidence of the artist's vigour in making it. The effect was dashed out with the paper still wet and the paint running freely. Turner was often described as working in a frenzy and this study seems to be no exception—the river spattered with thumbmarks, the paper scrabbled and soaked. In the second he opted for conditions closer to the finished watercolour, with a still summer morning shining out of a reflective pool of watercolour (TB CXCVI W, see p.92). The second problem he solved very simply. He asked the engraver to inscribe the words 'KIRBY LONSDALE' on a gravestone in the foreground, and even though Turner spelled it wrong, his audience can now have had little doubt where they were.

Turner had a remarkably anecdotal imagination, and his pictures are always full of interesting incidents. In *Kirkby Lonsdale Churchyard* a group of boys are waiting for the school to open. Some will no doubt already have walked a considerable distance to get here from their homes and farms in the valley. During the wait some horseplay has broken out. Two of the boys are harassing a third, and have tipped his belongings out on to a tombstone. To make matters worse they have piled up the books and ink bottle into a pyramid and are now proceeding to throw stones at it as if they were at a fair. The protesting victim, meanwhile, holds his one surviving book aloft while one of his assailants tries to grab it, no doubt to use for further target practice. Turner never introduced incident gratuitously. Every detail has its purpose, and the careful consideration of his details can reveal rich seams of atmosphere.

Ruskin, who liked to revisit Turner's sites and explore them for himself, was enraptured when he arrived at Kirkby Lonsdale: 'I do not know in all my country, still less in France or Italy, a place more naturally divine or a more priceless possession of the true "Holy Land' than Kirkby Lonsdale', and again: 'Whatever moorland, hill and sweet river and English forest foliage can be seen at their best is gathered there, and chiefly seen from the upper part of the town itself.' The view is signposted today as 'Ruskin's View', but it was Turner who had guided Ruskin there in the first place.

20. Weathercote Cave when half filled with water

1817-18, 301 x 423 mm
British Museum (Salting Bequest 1910 – 2 – 12 – 281)
Engraved by S. Middiman, paid £50 on account, 4 April 1821, and balance making 80 gns. 2 October 1821. Printed by H. Triggs. Publication date 30 October 1822.
REFS: W.580, R.188

Weathercote Cave is one of the best preserved of the original watercolours, and one of the most unusual subjects. 'Having entered the enclosure by a door', wrote Mrs. Hunt, 'you descend a number of steps to Turner's point of view, and see a circular pit overgrown with bushes, curious and uncanny, and in the face of the rock opposite, a hole with a stone at its mouth and a trickling of water descending from it to chasm of unknown depth below you, but there is no sign of anything like a large rejoicing torrent-fall as of some large stream pouring over the rock on the right, and the whole place, except for its depth, looks small in comparison with Turner's view. That view, however, will be found, when studied, to be full of truth and beauty. The shower which has 'half filled the cave with water' is flying along the sky. The hazels are wet and glistening with it, and the sunbeam brings out their shadows interlaced and quivering on the bare rock, wet and glistening also. A faint curve of prismatic colour plays in the drift which hovers over the truly sunless depth below. Exaggeration there is none, unless it be in the moorland above the thicket, which is too like a mountain side. The bushes, no doubt, did allow that background to be seen in Turner's time.'

Plate 1. Simmer Lake, near Askrigg (Semer Water)

Plate 2. Moss Dale Fall (Mossdale Falls)

Plate 3. Hardraw Fall (Hardrow Force)

Plate 4. Aysgarth Force

Plate 5. Merrick Abbey, Swaledale (Marrick Priory)

Plate 6. St.Agatha's Abbey, Easby

Plate 8. Aske Hall

Plate 9. Richmond, Yorkshire

Plate 10. Junction of the Greta and Tees at Rokeby

Plate 11. Wycliffe, near Rokeby

Plate 13. Egglestone Abbey, near Barnard Castle

Plate 14. High Force or Fall of Tees

Plate 15. Heysham and Cumberland Mountains

Plate 16. Crook of Lune, Looking towards Hornby Castle

Plate 18. Hornby Castle from Tatham Church

Plate 19. Kirkby Lonsdale Churchyard

Plate 20. Weathercote Cave when half filled with water

REFERENCES

ABBREVIATIONS

B&J,	Martin Butlin and Evelyn Joll, *The Paintings of J.M.W. Turner*, London 1977.
Dayes, 1805	*The Works of the Late Edward Dayes*, London 1805.
Farington *Diary*	K. Garlick and A. Mackintyre (ed), *The Diary of Joseph Farington*, London 1978, *et seq.*
Finberg, 1961, *Life*	*The Life of J.M.W. Turner*, Oxford 2nd ed 1961.
Gage, 1980	J. Gage (ed) *Collected Correspondence of J.M.W. Turner*, Oxford 1980.
R.	W.G. Rawlinson, *The Engraved Work of J.M.W. Turner RA*, London Vol I, 1908, Vol II, 1913.
TB	A.J. Finberg, *Complete Inventory of the Drawings of the Turner Bequest*, London 1909.
T.D.	C. Bruyn Andrews (ed), *The Torrington Diaries*, 4 vols., London, 1934 and 1970.
Thornbury 1877	Walter Thornbury, *Life and Correspondence of J.M.W. Turner* (1862), 2nd ed, London 1877.
Turner & Dr Whitaker	S. Warburton, *Turner & Dr Whitaker*, catalogue of the exhibition at Townley Hall, Burnley 1982.
Turner in Yorkshire	R. Green (ed), D. Hill, S. warburton, M. Tussey, *Turner in Yorkshire*, catalogue of the exhibition held at York City Art gallery 1980
W.	Andrew Wilton, *The Life and Work of J.M.W. Turner*, London 1979.
Wroot, 1923	Herbert E. Wroot, 'Turner in Yorkshire' *Miscellanies of the Thoresbury* Society,
VI,	Leeds 1923.
Y1	TB CXLIV
Y2	TB CXLV
Y3	TB CXLVI
Y4	TB CXLVII
Y5	TB CXLVIII
1819 Catalogue	*A Collection of Water Colour Drawings in the Possession of Walter Fawkes Esq.*, London 1819.

J.M.W. TURNER

Page 10, col I, line 27. Letter in Longmans' Archive, I, 102, No.207 H, dated 15 July 1834, from Longmans to Wordsworth.
II, l.2 Finberg, 1961, p.1
l.6 Thornbury, 1877, p.xv
l.9 cf. Thornbury, 1877, Chapter XXXV
l.11 W.P. Carey, *Some Memoirs of the Patronage and Progress of the Fine Arts*, 1826, p. 147
l.21 Thornbury, 1877, p.391
l.25 *ibid*, p.394
l.29 cf. TB CXCV (a) J and *Turner in Yorkshire*, No. 82
l.32 Thornbury, 1877, p.286
l.34 For Turner's will and subsequent litigation see Thornbury, 1877, p.369 ff. & p.620 ff., and Finberg, 1961. Chapter XXXVII
p.11, I, l.7. Thornbury, 1877 p.191. This story ties in with the chronology suggested below for the tour, which would have Turner arriving in Leeds on Saturday 13 July 1816.
l.30 *ibid*, p.242
l.34 *ibid*, p.127
l.44 Quoted by Finberg, 1961, pp.2-3
II, l.8 Finberg, 1961, pp.4-5
l.12 *ibid*, p.7
l.14 B. Falk, *Turner the Painter: His Hidden Life*, London, 1938
l.17-24 Quoted by J. Lindsay, *Turner, His Life and Work: A critical Biography* (1966), Panther Books, 1973 p.9 and p.7.
l.33 Finberg, 1909, p.xvi.
l.37. Oils listed by B&J, 1977
l.38. *ibid*, p.xvi
l.39 Watercolours listed by Wilton, 1979, though this catalogue is not complete.
p.12, I, l.9 J. Ziff, 'Backgrounds, Introduction of Architecture and Landscape, A Lecture by J.M.W.Turner', *Journal of the Warburg and Courtauld Institutes*, XXVI, 1963, p.144
l.12 Thornbury, 1877, p.180
l.17 Finberg, 1961, p.44
l.20 R.B.Beckett (ed), *John Constable's Discourses*, Suffolk Records Society, XIV, 1970
l.21 cf. (e.g.) Ernest de Selincourt (ed), *Wordsworth: The Prelude or Growth of a Poet's Mind (Text of 1805)*, Oxford, 1970
l.23 First Published in two volumes by Fenner, London, 1817.
l.37 Thornbury, 1877, pp. 127-8
l.43 see *Turner En France*, exhibition catalogue, Centre Culturel du Marais, Paris, 1981, p.146, n.34
II, l.2 cf. Mary Moorman (ed.), *Journals of Dorothy Wordsworth*, 2nd ed. Oxford U.P., 1971
l.10 *ibid*, p.109
l.24 cf. K. Coburn (ed), *The Notebooks of Samuel Taylor Coleridge*, London, 1957, *et seq.* K. Coburn, The Self-Conscious Imagination, Oxford U.P., 1974, and as an example of tracing the pathway of his imagination, J. Livingston Lowes, *The Road to Xanadu*, 1927.
l.35 Farington, *Diary*, July 1799

TURNER AND FARNLEY HALL

p.17, col. I, l.6 Farington *Diary*, 4 November 1812
l.20 Thornbury, 1877, p.352.
l.25 S.A. Byles, 'Farnley Hall', *Magazine of Art*, July 1887, p.285
l.26 Thornbury, 1877, p.237
l.32 see W.613, 616 and 617, and Thomas Shaw, *The History of Wharfedale*, Otley, 1830, p.149.
col.II, l.32 Farrington *Diary*, 6 December 1798
l.33 *ibid*, 4 March 1796. Sold Christies 28 June 1890, No.81.
l.35 cf. Dayes, 1805, p.333, and MSS notes on *The Farnley Collection* by Mrs [Edith Mary]Fawkes, 1890, at York City Art Gallery, p.1
l.38 cf. 19th. century list of the pictures at Farnley Hall, Yorkshire Archaeological Society, Leeds, (DD 161/26B)
l.39 Mrs Fawkes MSS, *op cit*, p.33
l.40 Gage, 1980, p.254
ll.43-5 TB LXXXIV 69, cf. W.366,367. No watercolour of *Mt Blanc from St Martin* of the same size as these has been identified (but cf.W.379).
p.18, col.I, l.3 Rev. Henry Forster Mills, *Elegiac Stanzas on the Death of Walter Fawkes Esq.*, Bristol, 1825. p.4.
l.5 Byles, *op cit*, p.298
l.8 W.365, 366, 367, 369, 371, 373, 374, 375, 376, 377, 378, 379, 380, 381, 382, 384, 387, 388, 389, 392, 396.
ll.11-12 B&J 59, 85, 95, 97, 103, 148
l.17 B&J 98, 99
l.19 TB CVII inside back cover and p.1
ll.21-22 TB CIII and TB CLIV A
ll.28-30 TB CLIV L,M,N,Q,R,S,T,U,V,W, see *Turner in Yorkshire*, Nos. 24-31
l.35 TB CIII inside back cover and p.52
l.37 W.615?
col.II, ll.1-2 At least two of the oils exhibited in 1803 remained unsold (B&J 48, 49). He opened his own gallery in 1804, and did not exhibit at all at the Academy in 1805. The Earl of Egremont bought 15 pictures between 1802 and 1812, B&J, 18, 53, 64, 71, 75, 77, 78, 88, 99, 108, 113, 119, 120, 149, 204.
l.4 TB CXXII - (4)
l.5 There is evidence for visits in 1808, possibly 1809, 1810 – 18, 1821, 1823, 1824.
l.8 TB CXXIX. Most others (eg TB CXXXIV) can now be dated to 1816 or later.
l.9 cf. eg. Gage, 1980, No.43
ll.13-21 B&J 126. Story quoted by Thornbury, 1877, p.239
l.22 A study for the figures appears in an earlier sketchbook, TB LXXXI 38, 39.
l.38 Mills, *op cit*, p.2
l.41 According to the Christies sale catalogue, 30.4.1863, No.271: 'Woodcock Shooting on the Chiver [sic], with portrait of Sir Henry [sic] Pilkington.'
p.19, col.I, l.3 Mills *op cit*, p.3
l.5 The first signs of Turner's domestic scenes at Farnley are in sketchbooks which can now be dated to 1816 (eg. T.B. CXXXIV).
ll.7-9 Gage, 1980, No.323
l.10 cf. Edith Mary Fawkes, 'Mr Ruskin at Farnley' in *The Nineteenth Century, a Monthly Review*, April 1900, p.619.
ll.12-17 *ibid*, p.622
l.25-27 W.538, 613, 616, 617, 612
ll.33-37 Thornbury, 1877, p.237. col.II, l.6 See *Turner in Yorkshire*, Nos. 74, 75
l.9 W.583
ll.11-12 TB CLIII 15a-16/17. *Shoeburyness*, B&J 85
l.13 W.592.
ll.14-15 B&J 137, 59, 95
l.17 W.1052-7.
l.19 J.G. Millais, *The Life and Letters of Sir John Everett Millais*, i, 1899, p.157
ll.23-24 Quoted by John Gage, *Turner and Watercolour*, exhibition catalogue, 1974, p.10
l.26 Byles, *op cit*, p.297
ll.34-35 W.499
l.37 Thornbury, 1877, p.239
ll.33-41 Edith Mary Fawkes Typescript, National Gallery, London, quoted by M. Butlin, *Turner Watercolours*, 1962, No.8
p.20, col.I, l.4 Thornbury, 1877, p.238, & Byles, *op cit*, p.299
l.6 B&J 138
l.8 W.494, and M.Cormack, *Turner Watercolours in the Fitzwilliam Museum, Cambridge*, 1975, No.14
l.10 cf. Mrs Fawkes MSS,*op. cit.*, pp.27-28.
ll.12-17 1819 Catalogue, p.7
l.22 Not in Wilton, *Turner in Yorkshire*, No.81
ll.25-30 Quoted by W.T. Whitley, *Art in England 1800-1820*, Cambridge, 1928, p.296.
ll.31-36 1819 catalogue, p.8
col.II, ll.2-12 W.P. Carey, *Some Memoirs of the Patronage and Progress of the Fine Arts*, 1826, p. 147
l.36 See Finberg, 1961, p.260 ff. and TB CLXXI ff.
l.37 B&J 228 and W.718 ff.
p.22, col.I, l.3 W.402, *Turner in Yorkshire*, No.95
ll.12-13 Thornbury, 1877, p.122. The sketch has not been identified, but the story would most likely relate to Turner's most recent visit, i.e. that of November 1812.
l.34 TB CLIV N, *Turner in Yorkshire*, No.29.
l.35 W.587, *Turner in Yorkshire*, No.64.
l.38 W.618
l.39 W.612, *Turner in Yorkshire*, No.67.
l.40 W.610
col.II ll.6-7 Thornbury, 1877, pp.121-22

TURNER AND THE NORTH OF ENGLAND

p.13, col II, l.30 The Lascelles account-books are in the Leeds City Archives Department, Sheepscar, Leeds. Harewood Mss 189-192 (Edward, *junior*), 211, 212 (Edward, *senior*). (Gift, 212).
l.37 British Museum 1958-7-12-402 (W.138). Often called 'St Erasmus in Bishop Islip's Chapel'.
p.14, I, l.1 For Lascelle's knowledge of Turner's work see C. Hartley: *Turner Watercolours in the Whitworth Art Gallery*, 1984, Nos 12-14 and W.182 ff.
l.6 21 November 1798 'To paid Mr Girtin for Drawings Lessons &c £17.17.0'.
II, l.3 TB XXXIV 'North of England' sketchbook and TB XXXV 'Tweed and Lakes'.
l.6 TB XXXV has a card frame inside the cover into which, no doubt, sample drawings could be slipped.
l.16 For sketches of Harewood see TB XXXIV 67 - 76, TB LI R,S,T,U,V,W,X
l.25 *op cit.* (189).
p.15, I, l.5 *Kirkstall* (W.224), *Norham*, see W.225, 226. Sketches for *Kirkstall*, TB XXXIV 16, for Norham, TB XXXIV 57.
l.16 see A Livermore: 'J.M.W. Turner's unknown verse-book', *Connoisseur Year Book*, 1957, pp.78-86.
ll.29-33 *Seasons*, 'Summer' 1647-54
l.38 TB XXXV 80
l.39 TB XXXV 7
II, l.3 TB XXXV 89
l.12 *Norham Castle* cf. W.225, 226
l.19 TB XXXVI V ?, see *Turner in Yorkshire*, No. 38 and W.282.
l.20 The last reference is to a watercolour of 'Fort Rock', *c.* 1808/9, price 60 gns, cf. TB CII 21, and *Turner in Yorkshire* No.93.
l.28 For Turner's 1799 sketches see TB XLV.
l.46 Quoted W.C. Monkhouse, *Turner*, 1879
p.16, I, l.2 There is no other record of Turner's watercolour.
l.17 Lomond, cf. TB XLV 28
l.18 *Bowland* cf. TB LXXXIV 67a
l.28. B&J No. 76
l.33 British Museum 1910-2-12-282 (W.532), *Turner in Yorkshire* No. 32.
l.43 TB LIII
II, l.1 cf. TB LIII 1-13, TB LII ('Guisb.Shore'), TB LXXXII 3-20 (possibly 21?), TB LIV 116a-83a, *Scarbrough Castle*, Leeds City Art Gallery 1369/38, W.317, 318.
l.2 TB LII
l.9 TB LII

A GENERAL HISTORY OF THE COUNTY OF YORK

p.23, col.I, ll.1-10 Farington *Diary*, 15 May 1816
ll.12-13 *History of Craven*, 3rd Edition, introd.
col.II, ll.17-19 T.W. Hanson, 'Edwards of Halifax', *Halifax Antiquarian Society*, 1912, p.178
p.24, col.I, ll.2-4 *ibid*, p.179
l.13 Related by Whitaker's son, Robert Nowell Whitaker, to P.G.Hamerton, *Life of J.M.W. Turner*, 1879
ll.14-19 Hanson *op cit*, p.182
l.23 cf. C.J. Weber, *Fore-Edge painting*, New York, 1966
ll.25-44 Hanson *op cit*, pp.181-2
col.II, l.33 Longman's Archive is housed at the University of Reading Archives Department. References to Whitaker's Yorkshire are contained in two ledgers, 2D pp.120-3, 252-4, and 1A 243, 426-34. Thoresby's *Leeds* (including Whitaker's *Loidis and Elmete*) in 1A 159, 410-15.
p.25, col.I, l.6 A Lister, 'A North Country Historian' *Country Life*, 29 September, 1955, p.676
ll.12-14 *Richmondshire*, 1891, p.xii, and Wroot, 1923, p.238.
ll.25ff. Longmans Archive, Correspondence-Books, I,100, No.266
col.II, ll.19-20 Hanson *op cit*,
ll.30-31 These were published by Hurst, Robinson & Co in 1820 as 'A Series of Views of the Abbeys and Castles in Yorkshire, Drawn and Engraved by W. Westall, A.R.A., and F Mackenzie, with Historical and descriptive Accounts by Thomas Dunham Whitaker, LLD, FRS FSA.'—though it comprised of only 16pp, all devoted to Rievaulx.
p.26, col.I, ll.20-22 Hamerton, *op cit*, p.174, names Turner, Tate and Whitaker, Mrs Hunt named her father, James Raine in the 1891 edition, p.x.
l.29 Gage, 1981, No.82
l.30 Many of the colour-beginnings, e.g. *Mill Gill* would have developed into finished pictures but for the cancellation of the agreement. A number of finished watercolours, however, e.g. *Mowbray Lodge*, (Wallace Collection, W.536), *Mowbray Vale* (sold Sothebys 7.7.1983 No.171) seem to have been intended for the project.—the subjects are dealt with in the text and they were sketched in 1816—but never engraved.
l.34 *Richmond from the Moors*, for example, seems, in terms of style and colour to be earlier than other *England and Wales* watercolours. In view of the fact that this watercolour is related to a colour-beginning made in series with the rest of the Yorkshire colour-beginnings—it is the same size and has the same fold down the centre, a date of *c.*1819 seems possible. Another *England and Wales* watercolour with a case for an early date is *Rivaulx Abbey* (Turner in Yorkshire, No.143).
ll.36-37 See E. Shanes, *Turner's Picturesque Views in England and Wales*, London, 1979, p.158.

THE SKETCHBOOKS AND THE TOUR

p.27, col.I, l.44 A.J. Finberg, *Complete Inventory of the Drawings of the Turner Bequest*, London, 1909, Vol. 1, p.415
l.45 A.J. Finberg, *Turner Watercolours at Farnley Hall*, London 1912, p.5
col.II, ll.36-38 Finberg, *Inventory*, 1909, p.426
p.28, col. I, l.9 Gage, 1981, No.65
l.19 Dayes, 1805, subscribers' list.
l.21 *ibid.*, p.91

THE TOUR

p.34 Friday 12 July 1816. Turner was still in London on Thursday 11th, when he wrote to Benjamin West (Gage p.64). His likely departure dates are therefore Friday or Monday, 12 or 15 July, but the latter would have left no time for Turner to sort himself out before leaving from Browsholme on Wednesday. The fare to Leeds for inside passengers was 3 gns. in 1785 – 7 (see T. Bradley: *The Old Coaching Days in Yorkshire*, Leeds 1889, pp 153 – 200). For names of coaches see Gage p.68. For bank notes see Y2 186a. Eton Socon TD IV 66. Stamford 1797 sketch TB XXXIV 86. For Grantham see D.Defoe: *A Tour through the Whole Island of Great Britain* (1724 – 6), London 1974, ii.103. and TD II 404 ff. IV 132.
p.35 For 1794 see Finberg, Life, p.25. *Grantham* watercolour, W.232, now at Yale, engraving, R.32. For Doncaster see TD III 28.
p.36 *Addingham* watercolour, W.548, where called 'Arthington Mill on the Wharfe'. Fawkes' letter of thanks, see Gage p.79, where letter dated Autumn 1818. For Skipton see John Bigland, *A Topographical and Historical description of the county of York*, 1812, p. 724 ff. Dayes 52. For Turner's first sketches at Skipton in 1816 see Y2 185 – 180a. Whitaker on Skipton see *Craven* p.406.
p.38 'Slight drawing', Y2 179a. For Browsholme see S.Jervis, *Browsholme Hall*, Derby, 1980 (antiquarian interior quote p.3), Anon (Thomas Lister Parker?) *Description of Browsholme Hall*, 1815. For Turner's first visit to North Lancashire see 'Lancashire and N Wales' sketchbook, TB XLV. Mitton sketch, f.1.
p.39 On Saturday 20 July 1816, Farington recorded that in London, at least, the change in the weather was dramatic: 'The weather has suddenly from damp & Cold to great Heat. The thermometer rose today to 78.-' *Diary*. Sketches at Hareden and Trough of Borland see Y2 174 - 172, Y5 22a. Clitheroe, Y2 171a, Sawley Y2 170a, 169a, Y5 21a-22. Whitaker on Sawley see *Craven* p.55.
p.40 For James Ward see E. Nygren: *James Ward's Gordale Scar; An Essay in the Sublime*, Tate Gallery, 1982.
p.41 Turner's sketches, Y2 169-168a, Y5 30a. For Ward's and Girtin's sketches see Nygren *op cit*, Figs 6,8. Thomas Hurtley: *A Concise Account of some Natural Curiosities in the Environs of Malham in Craven, Yorkshire*, London 1786. p.42.
p.42 Turner's sketches at Gordale, Y2 168 – 167a/166a, Malham, 165a. Whitaker on Gordale, *Craven* p.269. Turner's sketches at Gordale Y2 164-163a, 163, 162-161a, TB CLIV O.
p.43 Dayes, p.65, 66-67. Hurtley, *op cit* p.47. Turner's sketches at Malham Tarn, Y2 159a, 158a-159.
p.44 Whitaker on Dow Cave, *Craven* p.406. Sketches at Dow Cave, Y2 158 - 155, 154a?, 154. Y4 1a, 2.
p.46 Whitaker on Kilnsey, *Craven*, p.529. Sketches Y2 153a (i,ii,iii), 153, 152a, Y5 19a-20, Colour-Beginning TB CXCVII - O.

p.47 Sketches, Y5 18a, Y2 152, 151a,150a. Hubberholme, Y2 149a, Cray 148a. Dayes pp. 89-91
p.48 Sketches at Semer Water, Y4 2a-3, from Countersett, 3a-4, Other sketches Y2 147a, 147-146a. Dayes on Askrigg, p.91.
p.49 Torrington on Askrigg TD III p.86. Dayes pp. 92-3, 93n. Sketches at Mill Gill, Y2 146-145a.
p.50 Sketches at Whitfield Gill, Y4 4a,5, from Ellerkin, Y2 144a, 143a. Sketch at Mill Gill, Y5 18-17a.
p.51 Colour Beginning TB CCLXIII 133. Ernest de Selincourt (ed) *Letters of William & Dorothy Wordsworth* 2nd ed. Oxford 1967, Vol I p.278. Sketches Y4 6,7. Whitaker on Fors Abbey, Richmondshire, i.408. Sketches of Colby Hall Falls, Y2, 143-142a, 141a. Ure Bridge, 140a, Askrigg, 141. For Whitaker on Mossdale see Richmondshire, i.413.
p.52 Sketches at Mossdale, Y5 16-17,31a, 25a, 26a. On Hardrow see TD III 84-5. Wordsworth *Letters op. cit* pp. 279 – 280.
p.54 Sketches at Hardrow, Y5 15, 28a-15a. Sketches at Cotter Falls, Y4 8, Askrigg, Y2 139a.
p.55 For description of view over Askrigg see Dayes pp.93 – 4. Sketches at West Burton, Y2 138a, 137a, Y4 9, from Dove Scar Y2 136a, view of 'Wednesly dale' Y4 10.
p.56 Dayes on Aysgarth, pp.94 – 5. Whitaker on Aysgarth, *Richmondshire*, i.393 ff.
p.57 Sketches, Aysgarth Force, Y4 11, 12.
p.58 Middle Aysgarth, 12a,13. Church at Aysgarth, Y4 16. Other sketches see Y4 13a, 14, 15, Y2 135a - 128a.
p.59 Dayes on Castle Bolton, p.96 ff. Turner's sketches, Y2 127 - 123a, Y4 17,18. Sketches from Grinton road, Y2 123-122a, 122. View into Swaledale, Y2 121a. Panorama over Grinton, 121, Grinton church, 120a.
p.60 Marrick, Y2 119a, Y4 18a-19. Ellerton, Y2 119 - 117a, Y4 20.
p.61 Sketches, Y2 115a, 1797, sketch TB XXXV 9, c.1799 watercolour TB XXXVI - V (exh. York, 1980, No.38), &2 114a, 112a.
p.62 For Torrington's account of the King's Head in 1792 see TD III 62 ff - repr. of bill p.67. Mrs. Hunt describes the approach to St.Agathas, 1891, p.13. Sketches, Y2 113-112a, 112 (cf. 1797 sketch TB XXXIV 25 - the early watercolour in the Whitworth Art Gallery, Manchester, W.273, is unusually unlike the sketch), Y4 21,22. Y5 14a. TD III 64. Dayes, pp. 110 – 12. Turner used only his largest sketchbook at Richmond, suggesting the importance attached to his researches there, Y5 13a-14.
p.64 For 'Sweet Lass' see, e.g. E. Bogg, Regal Richmond, Leeds, 1909, p.151; D. Brooks, *The Story of Richmondshire*, Richmond, 1946, p.162; W.M.L'Anson, 'The Lass of Richmond Hill', in *Yorkshire Archaeological Journal, 25, 1920.*
p.65 John Ruskin, Notes to his Pictures exhibited at the Fine Art Society, 1878, No.27 (Works, XIII 430 – 1). Sketches at Richmond, Y5 41, 12a-41a
p.66 Sketches at Aske, Y2 110a, 111, Y4 23.
p.67 Sketches, Richmond from West, Y5, 11a-12, from path to Easby, Y5 10a-11. For progress on etching see commentary on Pl.3. Letter to Holworthy, Gage p.65 (BM Add MS 50118 fos. 44-5). For Holworthy see Gage pp.261-2. The reference to Sandycombe in the letter (i.e. Turner's house 'Solus Lodge', at Twickenham), shows that the Richmond connection (and thus the Sweet Lass) was in Turner's mind. Sketches at Ravensworth Y2 109a, 108a, 107a.
p.68 *Morritt Arms*: there were three inns to choose from at Greta Bridge, the *George*, the *Morritt Arms* and the *New Inn*, though identifying them is problematic, see e.g. A.J. Brown, *Fair North Riding*, London, 1952, p.15 ff. For Cotman at Rokeby, see Adele M. Holcomb (ed.), *John Sell Cotman in the Cholmeley Archive*, North Yorks C.R.O., 1980, p.24ff. For Turner's *Rokeby* illustration for Fawkes see York, 1980, No.77.
p.69 Sketches: 'Cave' Y4 24, Mortham Y2 105a, Meeting of Waters, Y4 25, 25a, Y5 29a. Another sketch at Rokeby, Y2 108.
p.70 Wycliffe sketches, Y4 26/27m 26a, 28/29, Y2 114, 104a (Whorlton). For Pye's reminiscences see Eric Shane's *Picturesque Views in England and Wales*, London, 1979, p.160, n.21. Brignall ref. Mrs. Hunt, 1891, p.80. Brignall sketches, Y2 106, Y4 29,28a, Y5 29,26a, Y4 30, 29a.

p.71 Egglestone Abbey, see TD III 68. Sketches Y4 31, 30a (cf. 1797 sketch TB XXXIV 28), Y2 104, Y4 31a (cf 1797 sketch TB XXXIV 27). Barnard Castle first sketches, Y2 103a, 103. Barnard Castle sketches, Y4 32 (cf. with 1797 sketch TB XXXIV 29), Towler Hill Y4 33. Sketches of Bowes, Y2 103 ii,iii, 105, i,ii. Cotherstone, Y2 107.
p.72 Middleton in Teesdale, TD III 69,71. Sketches at Middleton, Y2 107ii,iii, 105iii, Wynch Bridge, Y2 102a, 102.
pp.73-74 High Force, TD III 70, Sketches: Y2 101a, 101, 100a, Y4 34, Y5 9a.
p.75 Sketches Y5 8a,7a. Sketches *en route* to Cauldron Snout, Y2 100,99a. Cauldron Snout, Y2 98a, Y5 6a. *Chain Bridge over the River Tees* published 1838 (R.302), but very like the *Fall of Tees, Yorkshire*, published 1 June 1827 (R.214), in terms of colouring and handling. This might suggest that they were both made about the time of Fawkes's death on 25 October 1825. For the full text of the letter written after Fawkes's death see Gage 112. For letter of 11 September 1816, see Gage 68. High Cup Nick? Y2 97a, 98.
p.76 Sketches at Appleby, Y2 92a—89a. Y2 89 shows a panorama of distant hills possibly taken from Maulds Meaburn Moor. View from Orton Scar, Y2 94a. Lune Bridge Y4 24a.
pp.78-79 Whitaker deals with Kendale at length in the *Richmondshire* (ii.325ff). Sketches of Kentmere and Upper Kendale, Y2 88a, 87a,87,110,109, Y4 34a-35. Levens Hall Y2 95, Dallam Tower Y5 42-6. Previous visits to Morecambe Bay area in 1797, 1801 and 1809. Tide-tables published in Lancaster Gazette, 3 August 1816, p.3, col.5. Panorama from Milnthorpe sands, Y4 (35a-)36.
p.80 For early tourists accounts in Morecambe Bay area see J. Lofthouse, *The Curious Traveller Lancaster to Lakeland*, London (1956) 1981, p.55. The crossing to Meathop from Milnthorpe does not seem to have been an established route, and it would have been safer for Turner to have gone round *via* Levens Bridge. However the evidence of the sketch sequences (Y4 especially) clearly shows Milnthorpe—Castle Head—Witherslack—Whitbarrow Scar. Castle Head sketch Y4 36a-37.
p.82 Castle Head from Lindale sketch Y5 34a (cf. colour-beginning TB CCLXIII 350—hitherto known as 'Baiae'). On communications in the area see J.C.Dickinson, *The Land of Cartmel*, Kendal, 1980. View looking towards Witherslack from Newton Fell, Y4 38. Sketches at Witherslack, Y2 96a, 96-95.
p.83 Sketches at Whitbarrow Scar, Y2 94-93a, Y4 38a-39, 39a, Canal Foot Ulverston, Y5 33a-34, Conishead Priory, Y5 32a - 33. For Whitaker on Ulverston see *Richmondshire* ii 391. Conishead Priory sketches Y2 86, 85a. West quoted Dickinson *op. cit* p.46.
pp.84-85 Sketches made *en route* Ulverston - Lancaster, Y2 85 - 83a (84, Wraysholme Tower).
p.86 Y2 82a seems to be Turner's first impression of Lancaster. It would have been uneconomic to go into Lancaster first and then come out again to sketch the aqueduct. Sketches at the aqueduct, Y2 81 (details), Y5 35a. For Whitaker on Lancaster see *Richmondshire* ii 217. For 1797 sketch of aqueduct see TB XXXV 65. Final sketch at acqueduct, Y5 36-35.
pp.87-88 Sketches at Heysham, Y2 80a, 78a-79, Y4 40/40a-41, Y2 77a. Sketches at Lancaster, Y2 77,76a,75a (quay cf.Y5 36a-38a), 76 (old bridge cf. 1797 sketch TB XXXV 64), 75, 74a (new bridge cf. Y5 37a-38), 74,73a, 73-72a (two-part panorama). Wordsworth *Guide*, 1835, pp.3-4. Turner's route indicated by the fact that the first sketch at the Crook is taken from the road from Halton. For Whitaker on Crook, see *Richmondshire* ii.203.
p.89 Sketches at the Crook of Lune, Y2 72, 71a, 71, 70a, 69a (continuation of 70a to right) Y4 35a, Y2 69.
pp.90-91 Whitaker on Hornby see *Richmondshire*, ii.250. View from Castle Terrace Y5 4a. Sketches at Tatham, Y2 64a, Y4 41a-42. Sketches at Hornby Y2 64,63a,63,62a. Sketches at Tunstall/Thurland Castle, Y2 61, Y4 42a. For Whitaker's engraving of Thurland Castle see Longmans Archive, University of Reading, Ref: 2D, p.252: '4 [June 1822] Bonner, Engraving Thurland Castle 5.10.[0].'
p.92 For Whitaker on Kirkby Lonsdale Bridge see *Richmondshire*, p.279.
pp.93-94 Sketches, Y2 60-59a, 59.
p.95 It seems that Turner made two separate visits to the bridge, with a visit to the churchyard in between, since Y2 sequences show drawings of the bridge and then the 'continuation of K.L.Cyd view' (58a). Y5 has churchyard views then drawings of the bridge. Sketches, Y5 3a-4, 5a-3 (continued to right on &2 58a). K. Lonsdale bridge, Y5 5,4c, Y4 37a. Whitaker description *Richmondshire* p.277
p.96 Ingleton. First Impression Y2 58. For Torrington on Ingleton and his visit to caves see TD III 89 – 90. Turner's 1808 sketch of Chapel-le-Dale and Ingleborough TB LI - P (formerly known as 'Roadside church with distant mountain. Probably in Cumberland'). 1816 sketches of Ginglepot Y2 56a, Hurtlepot, 57, Weathercote, Y2 k3-12a, Y4 33a. Resketched 1808 view of Chapel-le-Dale Y2 39.
p.99 Sketches at Yordas, Y2 56 - 48a, Y4 43a. Ingleton, Y4 16a, 19a.
p.100 Sketches on the way to Kendal, Y2 41a,42 (Tunstall), Sketches at Kendal, Y2 34a-35, Y4 44, 45a and inside back cover, Y2 13a, 14. Sketches at Kirkby Lonsdale, Y2 34, 33a; Ingleborough, Y2 68a, 2a; Settle, Y2 32, 31a, 21a.
p.101 Sketches at Skipton 171, 170, 27a, 26a, 23, 22a, 14a-15, 11a, 8a, 4a, Y4 7a.
p.102 *Large Farnley* sketchbook, TB CXXVIII, basis of *Shooting Party* (W.610) f.10, *Grouse-Shooting* (W.535), f.8. This sketchbook, dated to c.1814-15 by myself, (*York*, 1980, No.46), must now be dated 1816 on the evidence of the Hackfall sketches in it (ff. 37,38) which were sketched on his tour of central Yorkshire at the end of August 1816 (see Y1 & Y3,). There is also a sketch of Kex Gill (f.7 cf. colour-beginning TB CXCVI O). Song inside cover of Y5.

INDEX